Remembering Arthur Miller

REMEMBERING ARTHUR MILLER

Edited by CHRISTOPHER BIGSBY

METHUEN *in association with*
THE ARTHUR MILLER CENTRE FOR AMERICAN STUDIES

First published by Methuen 2005

Methuen Publishing Limited
11–12 Buckingham Gate
London SW1E 6LB
www.methuen.co.uk

Copyright © 2005 The Arthur Miller Centre for American Studies

ISBN 0 413 77552 6

Methuen Publishing Limited Reg. No. 3543167

A CIP catalogue record for this title is available
from the British Library

Typeset by SX Composing DTP, Rayleigh, Essex
Printed and bound in Great Britain by
St Edmundsbury Press, Bury St. Edmunds, Suffolk

Disclaimer
Methuen Publishing Limited gratefully acknowledges the permissions granted
to reproduce the quoted extracts within this work. Every effort has been made to
trace the current copyright holders of the extracts included in this work. The
publishers apologise for any unintended omissions and would be pleased to
receive any information that would enable them to amend any inaccuracies or
omissions in future editions.

For Robert, Jane, Rebecca and all the grandchildren

Acknowledgements

All contributors to this volume have offered their work without fee but outside the context of this book the copyright is that of the authors.

Tony Kushner's remarks are reprinted with permission of the author and of *The Nation* magazine (portions of each week's magazine can be accessed at http:www.the nation.com). James Houghton's remarks which originally appeared in *Humanities, the Magazine of the National Endowment for the Humanities*, March/April 2001, Vol. 22, No. 2, are reprinted with permission of the author and of *Humanities* magazine. Dustin Hoffman's remarks originally appeared in *Arthur Miller and Company*, edited by Christopher Bigsby and published by Methuen Drama in 1990. Extracts from *The Ride Down Mount Morgan* by Arthur Miller, copyright © 1991, revised © 1999 by Arthur Miller and Inge Morath Miller. Used by permission of Penguin, a division of Penguin Group (USA) Inc., and reprinted by permission of International Creative Management Inc. © 1991 by Arthur Miller. Extracts from *Timebends* by Arthur Miller reprinted by kind permission of Grove/Atlantic, Inc., New York, USA. Copyright © 1987 by Arthur Miller. Extracts from *Timebends* by Arthur Miller reprinted by kind permission of Grove/Atlantic, Inc., New York, USA. Copyright © 1987 by Arthur Miller. The interview with Arthur Miller is an edited version of the programme broadcast in 1995, on BBC Radio 4, and is reproduced with the permission of the BBC.

Particular thanks also go to the United States Embassy and to Anne Cook, Tina Howe, Joseph Kane and Val Striker.

Methuen has forgone profits on this book, the proceeds of which, after costs, will go to students' scholarships in the name of Arthur Miller.

Contents

The Jewish woman goes to the psychiatrist for help with her eight-year-old son. He goes into fits of hysteria at the sight of kreplach.

Kreplach are meat dumplings.

The doctor advises so – demonstrate how a kreplach is made so that he can witness how harmless it really is.

She returns home and takes Sam by the hand to the kitchen table. 'Now watch. See this little square of dough?'

'What about it?'

'Nothing scary about it, is there?'

'Scary? Of course not.'

'OK. Now I'm going to put this little lump of chopped meat in the center of it, right?'

'What's this about?'

'Never mind, just watch. And now I'm folding over this corner of dough, OK? Good. And now I'm folding over this other corner, OK? And now I'm doing the third corner. How do you feel?'

'Me? I'm fine. Why are you doing this?'

'Just watch. Now I'm folding over the fourth corner .'

The boy throws up his hands and screams, 'My God! – kreplach!' And falls to the floor in a faint.

And they make such a fuss about Beckett.

Arthur Miller

Introduction

When Arthur Miller died, on 10 February 2005, it was fifty-six years to the day after the opening night of *Death of a Salesman* on Broadway and almost seventy years since he wrote his first play. That play, written in a rented room in Ann Arbor, as he struggled to earn grades that would keep him at the University of Michigan, had its origins in his own family. It linked private life to public issues as its characters struggled to retain the integrity of their identities while engaging issues which went beyond the personal. That nexus was to prove central to his subsequent work as it was to his life.

As a writer, he engaged with his times, registering the seismic tremors of his culture. As a citizen, he stood up to be counted, sometimes a perilous endeavour. The FBI opened its file on him in 1938, his last year at university. He was protesting his government's policy towards republican Spain. Thereafter, he signed documents, made speeches, was an advocate for what he believed and found himself declared un-American for doing so. He attended one of the first teach-ins over Vietnam, as he did rallies against nuclear weaponry. When a local man was falsely imprisoned he quietly worked for several years to secure his release, as he would work for the release of writers around the world when President of International PEN. Fernando Arrabal, Václav Havel and Wole Soyinka were among the many who benefited from his efforts.

He was, however, above all, a writer. It was at the centre of his being. He went each day to his desk. He persisted in the face of sometimes virulent attacks and an equally debilitating disregard, his international reputation not always being mirrored in the country which he celebrated in choosing to engage with its weaknesses no less than its strengths. That he emerged as the pre-eminent playwright of his generation would have surprised the young Arthur Miller, who in school had preferred sports to study and had scarcely seen a play before he sat down in Michigan to write his own. His pre-eminence, though, was undoubted and confirmed when, approaching the millennium, his fellow playwrights, along with actors and directors,

I

were asked by Britain's Royal National Theatre to identify the outstanding playwright and most significant plays of the twentieth century. He was placed number one while two of his plays featured in the top ten, the only writer for whom this was true.

What earned him this position? Above anything, perhaps, his ability to earth larger social, political and even metaphysical issues in the lives of ordinary people. For audiences, there was a shock of recognition. His were characters who lived on the pulse. Those who watched, read, studied his plays translated the hopes, despairs, betrayals, triumphs that he dramatised in terms of their own lives. He wrote about salesmen, dockers, warehousemen, doctors, policemen, lawyers, writers, actors, each precisely and convincingly rendered, but each, too, struggling with dilemmas that were entirely recognisable if seldom acknowledged. At the same time it was clear that there was a connection between such personal concerns and those of the wider society.

He was also, though, a man committed to language. Dustin Hoffman has spoken of the arias in his plays and there is a bruised poetry to the lives of his characters as there is a tragic drive to their struggles. Miller was at heart a poet and a number of his plays were written in verse, from his radio play *Juarez*, starring Orson Welles, to early drafts of *Death of a Salesman* and *The Crucible*. The one-act version of *A View from the Bridge* is a verse drama, but in all his plays his language is charged with lyricism. He had an acute ear capable of rendering the broken speech of Eddie Carbone and the vapid Madison Avenue cant of a television producer in *Resurrection Blues*. But he was not content with mimicking speech. When he attended the première of Tennessee Williams's *A Streetcar Named Desire* he felt vindicated and confirmed in his desire to liberate words from the merely prosaic. He was not, it seemed, alone.

At university in the 1930s he studied the theatre of ancient Greece alongside the drama of Henrik Ibsen, then seen as a radical. What he learned from both was that the theatre was a place for societies to debate with themselves, to explore the myths and values they embraced or traduced. When he began writing he thought the theatre a way to address the whole nation and to bring about change. Later in life he watched that audience fragment and accepted that change would be incremental, but never ceased to believe in the centrality of theatre nor the possibility of personal and social transformation.

He was aware of the flaws in human nature that could lead to betrayal and to the denial of such betrayals. He was drawn to the ideal while aware, like Ibsen, of the cruelties that can be justified in the name of the ideal. No wonder he saw the dark underside of American Utopianism, a Utopianism that celebrated the future at the price of the past, that committed the individual to the pursuit of happiness in a culture which too easily confused the spiritual with the material.

His characters compel because they are aware, at some level, of the insufficiencies of their lives. They have a tendency to shout out their names not because they are confident of who they are but because they are aware of the gap between who they would be and who they suspect they have become. Joe Keller, Willy Loman, John Proctor, Eddie Carbone, Quentin, Lyman Felt, there is scarcely a Miller character not conscious of failure but equally there is scarcely a Miller character not struggling to bring his life into alignment with his sense of himself. They are often not without their foolishness, their bafflement in the face of a life they never quite feel within their grasp. Yet they seldom surrender to the doubts which leave them staring into the past for an understanding of their present.

And what is true of his male characters is true in another sense of the women he creates. They are often, like Kate Keller, Linda Loman, Elizabeth Proctor, Beatrice Carbone, required to sustain a world precisely threatened by the anxieties and betrayals of those they love. Sometimes, as with Maggie in *After the Fall*, Patricia in *The Last Yankee*, Angela in 'Some Kind of Love Story', they begin to break under the pressure of a life whose demands seem too great. But they are no less committed to a search for meaning and there is a strength to most of his women characters, who are required to bear the burden of something more than their own frustrated hopes.

There were those who thought him a realist, in part because of *All My Sons*, but that had been written precisely because his earlier departures from realism had failed to find an audience. His instincts lay elsewhere. He experimented with forms and styles. In play after play he asked how the real is constituted. Willy Loman's dreams are real enough to dictate the shape of his life while John Proctor is damned for denying the existence of witches whose reality is affirmed by the state. The conceit at the heart of *The Archbishop's Ceiling* – that microphones may or may not be concealed in a room thus turning those within it into actors staging their lives for an unseen audience – underscores the extent to which performance underlies behaviour,

3

infiltrating the supposed integrity of the self, a dilemma no less at the heart of his last play, the aptly named *Finishing the Picture*.

Finishing the Picture looked back to the past and for him the past had always remained a living part of experience. In play after play he returned there, in part for lessons too casually ignored by those who believed only in that dream of tomorrow that seemed a national imperative, in part because for him the link between past and present is the basis of morality. Individuals and nations, he insisted, are responsible for their actions. The chickens, he never tired of saying, always come home to roost. Were it not so there could be no ethical system, no communal life. He lived through times when politicians insisted that social life should defer to an economic competition between individuals, that there was, in the words of the British Prime Minister Margaret Thatcher, no such thing as society. How could he believe that when the theatre constitutes that society with each performance, when its mutualities make possible an art which engages individuals who come together in part to understand themselves as private beings and social animals alike? There was something of Whitman about him both in his fusing of the self and the generality, and in his democracy as he dramatised the lives of those who might have seemed socially marginal but whose dilemmas were universal.

His awareness of human fallibility, a fallibility that could break relationships or lead countries towards some ultimate darkness, led him back to the figure of Cain. Not for nothing was he fascinated by the notion that the motor of human history had started with a blow, as brother turned against brother. He had lived, he acknowledged, through one of the most violent centuries in human history. Science and technology had been enlisted in the business of mass extinction. What to make of that? He certainly never closed his eyes to its reality or attempted to deny the complicity of those who declared themselves innocent the better to declare others guilty. Nor was history some abstract force rendering the individual irrelevant or innocent of agency, any more than he sanctioned the vision of the absurdists for whom humankind was a cosmic victim, the product of a cold irony as natural instincts rendered the individual more completely into the hands of an indifferent nature. This, he regarded as no more than a disinterested shrug, a casual dismissal not only of need but of possibility. He embraced Samuel Beckett as a poet but rejected his metaphysics. He was drawn to the tragic precisely because it turned on the wresting of meaning from defeat.

At the heart of individual actions, he acknowledged, was an all but disabling self-interest, sometimes frightening in its dismissal of the needs and rights of others. The struggle, it seemed to him, was always to discover a way of being that saw the urgency for brotherhood even as he recognised the impulse to betray that brotherhood. What else is drama but an attempt to inhabit the sensibility of others and invite the understanding of audiences for those who seem so different from themselves but who at some vital level are so similar? Why else would we reach out to Willy Loman, to John Proctor and Eddie Carbone, each locked inside his own distinctive necessities and yet each expressions of something more than unique anxieties? Miller's plays are full of people dreaming the wrong dreams but the energy, if also the desperation, with which they commit themselves demands attention, as does their awareness that at some level an uncommitted life is hardly a life at all.

He was conscious that in his youth he had given his loyalty to false ideals but never regretted the impulse that had led him to do so. He was bitter at the betrayals of the Marxism which once enthralled him but not at the impulse that had driven him towards it. It was, after all, a vision of human solidarity, of social justice that had urged him on and he never relinquished that. It had its residue. He retained his sympathy for those who worked with their hands or laboured at jobs that could not always be said to contain their own reward. He was always vaguely guilty at the money that came in through the box office, as he felt, without him having to do anything beyond write words in the wooden studio perched two score yards from the back door of his house. Yet he lived simply, his only indulgence the cars in which he took a guilty pleasure, driving the tree-lined Connecticut hills like some Jewish Natty Bumppo looking for meaning where nature intersected with man. And there is a natural existentialism to his plays. People are the sum of their actions, condemned to be free even as they imagine themselves in thrall to private needs and public necessities. For all his wealth he was dismissive of a president who cut his taxes on the assurance that wealth would trickle down to those who lacked both it and any purchase on political power. He was moved to anger at the thought of the children who went to bed hungry in a land of plenty, as at those who suffered oppression far beyond a New England that flamed with beauty every fall and wrapped itself in cold beauty every winter.

Until he married Inge Morath, he was not a great traveller. A post-

5

war visit to France and Italy had left him appalled not merely at the poverty and ruin but at what seemed a surrender of the spirit. He watched, uncomprehendingly, as survivors of the concentration camps pressed back into the shadows, kin, he knew, but not in any way he could as yet fully understand. It was to be Inge, Austrian-born, who had refused her father's suggestion that she should join the Nazi Party – not out of conviction but pragmatic politics – who led him to one of those camps, Mauthausen, not so far from her home in Salzburg. She felt the need to face her own demons and to show the man she loved, a Jew, what history meant in a Europe which, unlike the United States, could not wave it away as an irrelevance, a mere overture to the great symphony of the future. From that moment the Holocaust drew him. In 1964 he sat, with Inge, in a Frankfurt court room and watched the trial of Auschwitz guards. The camps, and what they meant in terms of human dereliction, would recur in his work, as fact and image, in *After the Fall*, *Incident at Vichy*, *Playing for Time* and *Broken Glass*.

They travelled widely – to a Russia that had always fascinated Inge, to China, South America, Europe, criss-crossing the planet. His plays reflected that fact – *The Archbishop's Ceiling* set in Czechoslovakia where his conversations had been bugged, *Resurrection Blues* set in a version of Colombia – even though the dilemmas these plays featured had an American dimension. He explored the world, indeed, not so much for its exotic differences as for the constancy of human need and aspiration that linked place with place and people with people.

At home, he and Inge were generous hosts. When they married she could barely boil an egg. Later, she could create stunning meals from the simplest ingredients. When she visited the local supermarket her shopping list could be in any of half a dozen languages (when I accompanied her it was in German), languages which at times she learned before one of their visits abroad the better to understand the culture. She had learned Chinese with the help of a tape recorder as she weeded the lettuces in their garden. She saw the world through a camera lens, he through a sensibility which registered the subtle shifts of language, thought, social assumptions. They complemented each other.

When the weather allowed, and sometimes when it did not, he and Inge would begin the day with a swim in the spring-fed pond down the slope from their house. Several of those gathered in this book will have swum there. 'There used to be snapping turtles,' he told me as I

6

trod water beside him, 'they can take your toes off. They're mostly gone now, though.' Mostly? In the winter, he and Inge would venture out on the ice, with its frost-glazed surface. Winters could be bitter in Connecticut. On his way to rehearsals for *Broken Glass* he had had to ease his car into the snowdrifts which lined the roads to slow his descent, brakes offering little purchase. But there was a beauty about this place that never ceased to compel, whatever the season.

Roxbury was, in truth, not without its dangers. For some reason snakes seldom slithered down on to the Miller property but there was poison ivy, which once necessitated his taking a prolonged cold shower, and it was wise to wear bright orange in the woods where hunters sometimes found it difficult to distinguish playwright from deer. He himself kept a rifle to hand, once shooting a groundhog for no better reason than that he could. That incident, and the guilt it fostered, spawned a film, *The Reason Why*, made at his Roxbury spread and featuring Eli Wallach and Robert Ryan, an allegory which features the needless shooting of a woodchuck to parallel the slaughter then under way in Vietnam. At first, the Wallach character explains, he killed a single animal but somehow that escalated and in the midst of a pristine countryside he began to kill ever more. The film was completed in a day, from sunup to sunset. The actors, too, were guests in a house to which actors, directors, academics would make their way and in which they were casually accommodated. One day Inge had to cater for a whole busload of Russians. I arrived late one evening, fresh off the plane, when they were out at neighbours'. Inge left me a snack, a beer and a bagel, then, doubtless remembering that I was British, left a note beside it with an arrow and the message, 'This is a bagel.'

Miller managed simultaneously to be a private man, guarding aspects of his privacy, and intensely sociable. There was a touch of the stand-up comedian about him and he would take pleasure in telling Jewish jokes, one of which opens this book. I asked him to send it to me and reproduce it as I received it. To sit beside him in the theatre was to see a man who laughed aloud at lines he had written decades before and must have heard hundreds of times. As one of the contributors to this book observes, he had the ability to respond to his own work as if for the first time.

Despite health problems in his later years, he was remarkably resilient. His eighty-fifth birthday was celebrated with the Freedom of the city of Norwich, in the United Kingdom. On the morning of the ceremony he tripped in the street and cracked three ribs. He refused the ambulance and went through the day – ceremony, platform performance at the local theatre, gala dinner – without mentioning the pain. When he returned to New York, though, he was in a wheelchair. At the airport he was greeted by a man holding up a sign saying, 'MILLER'. He duly went with him and was driven out of JFK. It was the wrong Miller. His actual driver had been looking for a six foot three man and had missed the wheelchair passenger.

It is startling to discover the disregard he suffered in his own country in the last thirty years of his life. He was celebrated for his early work but the new plays seemed to slip by invisibly. In a culture always in search of novelty he was too familiar, perhaps, too conscious of the past contained within the present. Critical attention had shifted to the European and American avant-garde, while there were still those in the critical establishment who associated him with political battles from another age, as if they had taken his measure long ago.

In the end, though, critics fade and writers last. Awards cascaded on him from Britain, Spain, Israel and, indeed, the United States. *The Man Who Had All the Luck*, his first failed play, came back in triumph, praised by the same newspaper (the *New York Times*) that had once dismissed it. In 1998 the Goodman Theatre, under Robert Falls, staged a major revival of *Death of a Salesman* with Brian Dennehy, while in that same year the Signature Theatre in New York, small, unfashionably located, staged a season of his plays, which included the première of *Mr. Peters' Connections*. It had the air of a homecoming, though in truth he had never been away. The American production of *The Ride Down Mount Morgan* seemed to signal a new receptiveness and where the world première of that play had been staged in England, his last works were staged in the United States, at the Signature, the Guthrie in Minneapolis and the Goodman in Chicago. The American theatre, which for him for so long meant New York, had changed. Broadway no longer seemed, and no longer was, where new plays could be born, as it had been half a century before when a young Arthur Miller left Michigan clutching the plays he had written there and ready to bring America the urgent news of its failed visions but still more potent possibilities.

Mr. Peters' Connections, written when he was eighty-three, presents a man looking back on his life, trying to make sense of its seeming arbitrariness and living in a society in which old buildings are torn down with a restless regularity and history is no more than a dream.

8

He shuffles through his memories in an attempt to discover the hidden history beneath a seeming contingency. His friends have died, yesterday's certainties dissolved as though they had never had true substance. Like Willy Loman, he feels 'kind of temporary', as Miller confessed to feeling about himself. It was an end of century, end of millennium play which also seemed like a final play, a Miller version of *The Tempest*, as if he were about to snap his magic staff and round off his career. Certainly it ends on a note of reconciliation, a celebration of love even in the face of knowledge that it could be snatched away on the winds. But even at so advanced an age he was not quite ready to bring down the curtain on a career whose last twenty years had been the most prolific of his life. Nor was he content to stay in his study.

Until late in his life he would ride a tractor to cut the fields around his home or play tennis with a vigour that could deceive his younger opponents. He could never see something broken without setting himself to mend it, as he did my car more than once. Indeed, auto-mechanic was the profession his sister had once confidently predicted for him. His mastery of croquet, though, attested to here by Frank McCourt, was surely nothing more than blind luck.

Later in life, stenosis of the spine slowed him down and encroaching deafness necessitated a hearing aid that would sometimes wail plaintively in the middle of recorded interviews. Beyond the trials and tribulations that flesh is heir to, however, he was what he had ever been – a worker of wood, a writer of plays, a citizen of something more than a small New England town and a country too often content to think itself sufficient unto itself.

He was not someone who could give up on life or on writing, the two braided together since he wrote his first story at the age of seventeen. In his final years he seems to have gone back through his files looking for unfinished business. *Resurrection Blues* opened in 2002. He had been working on *Finishing the Picture* since 1978. He completed it in 2004. 'The Turpentine Still' dated from his visit to Haiti many years before. It finally appeared in 2005. Here was a man putting his literary effects in order.

In his final days he asked to be taken back to his family home, having been cared for in his sister's apartment which looked out over Central Park, where he had once skated as a child in winter and raced with his older brother in summer. He had been born in Harlem, and raised there and in Brooklyn. New York remained, in his mind, the centre of the American theatre, but it was the countryside that drew him and where he lived for over half a century. It was where he chose to end the story of his life.

When he returned for a last time to Roxbury, he requested a glass of cold water drawn from the well sunk deep below that house in the Connecticut hills where he and his wife, Inge, had planted thousands of trees forty years before. It was from those trees, and others more ancient, that he had shaped furniture for his house. Once he even fashioned salad servers from a fallen apple tree from which his daughter had swung as a child – memories locked up in wood whose subtle striations marked the passing years as he had once worked in *Death of a Salesman* to slice down through time making past and present simultaneously visible.

He died with his family around him, a man who had once delivered bread at four in the morning and worked in an auto-parts warehouse to earn enough money to go to a university that offered prizes to young writers, a man who had once been told he was un-American but went on to become one of the finest writers that country has ever produced.

Sixteen years ago he explained about his plays and the audiences that saw them, 'I like to believe that the feeling that they have is that man is worth something . . . I think art imputes value to human beings and if I did that it would be the most pleasant thought I could depart with, apart from the fact that it entertains people . . . if it left behind that much value it would be great. What does a writer want? He wants to have left his thumbprint on the world.' Asked if that did not sound like Willy Loman he replied, 'Who does not want that?' Arthur Miller left his thumbprint on the world. It seems unlikely that it will ever be erased.

Christopher Bigsby, Norwich, June 2005

Remembering Arthur Miller

F. Murray Abraham

*Actor: **The Ride Down Mount Morgan**, Williamstown, 1996*

Arthur must have been in his late seventies when we worked on *The Ride Down Mount Morgan* at Williamstown, and women of all ages swooned when they saw him; a chick-magnet approaching eighty. His wonderful wife was still alive and I was deeply touched by the almost palpable connection between the two of them, and I remember feeling happy for this love he had found. I have good memories of the play, but my dearest memory is of them together. I also did a very successful reading of *Incident at Vichy* that he saw in Manhattan, and his generosity after the show was a tribute to his character.

Except for interviews or rewrites, Arthur was always present during rehearsals. His way of acknowledging good work was a little smile and a tilting back of his head. Best of all was when he told his wife about our discoveries; she would then quietly embrace us and tell us how surprised Arthur was to discover completely new aspects of his work, how delighted with the process he remained after all these years. The respect he had for his actors was repaid a thousandfold; we loved him. I wish playwrights everywhere could have witnessed his general respect for each of the several disciplines in the theatre and, as great as he was, his humility.

Edward Albee

Writer

Not long ago after Arthur Miller died there was a memorial in New York City – at a theatre, of course – at which a number of people in public life spoke, or had messages read: President Clinton, Senator George McGovern, the Reverend William Sloane Coffin Jr, the playwright Tony Kushner, the actor Daniel Day-Lewis, Arthur's daughter and film-maker Rebecca Miller, among others.

I spoke as well; here is the essence of what I said:

Shortly after Arthur died obituaries and evaluations of his career began appearing. Almost all of them were properly laudatory with the exception of a vile and sniggering unsigned editorial in the *New Criterion*, a ridiculously far-right magazine of arts criticism which attacked Arthur's talent, his politics and even – as I read it – his morality.

I used to think that the far-right diatribes were funny in their awful way until I began to see that our country was beginning to swing behind such attitudes, and I reminded myself that the United States has never been in any danger from the liberals or the Left, that it is the mindset of the reactionary Right that can bring democracy to its knees.

Arthur was a believer in the slow peaceful revolution that is the basis of the vitality of the American experience. His plays hold a mirror up to us, saying, 'This is who you are. If you don't like what you see don't look away. Change!'

There are many very talented writers in the United States whose work does not matter at all, for they are content to leave people's minds where they found them, offering escapism rather than social or political engagement.

These writers do not matter. We learn nothing from them except perhaps sloth and indifference. And then there are writers who matter. Arthur mattered. Arthur mattered a lot.

The *New Criterion* finally published a reply of sorts to my remarks, and I find their response just as vile and sniggering as their earlier effort. They referred to those of us who spoke as 'representative specimens of the left-liberal glitterati of yesteryear, a bit long in the tooth but present, preening and accounted for'. (Goodness! Poor Tony Kushner! In his forties and already passé!)

They went on to say, 'Before Mr Albee started tossing around words like "vile" and "sniggering" he ought to have reflected on the vile smugness of a playwright [Arthur's, I take it, not mine] whose career owed much more to his radical-chic political posturing than it did to his virtues as a writer.'

Perhaps I should add 'shrill' to 'vile' and 'sniggering'!

I imagine the whole brouhaha would have given Arthur a head-shaking chuckle.

Alun Armstrong

Actor: **The Crucible**, *Royal Shakespeare Company, 1984;*
Death of a Salesman, *Royal National Theatre, 1996*

I only once saw Arthur Miller get angry. It was during one of those
question-and-answer sessions, following a talk he had given. A well-
known playwright had asked a question from the back of the room,
which unfortunately I hadn't heard but whose tone sounded
inoffensive enough. Not to Arthur, however, who flew into a rage,
his basso profundo voice shaking the window glass. The playwright
kept trying to justify his position as Arthur's voice boomed ever
louder. I thought he was going to leave the platform and punch the
guy, which would have been very bad news for the playwright, since
Arthur's frame and fists were the size of a heavyweight. But then, so
were his words. Night after night, as John Proctor in a promenade
production of *The Crucible*, with the audience close enough to touch,
I watched grown men silently, yet unashamedly, weeping. I had
been an actor for twenty years but had never experienced anything
quite like it. It happened everywhere we took the play, including
Belfast and Warsaw.

You could be forgiven for thinking that working with him on one
of his plays would be a somewhat daunting experience. Not a bit of
it. In the autumn of 1996, two weeks into rehearsing Willy Loman
in *Death of a Salesman* at the National Theatre, I was flown to
Salzburg with the director David Thacker and the rest of the
Loman family, Marjorie Yates, Mark Strong and Corey Johnson.
For a week we lived in splendid extravagance at the Schloss
Leopoldskron, formerly the palace of the Prince Archbishop of
Austria and immortalised in the film *The Sound of Music*, as the
house of the von Trapps. Ostensibly we were there to participate in
a theatre seminar, 'The Power of Theatre', attended by seventy
actors, writers, directors and academics from forty-three countries,
but in truth it was a pilgrimage. From Nairobi to Singapore, from
the villages of India to the Andes mountains, participants had
moved heaven and earth to spend a week in the presence of the
seminar's special guest, Arthur Miller.

Arthur's mornings were taken up with *Death of a Salesman*
workshops, lectures, or play readings, leaving the afternoons free for
him to relax. No longer a young man, he suffered from constant and

debilitating back pain, but generously insisted that each day after lunch the five of us join him in his private rooms to work on the play. They were wonderful afternoons. 'What part am I auditioning for today,' he would ask, and we would select a part for him and start reading. By the end of the week he had played every character, male and female, coached us in Brooklynese and done impersonations of every Loman family he had ever seen, including the Chinese ones. He was warm, unpretentious and very, very funny.

As well as receiving a crash course in the history, culture and economics of his homeland, we were treated to hilarious tales of his childhood and family, whose colourful, sometimes crazy personas had inspired the characters we were to play. He would tease us about our funny English ways and we would tease him about his great misfortune in being born a Yank. It was like visiting your favourite uncle, an uncle who just happened to be one of the most celebrated and revered men on the planet. On the final afternoon, towards the end of an exhausting session and Arthur hoarse from reading Willy, he dropped his script and, sighing, said, 'I'm bored with this shit.' We all fell about. He looked at me quizzically. 'Actors are amazing,' he said. 'How the hell will you play this guy eight times a week without getting bored?'

I laughed. 'I have my ways,' I said.

'Like what?' he asked.

'As the writer, you really wouldn't want to know,' I replied, 'and besides, that's the sort of thing I'm only allowed to discuss with other actors.' He looked at me sternly for a moment, cocked his head to one side and narrowed his eyes, before allowing a grin to spread across his face, like an uncle who knew he should rebuke a mischievous child, but didn't have the heart.

I had always referred to him as Uncle Arthur, ever since that night in the summer of 1984 when I first saw his image on the cover of *The Crucible*. He bore an uncanny likeness to my Uncle Matt Southern who, despite looking every inch the urbane Harvard professor in photographs, was legendary, even in our family of religious puritans, for his austerity and rigid abstinence. He had had to emigrate to the USA to find a sect of ascetics severe enough for his tastes, thereafter devoting his life to the difficult task of spreading the Gospel and being miserable, in equal measure.

I had been cast in my first Arthur Miller play one Friday evening in 1984, in a Sainsbury's supermarket (the cheese section to be precise), when my agent Pippa Markham was doing a spot of late shopping and crossed trolleys with Joyce Nettles, the casting director from the Royal Shakespeare Company. Rehearsals were due to start the following Monday and they were still looking for an actor to double as John Proctor and Leontes in *The Winter's Tale*, and she was calling me direct from the shop. 'Darling, there's been a monumental fuck-up. Joyce checked your availability weeks ago and was told you were working. Great plays, darling. Great parts. Scripts being biked to you as we speak. Ring me at home when you've read them, whatever the time. Must dash, before the shop shuts.' A couple of hours later *The Crucible* arrived and there was the face of Uncle Matt Southern staring up at me from the back cover. It might have been a bad omen. In fact, it was the beginning of the most exciting theatrical adventure of my career.

One evening as I was leaving rehearsals, Nick Ham who, with Barry Kyle, was directing *The Crucible*, asked me if I'd like to pop over to the National Theatre with him, where Arthur Miller was appearing 'in conversation' with Christopher Bigsby. He was in town to celebrate the publication of his book *Salesman in Beijing*. The tickets were like gold dust but Nick had a spare. Minutes later we were in our seats in the Lyttelton auditorium, transfixed, as Arthur conjured up his adventures in China with the air of a college dean and the timing of a vaudeville clown. After the standing ovation and thunderous applause we retired to the foyer bar, which was a veritable *Who's Who* of British theatre. I bumped into director Bill Brydon, who asked me what I was up to. 'I'm rehearsing John Proctor for the RSC,' I said, 'and this is Nick Ham who's directing.'

'Would you like to meet Arthur?'

'Meet him?'

'I'm looking after him,' he said. 'He's in the hospitality room, come on.'

'But he won't want to be bothered by us,' I protested. He grabbed us both by an arm and began to steer us through the crowd. My God! What the hell did I think I was doing? I was phobic about turning up where I hadn't been invited, and here I was pushing my way past London's glitterati to gatecrash the private party of the greatest living playwright in the English language. Oh well, it would be excruciatingly embarrassing but as my old mum used to say, 'a shy bairn gets nae sweets'.

We headed towards a small room off the foyer. I'd worked at the National but never even heard of the hospitality room. A crowd had gathered at the door and rubbernecked furiously as it opened, hoping to catch a glimpse of the great man, who sat ramrod-backed, hands on knees, like that famous statue of Abraham Lincoln. Smartly dressed figures stood listening to him and sipping champagne. 'Arthur!' Bill called, 'this is Alun Armstrong who's going to be playing John Proctor, and Nick Ham, who's directing for the RSC, that's another of our theatres across the river.'

Arthur smiled. 'Bill, I know what the RSC is. I'm not senile. Come in, fellas.'

A woman sitting next to Arthur, whom I later discovered was his wife, Inge, came over to me and took my arm. 'You sit here, darling,' she said warmly. 'I've heard the old bastard's stories so many times before.' Arthur laughed, stood up, and shook our hands.

'I hope we're not disturbing you,' I stammered.

'Hell no, have some champagne.' He filled the glasses himself and handed them to us, beckoning us to sit next to him. 'So, *The Crucible*, at the . . . Barbican . . . is that what it's called?' We explained that it was just a humble tour and about the cathedrals and the cowshed. 'What, you're going to shout "God is dead" in a cathedral?' he asked incredulously. I nodded a yes. 'Well, that'll be a first,' he said, laughing and holding me by the arm. 'Tell me more.' He seemed intrigued by the idea of the promenade production and wanted to know exactly how different scenes would be staged, all the while refilling our glasses as soon as they were empty. Nick eventually said that he had to go to a production meeting and was already late. I stood up and said I'd better go too, as I had kept him from his guests long enough. 'Sit down,' he said, 'we haven't finished the champagne.'

I lost count of how many bottles we got through, but I stayed for the rest of that evening, hanging on his every word, learning how and why he had written the play and about his hearing before the Committee. He shared hilarious anecdotes with me about his research in Salem and flattered me by listening intently to my yarns about my father, a Durham coalminer, who was also a Methodist preacher, as was my mother. I told him about my childhood in a world not a million miles from Salem, hoping desperately that he'd see in me the makings of a passable Proctor.

Bill and Inge came to say that we had to finish up, we had drunk all the champagne and the theatre was closing. I stood, trying not to fall over, and thanked him for a magical evening. As we shook hands, he said, 'Well, Armstrong, you're going to make a fuck of a Proctor!' Yes! I was right. All those years, soaking up chapel politics, all those sermons; this part could have been written for me.

I laughed nervously. 'How do you know?' I said. 'Maybe I can't act.'

'I don't give a shit,' he roared. 'You've got a peasant's face. I'm sick of seeing this part played by a guy from the corps de ballet.'

Alan Ayckbourn

Playwright: Director of A View from the Bridge at the National Theatre, London, and the Aldwych Theatre in the West End, 1987–8

I first became aware of Arthur Miller's work when I was still at school. A friend and I joined the members-only theatre club at the Comedy Theatre, formed in order to stage banned plays which had, for some reason or other, fallen foul of the Lord Chamberlain. One was Peter Brook's production of *A View from the Bridge*, the memory of which was to remain with me for years. Nearly forty years later, I was asked by Peter Hall, then the Director of the National Theatre, to form a company and choose three plays to run respectively in the National's three auditoria, the Olivier, the Lyttelton and the Cottesloe. It was in the Cottesloe that I chose to direct *A View from the Bridge*. The years of waiting had paid off though my decision was slightly influenced, I confess, when Michael Gambon agreed to be part of that three-repertoire company and to play Eddie Carbone.

Rehearsals, as was often the case when Mike and I worked together, were sporadic and enjoyable. Sporadic because the church hall which the NT had allocated us for rehearsal was so cold that by lunchtime we inevitably chose to knock off early; enjoyable, because we worked, as usual, on the principle that the more tragic the play the more legitimate humour we needed to extract from the piece. Characters you can't laugh with you seldom love. Anyway, the principle seemed to work and by the time Miller arrived to see an early preview the production was already a big success.

I think he was genuinely surprised when he first saw it. For one thing the play was – due to the speed we played it, we cut nothing – a good hour shorter than a previous production Miller had seen in New York. It also inevitably, especially at the start, contained many more laughs. Actually, I was unsure what he made of it at all. Maybe he even disapproved. I sort of sensed he did – when authors tell directors their production is like no other they have seen before, you can't help wondering what they really mean. For instance, I know what I really mean by that because it's a phrase I've used as an author several times in my lifetime to various directors. It means, simply, what the fuck have you done to my play?

Certainly at the dinner the three of us had after that first preview, Mike and I on either side of the great man, Miller talked entertainingly and informatively throughout the meal, though the production was never referred to. I think it took him a second visit, on the press night, to come round completely to our version; not only to come round but to thoroughly endorse it. Maybe the ten-minute standing ovation helped.

After that second press night viewing, the three of us were once again in a restaurant, this time in separate parties, Mike and I at one table, Miller at another. Halfway through the meal the author marched over to us and, seizing Mike's hand and raising it high above his head like a boxing referee, shouted to the room in general, 'The best Eddie, EVER!' That was nice.

William Balcom

Composer: opera of A View from the Bridge with Arnold Weinstein. Also composed stage music for the New Haven/New York premières of Broken Glass

The trouble with so many tributes is that they are often less about The Great Man I Knew and more about The Great Man Who Knew Me. I'll try not to fall into that. All I'll say is that I had the luck to work with Arthur on a couple of occasions and it was an unadulterated joy.

When he, Arnold Weinstein and I worked on our opera built

from *A View from the Bridge*, Miller wasn't, like most writers, holding on to his original with sharp teeth. He was the first to know how an opera libretto must differ from a playscript; some of his suggested parings-down from the play (for that is what you do when you make a libretto; musical text just takes more time than the spoken word) we wouldn't have dared suggest ourselves.

This story is particularly mind-blowing: I needed to add a new aria for Marco, the older of the Sicilian brothers, to show us more of who he was, before the final scene where he is the agent of Eddie Carbone's death. I'd asked Arnold to write the text; nothing like what was needed existed in any version of *A View from the Bridge*. After a few days Arnold asked, 'Will you allow me to ask Arthur to write the aria for Marco?' (Would I allow him!) Arthur wrote the text in three days. I found in my sketches a melody I hadn't known how to use, which pre-dated his new lyric by about three years, and it fitted Arthur's words perfectly.

One winter evening at the Chelsea Hotel in late 1998, after Arnold and I had played the last instalment of *A View* to Arthur and Inge Morath, Arthur showed his pleasure by telling us stories for hours – all kinds of stories. That is what he was after all: a consummate storyteller.

Mark Bazeley

Actor: **Death of a Salesman**, *Lyric Theatre, London, 2005*

Prior to being cast, I had never read *Death of a Salesman* or seen it. I had seen a production of *The Crucible* at drama school and my initial reaction was to be surprised they were written by the same man.

In a world where the soldierly values of loyalty, courage and conviction are increasingly rare, Miller's actions during the 'Reds under the beds' era and his politics in the face of hostility cement his reputation as a true artist who responds to his conscience.

In our rehearsal room, Arthur loomed large. A picture of his face cracking a huge grin was always in the middle of the table. This served as a tonic during the fraught and insecure process of rehearsal.

After a week of working on the play, I thought it to be a beautifully crafted piece but was suspicious of it being 'a bit of a weepy', too saccharine if anything. As we progressed I realised its poetic force, its sense of nature's rhythms beating in the heart of man, the inevitability of death and decay and became fascinated by its operatic dimensions.

Having performed the play in front of an audience, I am convinced it acts as a cathartic experience. People seem to identify directly and sometimes weep for the situation of one particular character, or the family as a whole. Crying makes you peaceful, the dam has burst and the stocks are replenished. It is safer than anger, which I think Miller wants you to feel as well, and certainly less active. Miller was an artist not content with just an emotional response but hungry for change.

As with all great plays, and *Death of a Salesman* surely is one, it seems to resonate as the years go by to each generation who see it. You find yourself as an actor going back to the text many times, forensically trying to unpick the clues to the character and constantly being surprised by what you find.

Familial ties run deep and this play seems to resurrect the unresolved and often painful experiences of the audience. In *Conversations with Miller* by Mel Gussow, Arthur addresses the fact that many people are so emotionally overwhelmed at the end of the play. He expresses his unease at this emotion and suggests that he consciously sought to steer clear of it in his future work. Nevertheless, the emotion is understandable in a play that is about losing and loss.

Elizabeth Bell

*Actor: **A View from the Bridge**, National Theatre, London, and the Aldwych Theatre in the West End, 1987–8*

Arthur Miller was a dish, he was crumpet. This was the most surprising thing about him. In the famous photos with Marilyn Monroe he looked like a thin, slightly stooping academic and one imagined she married him for his brain. Well, I suppose she did, because it was a tremendous brain, but he was also incredibly handsome and sexy. It was of course over twenty-five years later when I met him and maybe he'd muscled up in the meantime, but he was a gorgeous man, like a golden eagle – tall, broad, with golden eyes that stared right into your feeble mind. All this rendered me speechless, so I had very little conversation with him. Anyway, the men monopolised him, all longing to ask about Marilyn, but just well-mannered enough not to; and, too, they were afraid of him because he was so impressive and much taller than nearly all of them. For most of the dinner that we all had together Suzan Sylvester (Catherine) and I talked to his wonderful wife, Inge, and it seemed to me that if he had such a wife he must be as good, as well as talented and wise, as he seemed.

The production was one of those blessed things that come along only very occasionally. It was marvellously directed and Michael Gambon was stunning. Everything and everybody who had anything to do with it seemed to fit. We had no idea it was anything special, so absorbed were we in our world of the play, but audiences were surprisingly (to us) deeply moved, and Arthur Miller liked it as well as any he'd seen. He did say he didn't quite recognise our Brooklyn, but wherever we came from we all came from the same place and he gave us his unqualified approval. This was thrilling. It was an enormous privilege to have met him, and one of my most treasured possessions is a copy of *Timebends* which Arthur Miller signed.

Michael Blakemore

*Director: **All My Sons**, Wyndhams Theatre, 1981; **The Ride Down Mount Morgan**, Wyndhams Theatre, 1991; **After the Fall**, Royal National Theatre, 1990*

Arthur Miller was full of surprises. He first surprised me when I met him in 1981. He'd just flown over for the opening night of *All My Sons* at the Wyndhams Theatre and at the end of a day's rehearsal I set off to his hotel to welcome him to London. Familiar with that impressive head from a hundred photographs, with his reputation for moral courage, it felt a little as if I was about to ascend Mount Rushmore. Instead, I met someone genial, curious and, what was most surprising, shrewd, assessing me the way a businessman might a new colleague. I soon learned that he also liked company and didn't want to waste a night alone with jet lag in a hotel room. 'What's playing at the moment?' he asked, and after a couple of phone calls we were setting off to the Piccadilly Theatre to see *Educating Rita*.

Walking along a London street with Arthur was like keeping company with a film star. Everyone recognised him – some as the great American playwright, others as the husband of Marilyn Monroe – and he accepted this attention with uncomplicated satisfaction. The regard with which he and his work were held in Britain saw him through periods of wounding neglect in his own country. A film crew arriving at his front door to interview him, especially if it was from the BBC, was something he could never resist; and no wonder, because talking well was another of his talents and he enjoyed exercising it. As a very young man he had tried singing in a radio programme and he always retained something of the performer. The singer had become the sage.

Over the next twenty years I directed three more of his plays and we became friends. When we were planning a new production I'd stay with him and his wife, Inge, in Connecticut, and I'd see a great deal of him subsequently in London as the first night approached. Having Arthur in a rehearsal room was a mixed blessing, not because he was in the least difficult, but because he was such a huge presence. He also couldn't keep his mouth shut and rehearsals were often like a tennis tournament as the actors looked first to their left at the director, then to their right at the author, wondering whom they should heed. Nevertheless he once paid me the greatest compliment I've ever had from a playwright: 'The things you say to the actors, they're exactly the things I'm about to say myself.' The trick was to get in quick.

Like most artists Arthur was self-centred, but with a certain size to it which made it something else, almost an innocence. No stranger to self-absorption myself, I sometimes engaged him in a kind of tit-for-tat. He'd give me something to read, so I'd retort by giving him something of mine. His face would drop for a second, but he'd go away with it and often respond with a thoughtful, generous letter. In his local community he'd take on causes and see them through with time-consuming thoroughness. Though first and foremost a writer, you sometimes caught sight of another dimension to him altogether, something practical and resolute like his carpentry, and it was very impressive.

His work was also surprising, never quite what it was assumed to be. Commentators tried to pin him down with unverifiable assertions. You'd read that he had no sense of humour. Yet there is a scene in *The Price* that if played properly is as out-loud funny as a vaudeville sketch. Others said he was trapped in the left-wing humanism of another time. But *After the Fall* dares to suggest that human beings, far from being on the whole good, may on the whole be bad, and that loyalty and love drift remorselessly towards their opposites, betrayal and murderous indifference. The plays he wrote near the end of his career are particular and quirky and defy categorisation.

When Arthur was in his eighties I visited the Millers at their small New York apartment. I was about to catch a plane to London and this was simply a chance to say a brief hello. The time came for me to go. Arthur rose from his chair on stiffening knees, something which, though his junior by several years, I was just beginning to experience myself. He and Inge waited by the open front door as I went towards the elevator. I looked back and realised we all shared an unspoken thought. Would this be the last time? The shows Arthur and I had worked on had slipped into the past. A dustpan and brush had disposed of all that fervour and precarious hope, the sense of being truly alive that theatre people feel mostly through their work. It was tied up in black plastic bags and out the door. Next in line, presumably, were ourselves. Even for Arthur's great reputation there was an open bag waiting. His face expressed all this, but realistically and with acceptance, as if that was the way things were and there wasn't much we could do about it.

Life, however, isn't interested in our tidy conjectures, whether hopeful or full of dread, and I would see them both on many more occasions. Shockingly unexpected was Inge's death, but Arthur would press on as before, writing new plays and seeing them into production. At the end of his life I was amazed to hear that he was in a new relationship with someone much younger. Then one day I read in the paper that he too had died. But I felt I'd already made my farewell to him that day waiting for the elevator, because there was something so perfectly shaped about it, as in a play.

Enoch Brater

Professor of English and Theater, University of Michigan, Ann Arbor, author of Arthur Miller: A Playwright's Life and Works, 2005

More than 1,500 people attended the large public memorial in honor of Arthur Miller held at the Majestic Theatre on West 44th Street in New York on Monday, 9 May 2005. They were lucky to get in: the line for admission in front of the theater, where *The Phantom of the Opera* was still playing, wrapped around Schubert Alley and spilled over past the now renamed Booth Theatre on to West 45th Street. Not everyone could find a seat and some members of the public had to be turned away. There were, of course (as might be expected), any number of A-list personalities in the front rows to witness a dignified ceremony moderated by Miller's long-time friend from Connecticut, the Reverend William Sloane Coffin, Jr. The actresses Marian Seldes, Laura Linney and Lauren Bacall, the novelist Philip Roth, the playwright John Guare, the actors Martin Sheen and Brian Dennehy, and former mayoral candidate Martin Green might have, under other circumstances, attracted the attention of the paparazzi, but on this spring morning the publicity seekers were uncharacteristically respectful and restrained. The carefully choreographed event included rich presentations by Tony Kushner, Edward Albee and George McGovern, as well as moving ones by family members Rebecca, Robert and Ross (Miller's nephew). Daniel Day-Lewis, the playwright's son-in-law, read a passage from a short story full of autobiographical references to Miller's short career as a bakery-goods delivery boy in Brooklyn and Miller's sister, the actress Joan Copeland, performed a Depression-era scene from *The American Clock* featuring the figure of Rose Baum, the stage character based on their mother Gussie. In the background were many black-and-white photographic images, the best of them taken by Inge Morath, documenting a life well spent. Estelle Parsons read Linda Loman's farewell speech to Willy from the famous Requiem in *Death of a Salesman*.

On that morning, however, my sights were set on another, quite different auditorium, some 700 miles away, and a ceremony that took place more than two decades before. In 1981 Miller, on one of his many visits to the University of Michigan, traveled to Ann

Arbor this time to offer the keynote address marking the fiftieth anniversary of the Hopwood Awards. What I remember most about that October day was the flock of undergraduates who rushed to the podium of the Rackham Auditorium immediately following his comments, urging him to autograph dog-eared paperback copies of *Salesman*. Even more so, I remember his winning smile. Here was Miller, class of 1938, enjoying a nostalgic moment in the presence of so much youthful adulation. One student had forgotten to bring a pen; Miller presented her with the gift of his own.

That day marked a turning point in Miller's relationship with the University of Michigan, and of mine with him, though neither of us recognised it at the time. His strong contacts with faculty members like Paul Mueschke, Arno Bader and Erich Walter, who had been so supportive during his formative years as an aspiring student playwright, had long been undone by time. Kenneth Rowe had long ago retired; Miller spent an hour visiting his old professor at his house on 2061 Day Street, but both knew this would be the last time they would meet. It was a long day of many memories and far too many interactions. Miller and Morath quickly accepted the invitation my wife (now Senator Liz Brater) offered to spend a quiet evening with us at our house on Wells Street.

That's how our friendship began, spontaneously and informally, and that's how it would remain over the next twenty-five years.

Miller loathed pretension, especially of the sort easily generated by a visiting celebrity in an academic community. New Yorker to the core, and proud of it, what he liked best was straight talk: the good story well told, combined with a compelling (preferably ironic) anecdote, a winning sense of humor, and a warm, sharp and flexible mind, all of which he displayed in abundance. He could never quite understand my passion for Beckett, and he was even more baffled by any serious interest in experimental theater, which he felt was essentially after a 'minimalist conceit'. I consistently avoided calling him 'Arthur'. But why he insisted on calling me 'Professor' remained a mystery, especially as I was the same age as his two children by Mary Slattery, Jane (b. 1944) and Robert (b. 1947). Only in his very last years, encouraged to do so by his wife Inge Morath, did he feel comfortable calling me by my first name. But by that time we had talked many times, mostly in Ann Arbor, but occasionally in London and New York.

Those conversations took on a new urgency as we began to

formulate plans for 'Arthur Miller's America: Theater and Culture in a Century of Change', the international symposium held in Ann Arbor on the occasion of his eighty-fifth birthday in October 2000. Initially, Morath seemed more excited about this than Miller, and she generously agreed to an exhibit of her photographs 'all about Arthur', which was successfully mounted at the University Museum on South State Street. 'We'll be there,' she said. As things turned out, that visit was not to be – at least not in the flesh. Two weeks before the event Miller fell on a sidewalk in Norwich, in the UK, and cracked three ribs. On his return to his farmhouse on Tophet Road in Roxbury, Connecticut, his doctor told him a journey by air to the Midwest was out of the question. Undaunted, Michigan arranged for a 'live feed' with a local television station: Miller appeared in the Rackham Auditorium once again, this time on three larger-than-life MTV screens.

That remarkable event would never have taken place without the enthusiastic support of Lee Bollinger, now President of Columbia University in New York but at the time Michigan's chief executive officer. Bollinger had the idea that Michigan needed to celebrate what it always did best: as one of America's great public institutions of higher learning, it provided opportunities based on merit, not on legacies, elitism and other corporate connections. Miller, whose family lost (not quite) everything when his father's coat-manufacturing business went bust during the Depression, was a prime example of what Bollinger had in mind. A year before the symposium took place I met with Miller and his son Robert at Inglis House, overlooking the Nichols Arboretum; I told him that as part of the event we would announce the naming of a new theater in his honor. 'Whoever thought,' he wrote a few weeks later, 'when I was saving $500 to come to the University of Michigan, that it would come to this.' The ground-breaking for the Arthur Miller Theater took place on the North Campus on 14 October 2005, three days short of what would have been his ninetieth birthday.

Much of the time I spent in conversation with Arthur Miller concerned our mutual attachments to the University of Michigan, his as alumnus and mine as long-term professor of dramatic literature and theater. I had been teaching his plays to Michigan students since 1975; in fact, the very day he died, 10 February 2005, I was five weeks into a seminar devoted entirely to his life and works. The book based on the 2000 symposium, *Arthur Miller's*

America: Theater and Culture in a Time of Change, had been
published only two weeks before. When the phone call came
announcing his death, I sent a quick e-mail to my students. They
were overwhelmed. They did not know, as I did, that he had been
deathly ill for several weeks.

Miller, who was born in 1915, worked as a ship fitter alongside
my father, one year older, at the Brooklyn Navy Yard during World
War Two. I wanted to know if they ever encountered one another
among the thousands of men and women who kept those ships
afloat. I never found out.

I was proud when Miller accepted me as his 'last official friend' at
the University of Michigan, the 'only one', he said, 'I have left.
Everybody else is dead.' He was proud, on his part, that both of us
were graduates of Abraham Lincoln High School on Ocean Parkway
in Brooklyn, albeit more than thirty years apart. 'You, I'm sure, had
the better record,' he said.

I countered with this: 'That's as may be, but you're the one who
became *Arthur Miller.*' How we both ended up at Michigan, and
how our friendship blossomed there, is quite another story.

Arvin Brown

*Director: A Memory of Two Mondays, Long Wharf Theatre,
1976; A View from the Bridge, Long Wharf Theatre 1981; All
My Sons, Long Wharf Theatre, 1987*

My experience directing an Arthur Miller play came with my
production of his brilliant one-act *A Memory of Two Mondays* on a
double bill in New York with Tennessee Williams's *27 Wagons Full
of Cotton.* Because of the supposed rivalry between America's two
most important living playwrights (a rivalry lovingly created by the
press), it was decided that Arthur and Tennessee would not attend
the opening night together. Arthur would come to the final dress
rehearsal and Tennessee would tackle the first night.

I was, of course, a nervous wreck before that final dress,
wondering how Arthur would respond to my work on a play very
dear to his heart. About an hour before Arthur's arrival the actress
understudying Meryl Streep in both plays came up to me to get my

permission to ask Arthur if he would draw a frog. It seemed that she had a collection of frogs drawn by the celebrities she happened to encounter. Trying to hold myself together, I suggested there might be a better time and place than the rehearsal that I felt would determine my fate in the theatre. Off she went, in came Arthur and the rehearsal began.

It could not have gone more perfectly. Arthur was misty-eyed, remembering his youth in the auto-parts warehouse that serves as the setting for the play, and very complimentary about all the actors and, to my great relief, the direction. Before the glow had even begun to fade, and just moments after we all said goodbye to the great man, the understudy came up to me and proudly thrust a sheet of paper in my face. It was a drawing of a strange, ugly little creature and signed by Arthur Miller. 'One of my best frogs,' she said.

The next night was the opening, with Tennessee and a small entourage in attendance. *27 Wagons Full of Cotton* was first on the bill, with Meryl Streep giving what was to be a Tony-nominated performance. Tennessee couldn't contain his excitement. 'That girl is superb, unbelievable – I have to meet her after the show.' So I waited for Tennessee backstage when the curtain came down on *A Memory* . . . to introduce him to the cast, excited because he had told me at intermission how much he loved them all and how happy he was with the production of . . . *Wagons*. He never appeared.

Early the next morning Tennessee's agent, who had been with him the night before, called to tell me that indeed Tennessee had thought the evening a great success and was headed backstage when a very large woman confronted him in the lobby, muttering something about a frog. Tennessee ran for his limousine and now was sending me his heartfelt apologies that a madwoman had kept him from a meeting with Meryl.

In the years after, as my career seemed more and more dedicated to the plays of Arthur Miller, I would often think back on that fateful dress rehearsal. I'm very proud to have devoted so much of my theatre career to the work of a man who never shied away from drawing the ugly little frogs of the world just as he saw them, but always with compassion and always with the utmost respect for the pain and resilience of the human condition.

David Burke

When the famous pass on and their obits appear, you find yourself searching for a moment when you might have crossed their path. As a four-year-old I waved a tiny flag as George VI was driven through the streets of Liverpool. Churchill came to a Shakespeare play I was in. Einstein I never met. Arthur Miller I did. I can offer no new insights into his plays, just a couple of shared moments, tourist snaps kept by me.

I first encountered the power of Miller's words as a young actor in Richard Eyre's production of *The Crucible* circa 1970. Those words moved me like nothing I have encountered before or since. They felt totally personal: a catalyst for all the pent-up emotions I had gathered during my childhood and adolescent years. So, when years later I met the man himself it was like coming face to face with my father confessor. He came to London for the opening of the National production of *The Crucible*, and sat in on some of the rehearsals. It felt a bit like doing *Hamlet* with Shakespeare in the stalls.

There were a couple of sessions where we sat in a circle and he answered our questions. What did he say? Alas, I can't remember. I didn't write it down, and no one had the forethought to bring a tape recorder. I recall a handsome man with very long legs talking to us about his life in a voice rich in experience.

One moment does sit up from those informal seminars. Tom Wilkinson (who is the sort of person brave enough to tell the Holy Ghost to pull himself together) suddenly said, 'Arthur, next time you publish this play, if I were you I'd leave out all those stage directions. They go on too long.' I think my mouth fell open. The printed notes he was referring to are Arthur Miller's summary of the historical background to the play. He writes in detail about Salem, John Proctor, Giles Corey, etc. For me as an actor preparing a part they were invaluable ammunition, both on that occasion when I was playing Hale and years before as Proctor. That text was my bible and here was a wild heretic proposing to destroy it. Miller must have caught the look on my face for, without looking in the least put out, he nodded in my direction and said, 'What do you think?' I stuttered my defence of the stage directions and he smiled his thanks, leaving me proud to have shared this fleeting alliance.

Some days later I found myself sharing a bench with him in the foyer of the theatre. Just the two of us. I was paralysed with shyness. He, on the other hand, appeared relaxed and happy to be quiet. At last I could bear the silence no longer. 'You once wrote me a fan letter,' I said.

He turned very slowly to look at me. 'Really?' was all he said, but there was no mistaking the polite incredulity in his eyes. At that moment someone approached and he was called away. We never spoke again.

I was left feeling foolish. I had had no time to explain. I had not been fantasising. He had written me a letter. Some years earlier I had acted in James Saunders's *Bodies*. Miller had come to see it and, much to my delight and astonishment, had written me a very flattering letter on Savoy Hotel notepaper. I still have it.

So that's it. Two snapshots. One smiling thanks. The other in retreat looking embarrassed. Me the stranger with a camera. Thanks, Mr Miller.

William Sloane Coffin, Jr.

Former Chaplain of Yale University

Remarks delivered at the funeral of Arthur Miller: Roxbury, Connecticut

I'm Bill Coffin, a sort of 'spiritual MC' for this occasion. Clearly it is right that all of us should gather here together this afternoon. To borrow a line from Edna St Vincent Millay: 'His absence is everywhere present.' During the last two weeks all of us have wept, some of us profusely, and that's good. As Melville reminds us, rainbows don't visit the clear air, they irradiate vapour. Yet all the while I was grieving I thought of what I said three years ago this very month of Inge: Arthur too would not wish to be held close by grief. And actually, I see him best when I grieve him least.

I see him as a genius writing plays and all manner of other things across seven decades. I see him vividly, dressed to the nines, at the fiftieth anniversary of *Death of a Salesman*. In the whole theater that night there were only two men without black ties – myself and Tom Doyle [Arthur Miller's son-in-law]. Before the curtain went up, I wandered over to ask Tom if he felt underdressed. 'Yeah,' he replied, 'but look at Arthur (at that moment charming Lauren Bacall); no matter what he's wearing he looks as if he had gotten dressed in a hardware store.'

That's really how I see Arthur best – in blue jeans and boots because, for all his being a giant of a man, like the rainbow, an overarching presence, he was wonderfully down to earth, wonderful company. So, like many of you, I see him best at the house, in his studio, at the workbench, by the pond, always with Inge, earlier with Titi [Inge's mother] too, and Nina and Bella, the two big dogs, and with that slip of a kid still to become the radiant wife and mother, painter and writer and movie maker Rebecca is today.

In the spring of 1976 I arrived for a weekend and as Arthur loved to relate, 'six months later he was still here'. I remember at breakfast, that first morning, Inge complaining, 'Arthur, the coffee pot is leaking.'

Says Arthur to me, 'Willie, do you know how long I've had that coffee pot?'

'No, but I'm sure I'm about to find out, after which I suggest we go to the shop where you can show me how beautifully you solder.'

Inge shot me a grateful look. At the workbench Arthur comments, 'The trouble with you, Willie, you don't live in touch with your environment.'

The next morning Inge announces, 'The coffee pot is not leaking.'

Says Arthur to me, 'Do you know how long that coffee pot will last?'

'Arthur,' I said, 'you're making a tight-fisted Scot look like a big spender. But you're also making me understand your great writing gift of putting an abundance of wisdom in an economy of words.'

Mornings were for writing. In the afternoon he and I planted potatoes and tomatoes. Actually, I did most of the work while Arthur lectured me on Archimedean principles. Dinner time, we gathered, often with some of you, to praise Titi's goulash and to listen to Arthur say, for example, how people are forever attributing informed wisdom to power, whereas wilful ignorance might be closer to the truth. From him I learned that all wise people think tragically because tragedy teaches us less to indict than to reflect.

I knew Arthur for forty wonderful years and never, in all changes of fortune and down to the gates of death, did I see a lifeless expression in his eyes. For such a spirit I'm so grateful and grateful too for the special care he received from Agnes [Barley]. Grief and gratitude don't compete; they are lifelong companions – 'Joy and woe are woven fine.' So while mourning its passing, let's remember Arthur's incredible life. This hour will be a healing time for all of us.

In the hospital a few days before he died, I said to Arthur, 'You may think you're headed for nowhere, but I'm better informed than you. There's a distinguished chair awaiting you. It's for God's favourite atheists. Your heavenly assignment will be to keep the Christians honest.'

Arthur, like Inge, is now in a good place and for us who remain there is a good prayer: 'O Lord, support us all the day long, until the shadows lengthen and the evening comes, and the busy world is hushed, and the fever of life is over, and our work is done. Then in thy mercy grant us a safe lodging, and a holy rest and peace at the last.'

Arthur Miller tribute – Majestic Theatre, 9 May 2005

It was in Roxbury, Connecticut, during the Vietnam War, supper was over but the guests were still sitting around the table. His feet were somewhere off the ground and he was picking his teeth. Later I asked Inge how an Austrian of her refined tastes could possibly fall for Arthur. Without hesitation, she replied, 'It was his integrity of mind.'

I fell for Arthur for the same reason as I'm sure many of you did too. He loved the countryside and the human species if only we would stop killing each other. It impressed him that the first murder in the Bible was a fratricide. He knew so much about the power of evil, and the evil of power, and especially about our own complicity in the very evils we abhor. He carried on a lover's quarrel with the world, writing once, 'I could not imagine a theater worth my time that did not want to change the world.'

In the literary woods, he was a sequoia. Nadine Gordimer claimed, 'You don't become a better person because you are a splendid writer.' Still, there is a transforming power in splendid words and I believe Arthur's own words helped make him such a friend to so many of us. He was brilliant, so funny, and, upon occasion, strangely tender. I loved him for forty years so today, in the words of Edna St Vincent Millay, 'His absence is everywhere present.'

But 'joy and woe are woven fine'. Grief and gratitude are not opposites, they are constant companions. So let's let them freely mingle in this hour, as we remember a brother, father, mentor, friend, a lovable and great man, Arthur Miller.

Tom Cole

Writer (who lives now in the house where Arthur Miller wrote **Death of a Salesman** *and* **The Crucible***)*

A man as great and celebrated as this one always threatens to disappear into his own legend, while we fiercely try to hold on to the man himself through an image or two, or the sound of his voice, remembered.

I knew Arthur Miller as a companion in the New England countryside for almost thirty years. In the last decade or so we were close neighbors, just down the road in Roxbury where I could always count on finding him, if he wasn't in London or Beijing – the dearest of friends, a keen listener, an addict of jokes and sports and (especially) of absurd human behavior, and vegetables dug up from the garden, and making things by hand, including a better bird feeder to combat the squirrels (Emerson would approve), and an elliptical Olympian dinner table, which he also designed and to which all the civilised world seemed to beat a path to enjoy Inge Morath's dinners and to trade stories, both tragic and comic. Arthur never seemed to run out of stories and we always assumed, blithely, that he never would.

The public Arthur Miller, whom I knew chiefly through photographs and above all from Inge's amazing gallery of black-and-white portraits taken over the forty-five years that they knew each other, beginning with the time of *The Misfits*, engaged with Russia, China, Greece, Italy, Washington DC and in ideas and theater everywhere, with Ilya Ehrenburg, Elia Kazan, Pablo Neruda, Saul

Steinberg, John Huston, Ralph Ellison, Bella Akhmadulina, John Steinbeck, Ying Ruocheng, etc. This man seems to my eye always moving forward behind his ship's prow of a profile, leaning into the wind of controversy, considering, weighing, assessing, accepting that it may well be his responsibility, yet again, to express some distilled essence of this moment either on our stage or in the heat of journalistic debates, to the extent that we still have them.

But the private man, the one I was lucky enough to know, close to his beloved earth at home in Roxbury, Connecticut, always seemed to find a curious repose, as if the tall, restless athlete's body became restored and whole, like Antaeus, the moment his feet touched that ground. Whether quiet at his writing desk, or with a baby daughter on his lap, or laboring on his tractor or with shovel or carpentry tools or his own hands, he was a man who seemed always able to find rest there, physically and metaphorically.

After some of the most painful public chapters in his political/marital/movie/theatrical fields of combat, it was here on these grounds that Miller and Morath forty years ago began their new life by planting together, day after day, perhaps a thousand young trees. That was an image I did not see and yet I find it often in my mind. Those seedlings of 1962 became a kind of enchanted forest through which Arthur loved to stroll almost to the very end, in 2004; he loved the thought, as Chekhov did, of planting his own trees that would long outlast him.

Another image springs to mind, this one more recent (June 1999), produced not by memory but by the pen of our great theatrical caricaturist, Hirshfeld. On the front page of the *New York Times* Sunday Arts supplement, anticipating the 'Tony' Awards for the century's last Broadway season, sprawled a grand cartoon of all the season's dramatic playwrights centering on our twentieth-century triumvirate – Eugene O'Neill, Tennessee Williams, Arthur Miller – each of whom unaccountably had a serious revival running that season in Broadway theater. Miller's *Death of a Salesman*, of course, walked off with all the honors exactly *fifty years* after its tumultuous opening season, which changed the scope of American theater for ever. The cartoon's panorama is built around a triangle of Arthur and O'Neill and Williams, the latter two already long gone, alas, from earth and so watching from the sky, O'Neill glowering like a thunder cloud and Tennessee Williams finally at ease again, reclining in nebulous comfort with long cigarette holder and sunglasses. But down below, at the apex of the inverted triangle, very solidly on the ground, or at least pavement, amid all the furore of living playwrights one or two generations younger, stands Arthur. He, indeed, looks younger and springier than his eighty-four years and he has a rather devilish private smile spreading across his face.

Why is he smiling? Because he was still alive and kicking to enjoy all this? Because he had as many *new* plays the past few seasons as any of the other young writers in London and New York? Plausible, but wrong. No, Miller is smiling because he is thinking of a story. When a story dawned upon Arthur's mind, either in the telling or the hearing – for gladly would he tell and gladly listen – first his eyes lit up and then the smile of wicked anticipation would spread, then the eyes crinkled with the internal deliciousness of the tale and would virtually disappear: a wine taster at a moment of ecstasy. This is what Hirshfeld caricatured, gleefully – that image, that moment of incipient internal mirth that meant some kind of story was brewing, no doubt concerning human folly in one form or another, and it would enter the capacious Miller repertoire and never be forgotten and, again like great wine, just get better with age.

Of course, *Death of a Salesman*, *The Crucible* and so many of his other plays are first and foremost stories, of human destiny, that can play almost anywhere in the world and seem peculiarly local in their significance.

I had to move to California for a while in the 1990s, which proved to be another lucky stroke in our friendship as Arthur wrote letters that I could hold on to for ever, with the sound of his voice wonderfully built in – a tone of ironic bemusement and at times a startling modesty that I think the world seldom heard. And of course the most delightful zingers. On 12 November 1995 he thanked God that he only had to turn eighty once. He'd had four parties, two in England at the National Theatre and the University of East Anglia, one at home and one in the Town Hall. 'I have run out of virtues and may now return to my sins.' He found the Town Hall thing especially touching, he said, 'because American writers so rarely have anything good to say about one another, at least while alive'.

On 6 April 1997 he announced that he was returning to a play he'd turned away from months ago – and in fact there was another one stacked up behind it which he'd also abandoned and was suddenly crying out for his 'ministrations' again. 'Why do I, at eighty-one, take time to do this? I have no idea. I could be anywhere watching the girls go by.'

On 16 March 1994 he was responding to something I had said about the year 1938. He pointed out that 1938 was also the year of his graduation from the U of Michigan, the year of the *Anschluss*, and the year he rented a room on 74th Street between Madison and Fifth for five dollars a week. He spoke of Time as the mystery with which he could not deal. 'I started writing plays in 1935, almost sixty years ago, *and I still don't know how to do it!*'

It's the '*I still don't know how to do it*' which fascinates. A cry of honest humility, or modesty, in a man who certainly knows his worth and the power of his celebrity. The truth underlying this apparent paradox comes, I believe, from the 'handmade' quality of his life and work, and the standards implied therein. Theater is 'handmade' and always has been – certainly through the time of Miller's rich career. An imagined action comes from the hand of a playwright, and a place to house it is built by the hands of craftsmen, in rather medieval fashion. Anyone so deeply involved as Miller is with the work of hands knows it is never good enough, it *can always be made better*. A different design, a better finish always beckons around the next corner. It is a source of genuine humility, or modesty, tested by facts, and for the most part denied to clerks and intellectuals. When Miller moved to the country to hammer together the elusive ideas for *Death of a Salesman*, he felt driven first to build a shack, by hand – floor, walls, windows, roof – to write in, and only then did Willy Loman walk in, mystically alive: 'It's all right. I came back.' Half a century later the play still stands and so does the shack, although Arthur liked to point out to me that he should have put two-by-sixes in the floor instead of two-by-fours and he's lucky the whole thing didn't fall through.

This paradox of pride and modesty is only one of a number that made up this paradoxical man: like the striking extremes of public and private in his geography. Born in Harlem, raised in Brooklyn, rampant on Broadway, immersed in Manhattan's fierce ideological debates of the 1930s, Miller would seem the quintessential New Yorker – and yet he has been a deeply rooted countryman, in Roxbury, since 1948.

And was he really, as the world thinks, *The Man Who Had All the Luck*? This was the title of his first (and misunderstood) Broadway play, revived only after a half-century, whose biblical themes of father/son and brother/brother, and the poetic, playful vision on subjects like baseball and the business of mink farming foretold certain dreamlike aspects of *Death of a Salesman*. Is the title prophetic? Miller could well be seen as the Luckiest Man in America, in achievement, fame, the women he married, his longevity, his independence . . . and yet to study his face as I knew it or in Inge Morath's long gallery of pensive portraits is to see, paradoxically, a Man of Sorrows. Of course he has had to bear personal grief, family break-ups, the ravages of illness, years of attacks upon himself from the political Right and avant-garde Left; but, beyond that, I believe the sorrow that shows through is the sign of his rage and misery at the horrendous oppressions and injustices of the century he lived through – our century of Franco, Hitler, Stalin, Mussolini, and Joseph McCarthy and J. Edgar Hoover, and Pol Pot, and Milosevich. Arthur Miller was one who felt these grotesque human tragedies not only in his heart but in his nerves, his bones. It is part of what made him a necessary playwright.

And yet, again . . . the mere mention of certain men like Nelson Mandela (whom he knew, of course) or Václav Havel, would make the corners of his eyes light up. It was their clear-headed stubbornness in standing so long and so well against oppression that ignited both the light in his eyes and a better story in his head.

Arthur himself was a stubborn man. I once asked him how he kept his extensive lands in such good shape, and did he have any suggestions for the rest of us? He answered, after a pause, 'Good equipment.' Well, yes, of course, he always loved tinkering with tractors and old jeeps, proud of keeping those engines going. But pondering on this parable, I've come to think that this 'good equipment' was actually within himself, his insides, a patient durability, a clear lasting power. He may have been gifted with it from birth but was also willing and able to tinker with it for ever, so that he could be hit with the sharpest blows and still come out standing. And that is the way I will think of him, always: on his feet, on the earth, with that smile just beginning, which means a story is about to happen.

Brian Cox

Actor; director: **The Crucible,** *Moscow Art Theatre*

The association with the 'great American Play' was very much a double-edged sword for Arthur Miller. And I believe like all great writers, particularly of the twentieth century, his other writings suffered detrimentally at the expense of his more so-called classical plays. An example would be his 'self-ironic' late comedy *The Ride Down Mount Morgan*, which I believe needs some serious reappraisal.

The subject is bigamy, of which there are very few significant examples in dramatic literature. In fact, I can't think of one, apart from perhaps some minor examples in late nineteenth- and early twentieth-century boulevard farce. But it doesn't immediately spring to mind as a subject that attracts such Ibsenesque themes as Man, the rootless wanderer; the pursuit of the sacred and profane; innocence and guilt and the destructive nature of veracity.

The Ibsen analogy can be taken even further. *Mount Morgan* is very much in step with the late great plays of the Norwegian bard, *The Master Builder, John Gabriel Borkman* and *When We Dead Awaken*, and the hero Lyman Felt is very much a distant cousin of Solness, Borkman and the sculptor Rubek. In Miller's play, Felt is bedridden in hospital, under the care of Nurse Logan who is black. He is recovering from a bad car accident, a result of his ride down Mount Morgan. Lyman, we soon discover, is a bigamist, and both of his wives, Theo and Leah, turn up, each unaware, until now, that the other existed. Refusing to accept that he has done anything really wrong, Lyman tries to salvage the situation and keep them both happy. He largely fails in this attempt, as he is perceived to be selfishly motivated, something his daughter, Bessie, tries to teach him. He ends the play alone; even his lawyer and admiring friend Tom cannot continue to support his actions.

Miller was in his late seventies when he wrote the play. And again in keeping with a late play, as with Ibsen, his style is suggestive and metaphorical. Arthur described the play as being the closest he came to writing a work of an autobiographical nature. Now as far as we know Miller was not a bigamist! So what did he mean by that? Clearly the themes of the play were the themes from Arthur's life.

At one point, early in the first act, when Lyman is about to marry wife number two, Leah, he says to her, 'Feeling is all I really believe in, Leah . . . Feeling is chaos, but any decent thing I've ever done was out of feeling, and every lousy thing I'm ashamed of came from careful thinking.' A struggle, between the intuitive and the intellectual! For Arthur, clearly this was a lifelong struggle: the successful younger writer, caught like a deer in the headlights of his own lust, with the most sensuous 'arm candy' a quietly libidinous fellow could ever hope for; caught in the glare of the world's media as he contemplates his own metamorphosis. Oh! the joy of feeling and the despair of having to think about it. The veteran playwright had a huge reservoir to tap into, which continued till his last breath.

Lyman's ride down Mount Morgan. Is it a suicide attempt? A cry for attention? Or a means to an end, where the dramatis personae can gather, in the debating chamber of Lyman's hospital room, to wrangle over the nature of truth? Again, as Lyman says to his partners in his summation, 'The truth is terrible! It's terrible because it's embarrassing but the truth is always embarrassing or it isn't the truth!'

Truth was Miller's yardstick, the moralist's prime tool in his theatrical armoury. At times it became a stick to beat his own back, particularly during the unfashionable period of his career, when his despair with Broadway exacerbated his need to maintain principle in the face of theatrical apathy.

As with Ibsen, the monogamy debate rears its head, the sticking point for many a sweet old-fashioned heterosexual moral classicist. Ibsen, the nineteenth-century playwright, is inferential and downright obtuse. Miller, the twentieth-century writer, is much more prosaic. At the point in the play where he decides to marry wife number two, Leah, Lyman takes his first family – wife number one, Theo, and their daughter Bessie – on safari in Africa. They are watching a pride of lions.

BESSIE   Daddy! Why do you look so sad?
LYMAN   Just thinking. (*To his wife Theo.*) About monogamy – why do you suppose we think of it as a higher form of life?
   (*Defensively.*) . . . I mean I was just wondering.
THEO   Well, it implies an intensification of love.
LYMAN   But how does that make it a higher form?

THEO   Monogamy strengthens the family; random screwing undermines it.

LYMAN   But as one neurotic to another, what's so good about strengthening the family?

THEO   Well, for one thing it enhances liberty.

BESSIE   Liberty? Really?

THEO   The family disciplines its members; when the family is weak the state has to move in; so the stronger the family the fewer the police. And that is why monogamy is a higher form.

LYMAN   Jesus, did you just make that up?

In all the late plays of both writers, the women come in pairs: Aline and Hilda in *The Master Builder*; Ella and Gunhild in *Borkman*; Irene and Maja in *When We Dead*. And in Miller's *Mount Morgan* Theo and Leah. The female characters embody the organic nature in all these plays. And usually, *Borkman* aside, one is older, and one younger.

The genesis of *Mount Morgan* began some twenty-seven years earlier. In 1964 Miller's autobiographical play *After the Fall* was produced at the Lincoln Center in New York and the progenitors of Theo and Leah first appeared in the form of Louise and Maggie. Though *After the Fall*, like *Mount Morgan*, is a dream play, it is ambitious and tangential in its nature, and its themes are myriad and diffuse, deliberately creating a much more fractured construct, provocative to its audience. As a result the balance of the play lies very much in the direction of the childlike Maggie. The consequence of this is to isolate the character of Quentin (Miller's alter-ego in the play), who already exists in a state of withdrawn isolation. And again this is clearly a deliberate choice of Arthur's. I would I contend it is a choice founded in guilt.

Which brings us to *Mount Morgan*, twenty-seven years later. The now older, maturer playwright revisits once well-trodden territory. But now he hews the ground focusing on an essential yield; allowing growth for his protagonists. Maggie transmutes into Leah, a sensual, self-sufficient careerist and closet anarchist, a woman seemingly in charge of her own destiny, and, like Lyman, Jewish.

LYMAN   You know? I have never before with a Jewish girl.

LEAH   Well, you're my first Albanian.

LYMAN   There's something venerable in your eyes. Not old–
ancient. Like our people.

Lyman's kindred spirit, Louise, has now become Theo, the
quintessential WASP, principled, motherly, noble, idealistic and
courageous.

THEO   There was a strange interview some years back with Isaac
Bashevis Singer, the novelist? The interviewer was a woman
whose husband left her for another woman, and she couldn't
understand why. And Singer said, 'Maybe he liked her hole
better.' I was shocked at the time, really outraged – you know that
he had gotten a Nobel; but now I think it was courageous to say
that, because it is probably true. Courage . . . courage and
directness are always the main thing!

Quentin, the humourless passive-aggressive lawyer, flowers into
Lyman Felt, poet-turned-businessman, passionate in his pursuit of
his own humanity, with a fine degree of self-irony; and a
determination to assuage his guilt. In the earlier play Miller's own
guilt pulverises his central protagonist to an apathetic standstill. In the
latter, Miller takes the guilt of his younger self and consciously trails it
like a weed through fertile ground. To surprising comic effect.
     Lyman stands before the window of wife number one, Theo. He
stares at the departing figure of wife number two, Leah.

LYMAN   Why is it, the happier Leah is the sadder I get. It's this
damned objectivity! – Why can't I just dive in and swim in my
happiness!

Now he looks up at Theo, and his heart sinks before he leaps up
with violent determination 'Idiot! – love her! Now she can't deprive
you any more let love flow to your wise and wonderful wife!' He
rushes towards Theo, but then turns away in terror, walking around
in a circle and blowing air and covering his face. 'Guilt, burn in
hell!'
     As with all of his Ibsen cousins, Lyman's guilt clearly masks a
much deeper fear that can only come from the procrastinating spirit
of an elderly writer, something both Ibsen and Miller clearly
understood, and with which Arthur, in his twilight hour, visibly

43

danced a sensual jig. Just as he is about to ask Theo for a divorce, Lyman, in a moment of total blockage, suddenly lets out a giant howl to the heavens. He comes face to face with his own truth.

LYMAN   No! I know what's wrong with me – I could never stand still for death! Which you have got to do by a certain age, or be ridiculous – you've got stand there nobly and serene and let death run his tape out your arms and around your belly and up your crotch until he has got you fitted for that last black suit. And I can't! I won't . . .
    So I'm left wrestling with this anachronistic energy, which . . . crying out to the world God has charged me with and I will use it till the dirt is shoveled into my mouth! Life! Life! Fuck Death and dying.

The final autobiographical note, which rings loud and clear and true, is Arthur's yearning for the simplicity that prevailed throughout his life, a longing which, I suspect, caused him great pain. It was as though the burden of his morality maybe, just maybe, secretly seemed somewhat bogus.
    Lyman, in one of the early scenes with his lawyer, Tom, is drawn by the memory of his father.

LYMAN   I keep thinking of my father – how connected he was to his life; couldn't wait to open the store every morning and happily count the pickles, rearrange the olive barrels. People like that knew the main thing. Which is what? What is the main thing do you know?

Throughout his work Arthur Miller was fuelled by his sense of disconnectedness and a desire to discover that ever-elusive 'main thing'. In the dying moments of the play Lyman is alone with his black Canadian nurse, Logan. At the beginning of the play she mentions that she often goes ice fishing with her family. Lyman asks her what they talk about when they are out on the ice. She tells him that recently they have been talking about the big Knapp Shoe Outlet, where they buy seconds that you can't tell old from new. She exits. Lyman is alone.

LYMAN (*painful wonder and longing in his face his eyes wide alive*)

44

... What a miracle everything is! Absolutely everything! ...
Imagine ... three of them sitting out there on that Lake, talking
about their shoes! (*He begins to weep, but catches himself.*) Now
learn loneliness. But cheerfully. Because you earned it, kid, all by
yourself. Yes. You have found Lyman at last! So .... cheer up!

Howard Davies

*Director: **The Crucible; All My Sons**, Royal National Theatre,
2000*

I first met Arthur in his New York apartment, which was too small
for such a big man. He really had no need to see me – there had
been countless productions of *The Crucible* – but I got the sense that
he would give of his time generously to whomever asked for his
help. The chair I sat in had been made by him and was wonderfully
crafted, with no ostensible stylistic flourish. His plays are like his
furniture; and the man I met was clearly the author of both. I spent
two hours with him drinking his appalling coffee and wondering
how a man with such a large frame and a head like an American
eagle could be so delicate in his thinking. He also made me laugh a
lot. And that surprised me because the rich vein of irony in his work
surfaces at times when the plays are at their darkest.

I was five weeks into rehearsals for *The Crucible* when Arthur
turned up in London. He came for Sunday lunch; and later I
watched him play in the garden with my two young daughters. He
had introduced himself to them as Arthur – and the man called
Arthur was a big hit. He took them very seriously and played very
hard, making no apparent concessions to their age. He was much the
same when he came to address the cast. Tom Wilkinson and Zoë
Wanamaker, who played the Proctors, were near silent with awe.
But some of the younger members of the company were bemused by
the paradoxes of his writing – the heroism of the weak, or the
impossibility of moral certitude – and questioned him at length.
Direct answers were asked for, but he never gave any. Always ready
to contextualise a question, he managed to engender a debate with
every response he gave. We were deeply impressed.

Some years later I tackled *All My Sons*, a play that many

academics and critics have found wanting. Too like Ibsen, too Greek – by which I assume they mean that you can see it coming, and that the politics of the piece overwhelms the characterisation. That wasn't my experience. As with *The Crucible* I had a wonderful cast – Julie Walters, Jimmy Hazeldine, Ben Daniels – and we set about creating a family in crisis. None of Arthur's characters in this play is very special. In the so-called real world they would not command our attention and some of them are not even very likeable. But night after night the audience sobbed audibly as the play finished. They had watched a tragedy born of human failing – indeed, more than that: born of criminality. For the audience to be so involved and so shaken by the breaking of ties of love and loyalty, by the failure to place morality above self-interest, meant that the writing had poked an insistent finger into our hearts and into the core of our humanity.

Arthur, without my knowing, came to see the production. He wrote me a letter on a very old typewriter with a lot of crossings-out and corrections in pencil. Thankfully, he was very complimentary. But he spent much of his letter analysing his play as if it was new to him, as if it had been written by someone else. His analysis was fearsome, and unforgiving. I was amazed – he was still in the process of teaching himself what to write and how to write it. His eagle intelligence was engaged, after all those years as the leading dramatist of his generation, in an act of pitiless self-scrutiny.

Brian Dennehy

*Actor: **Death of a Salesman**, Goodman Theatre, 1998; Broadhurst Theatre, New York, 1999*

Salesman was written in 1948, at a time when America was literally at the apogee of its self-regard. We felt we had won the war and not only that. We had come out of it unscathed. Of course, we had casualties, but the main contribution was our economy, which was now a huge, deep, wealth-producing machine. In that context of self-congratulation and success, here come a couple of voices saying that the American system does not work – one was O'Neill in *The Iceman Cometh* and the other was Arthur Miller with *Death of a Salesman*. I thought this was very brave, and it was also pretty brave for the American audience to accept it the way they did, and to understand it and to take it to their hearts.

It is about a man whose nose is pressed up against the window of the American dream. He sees it happening on the other side of that window. He understands that he should have been invited to the party but for some reason never did get invited. He fails to realise that he is a success. He has worked hard all his life. He has bought his house. But he doesn't see it that way because he hasn't had the huge success that America expects. America is a system of winners and losers, and the winners do well and the losers feel like losers. Willy is a loser and cannot bear that knowledge. He keeps pushing that knowledge of himself away. And he keeps selling this bogus American dream to his sons.

The play continues to be performed because people around the world understand and recognise the relationship between Willy and Biff – the huge expectations that he places on Biff, the sense that with a golden childhood he is bound to have a golden future, that all that is required is a little personality, a joke, a smile. It turns out that though this is an American story, those failed expectations, those failed attempts at life, the failure of the family and its communication are universal. Willy disappoints Biff. He cannot live the life his father thinks he should. That relationship has touched a chord around the world that resonates fifty years later. It is powerful and profound.

I don't think it makes the slightest difference whether the part of Willy is played by a small man or a large one. Chinese actors have played him, young actors, old actors, black actors. It has been played in virtually every country in the world. It is not about that. For my part, though, I have to play him in a certain way. I play him as a man who has been large and expansive, and who has used his size and his big, booming happy salesman's voice to dominate his home and to some extent his clients. Now his mental health is uncertain, his physical health is uncertain. His confidence is waning. He is terrified that Biff has come home to force some kind of confrontation. All of his powers are draining away. And there is something really sad about a big, strong, capable man who is no longer any of these things. That is the way I play him. Dustin Hoffman was great in what he did, a small guy, fussy, whose fussiness is part of his neurosis. To me, though, he is a big guy who loses everything.

47

When I was doing *Salesman* in New York I had a little episode
with my health. My blood pressure spiked and I went to the
hospital. They gave me drugs and lowered my blood pressure. I was
resting in the hospital, in a quiet room, when I heard a disturbance
in the hallway. The door opened and there was this guy standing
there, in a suit, with an attaché case, whom I had known twenty
years before. I said, 'How are you?' through the tubes in my nose.

He said, 'How are you feeling?'

I said, 'Well, considering that I've got tubes in my nose and my
arms I feel pretty good.'

He said, 'I heard about it on the radio.'

I said, 'Well, thank you, but I'm not supposed to have any
visitors, but thank you for coming.'

He said, 'Yes, well, I just wanted to let you know about this great
investment opportunity. This is probably not a good time to talk to
you about it but what I want to do is leave this stuff and when you
get a chance, look at the material and give me a call.'

Then he leaves and I turn to my wife and say, 'It's Willy Loman.
The guy is a sensational salesman!'

Joe Dowling

*Former Artistic Director of the Abbey Theatre in Dublin and
founder of the Gaiety School of Acting in that city. He is currently
Artistic Director, Guthrie Theater, Minneapolis*

'Mr Miller, as a student of gerontology, I would like to know to
what do you ascribe your remarkable longevity.' The voice came
from the back of the Guthrie Theater, where Arthur was fielding
questions after a ninety-minute public conversation I had conducted
with him.

Arthur paused, ruminated for about ten seconds and then replied
in that characteristic throaty drawl, 'I've eaten a lot of Hot Dogs!'
The roar of approval was genuine and extended as the unexpected
answer struck home with the capacity audience. Once again, and
with typical humour, Arthur Miller had undercut pomposity and
avoided pretension. During the course of that session, which
followed the world première of his play *Resurrection Blues* in 2002,

Arthur demonstrated his great storytelling ability, his anger at political hypocrisy and his overwhelming intellectual command of contemporary issues. It was all offered with a sense of humour and a keen eye for the ridiculous. Then eighty-seven, he gave no hint of slowing down or being counted out. His loss earlier this year is still a shock. It is hard to believe that I won't ever again pick up the phone and hear that inimitable voice: 'Hello, Joe, Arthur here.'

To say that Arthur Miller was the most impressive person I have ever met is to underestimate his impact by several degrees. Growing up in Ireland as a stage-struck kid, much of my pleasure came from reading plays borrowed from the local library. For a long time I focused on Irish writers and I revelled in the poetry of John Millington Synge, I was excited by the furious intensity of Sean O'Casey's Dublin plays and admired the acerbic genius of Bernard Shaw. But forty-some years later, I can still remember the excitement of reading *The Crucible* for the first time. I was about fourteen and madly interested in theatre and in history. I was also eager for the end of formal education so that I could pursue my dream of joining the professional theatre. This play had everything I could imagine in a great play: memorable characters, a great story, an historical theme that spoke of contemporary issues in an immediate way. It had dialogue that was both literate and thrilling to speak. I read the play aloud in the privacy of my bedroom, playing every part, male and female, young and old. Then I moved on to *Death of a Salesman*, *All My Sons* and anything else by this vibrant American writer whose dialogue and characters fired my young imagination.

His own biography was as exciting as anything in his plays. Like everyone else, I was fascinated by his intimate connection with the Goddess of Glamour, Marilyn Monroe, deeply impressed by his unwillingness to accede to the forces of McCarthyism and thrilled by the journey of his immigrant family whose travails mirrored the progression of twentieth-century America. In my wildest dreams I never imagined that I would meet him and become a friend. Yet that is exactly what happened many years later, when I became artistic director of the Guthrie Theater in Minneapolis and, after a while, it seemed *almost* normal to spend time with him and to call him Arthur.

The first time I met him was when he came to the Guthrie Theater to see *The Price* during my first season in 1996. He agreed to do a talk from the stage on the Sunday afternoon following the performance. Before the event, my wife, Siobhan, invited Inge and himself to our home to relax over a family brunch. Our children, Susanna and Ronan, were both studying his work at school and their excitement at the prospect of meeting him was infectious. The whole household was turned upside down waiting for our special guests. Of course, both Arthur and Inge relaxed us all immediately and the conversation flowed easily. Great stories were told, we laughed a lot and Inge took some special photographs. It was a joyous event and unforgettable for our family. Recognising that Arthur might be tired before the stage appearance, Siobhan asked him if he would like to stretch out on the sofa. He did not wait to be asked twice but stripped to his braces, lay down and promptly fell asleep. We all tiptoed around as the great man rested. Much to our horror, the phone rang. It was a good friend calling from London. 'Sorry,' I whispered, 'I can't talk now; Arthur Miller is asleep on the couch.' To this day I am not sure she believed me.

Arthur spent some time in Minneapolis when we were rehearsing *Resurrection Blues* in the summer of 2002. He stayed in the home of Jim and Joann Jundt, two wonderful supporters of the theatre. Their beautiful home out at Lake Minnetonka was an ideal place for him to relax and work, and he became very fond of it and of his hosts. It was a twenty-minute drive from the theatre to the house and, as often as possible, I drove him there so that I could spend time with him and enjoy his company. One evening as we sped along the 394 West, a car shifted lanes without warning, causing me to brake suddenly. There was no danger to either of us, but I could not help imagining the consequences of a serious accident. At that moment I could see the front pages of every newspaper in the world. It was not among my ambitions to be remembered as the person who killed Arthur Miller!

I had the joy of directing *All My Sons* at the Guthrie Theater in 2002 and subsequently in the Abbey Theatre in Dublin in early 2003. When we opened in Minneapolis, the media was filled with the corporate scandals that rocked the business world in the United States. Audiences were not slow to see the parallels between the mendacity of the contemporary CEOs and Joe Keller's treacherous behaviour during World War Two. On the day we opened in Dublin in February 2003, half a million people marched through the city protesting the anticipated invasion of Iraq. Again, the play, which illustrates so poignantly the corrosive effect of war on families and individual lives, seemed to have a special resonance for the times.

Although he had seen and participated in countless productions of that early play, Arthur paid kindly attention to our production, sending us a heart-warming message when we opened in Minneapolis and, astonishingly, turning up at the Abbey Theatre to see the show. Visiting his daughter Rebecca and her husband Daniel Day-Lewis at their home in Ireland, he heard that the production was playing at the Abbey and made the trip to see it. The cast, which included Peter Michael Goetz and Helen Carey, two magnificent American actors, was stunned to see him there and overjoyed when he stayed after the show to entertain them over drinks with his customary graciousness and humour.

Among many other things, Arthur Miller was a passionate advocate for the art of theatre. He consistently argued that American theatres should have the same investment from the public purse as their counterparts in Europe. Such subsidy, he argued, allowed writers to explore ideas and forms in a way that was true to their own imaginations if not always linked to broad popular appeal. Theatre that depends on commercial success and private fund-raising will always be conscious of the need for immediate popularity. Serious playwrights need the freedom to experiment and to stretch their audiences' appreciation of new forms and approaches.

Arthur never compromised in his pursuit of different dramatic forms to express his ideas. There is no such thing as a 'typical' Miller play. From the early Ibsen–influenced naturalism to the introspective self-laceration of *Mr. Peters' Connections*, he always found the form to suit the material. It was a source of disappointment to him that, for much of his later career, he seemed out of step with theatre in his native city and more attention was paid to his work abroad than at home. It is a real disgrace that neither of his last two plays, *Resurrection Blues* and *Finishing the Picture*, had productions in New York during his lifetime. Nervous producers, always conscious of the bottom line, are denying audiences in the cultural capital of the United States the chance to examine the entire canon of one of the world's greatest writers. In so doing, they diminish the art form they are supposed to lead. It is inconceivable that new work from Tom Stoppard, Harold Pinter,

David Hare, or other major British writers would fail to get a London production. The neglect of Arthur's important legacy proves his case for increased national subsidy for theatre in America.

Arthur Miller was a remarkable man whose extraordinary talents were matched by his deep and abiding humanity. He had a simplicity and a directness that both charmed and disarmed. He was a unique American figure who brought honour to his country and to the profession he so brilliantly led until the end of his remarkable life. As one whose life he touched in so many ways, I salute his memory and know that we shall never see his like again.

David Edgar

Writer

Consisting as it does of cycles of renewal, hope, betrayal, denial and disillusion, the history of the progressive Left in the last century can be charted as a war between generations. This was made clear to me when I met Arthur Miller at a conference at the University of East Anglia. Like everybody who came of age in the 1960s, I felt that the preceding generation had failed in its historical task (in Germany by succumbing to Hitler, in America by giving in to Senator McCarthy, in Britain by failing to build the new Jerusalem sufficiently robustly after the war). Miller was ever gracious, but he put me right.

Arthur Miller was part of the golden American generation which was brought up during the Depression but who benefited from and contributed to the New Deal before going on to win the war against Nazism. For those who saw that progression as a political narrative, there were three variants: one was the heroic version, which saw the Depression and Hitlerism as two dragons for the American Dream to slay, and the fifties as its victorious homecoming. The second was the disillusionment narrative, which converted pre-war and wartime Trotskyites to Cold War liberals to neo-conservatives. The third group said 'hang on a minute', calling American post-war triumphalism to account. Miller was one of those, and he did it boldly. He took on America at its own face value and its highest point, and he told it its system was corrupt (*All My Sons*), that its dream didn't deliver (*Salesman*), and that it was turning into the very thing it had set out to destroy (*Crucible*). What's more, he did all that in the commercial theatre.

In *Timebends*, Miller wrote that 'somewhere down deep where the sources are was a rule if possible never to let an uncultivated, vulgarly candid, worldly, loving bleached-blonde woman walk out of one my plays disappointed'. Because what Miller had to say was important, he wanted to say it in language that everyone could understand. This accounted for his hostility to the Continental experimentation of absurdism and the domestic upheavals of the theatre in the 1960s ('The theatre's serious work now was all about devastation, which is not the same as tragedy'). But his hostility to the sixties went deeper. Miller's refusal, as he put it, 'to join the dance around the maypole' was an expression of his belief that deep down the politics of the sixties wasn't serious. Speaking at his alma mater in Michigan at the height of the anti-Vietnam War protests, Miller noticed 'something like a festive air among the students', which he felt he had to break, reminding them that the FBI was among them, and 'some day you may have to account for being here'. Which, of course, he had reason to know (it is worth remembering that Miller was sentenced to jail for refusing to name names).

I think that Miller confused the style of the sixties with its content. Although its (white) activists had grown up in prosperity, many of their parents had been victims of the very McCarthyism that Miller had fought so bravely. But his suspicion of the politics of festivity, like his suspicion of the theatre of despair, arose out of the seriousness of his mission, and the fact that he had undertaken it at such an important time.

It is because of this that I find it hard to accept the thesis that Miller was an anterior postmodernist, that what is enduring about even the early, superficially realist plays is their challenge to the notion of reality, that *Salesman* is a play about delusion rather than betrayal, that *The Crucible* questions truth rather than asserting it. For me, the opposite is true: throughout his career, Miller demonstrates how public events impinge on and destroy private lives, from the line of Jews awaiting deportation in *Incident at Vichy* to the flawed East European intellectuals of *The Archbishop's Ceiling*, from his excoriating self-portrait in *After the Fall* to the comfortable and safe American Jews responding to news of Kristallnacht in *Broken Glass*.

The big question that all of these plays ask is whether individuals can live up to the challenges that history offers them. At East Anglia, Miller answered that question with wryness and clarity. The big problem with Socialism was not the command economy, or even the secret police. It was the emancipatory project of Socialism itself: the idea that people can break free from their past and build their lives anew. For Miller, the past is 98 per cent of what we are, the irony being – of course – that breaking free from the past and building lives anew is not just a definition of Communism, it is also (in individualised form) a definition of the American Dream, whose limitations Miller exposed so definitively.

Like Brecht, Miller's beliefs tussle with his plays. Miller's heroes are often mired in delusion, some act badly and many act well too late. But for most of them there is an honour in their motives and, for all, a grandeur in their striving. At Ann Arbor, Miller went on to tell the students that

> despite the presence of spies and the possibility that people might one day be called on to renounce and condemn the passions they were feeling today, it was the essential risk of living at all to feel what they were feeling now. And more: that even if this movement should end, not in some climactic thunderclap of victory but in pale distraction and remorse for wasted time, it would not be the occasion for disillusion, because we must go on groping from one illusion of virtue to another; the fact was that man could not act at all without moral impulse, however mistaken its identification with any particular movement might eventually turn out to be.

I quote that passage from *Timebends* at length because it shows why Miller did not follow the neo-conservatives on the primrose path to the Right, but also because it hung over my desk while I was trying to write about the legacy of the sixties in contemporary American politics, a legacy which sometimes seems invisible and more often trivial. Miller's characters may be trapped by the past, and a man whose prime was mid-twentieth-century America has a mighty past to be trapped in, but throughout his work the axis is entrapment and the urge to break free. 'We must go on groping from one illusion of virtue to another', because by doing so we make the moral impulse real.

David Esbjornson

Director: **The Ride Down Mount Morgan**, *the Public Theatre, New York, 1998;* **Resurrection Blues**, *Guthrie Theater, 2002*

If someone had told me earlier in my life that I would work with Arthur Miller some day I would have told them they were dreaming. The difference in our ages alone would have made this deeply unlikely. And yet, in my mid-forties, I found myself sitting opposite Arthur in his East Side apartment. I had come to interview for his new play *The Ride Down Mount Morgan*.

I don't remember many specifics of our conversation. I was busy trying not to be overwhelmed or say something that would betray me. The play had not been well received when it was done in London, or at the Williamstown Theatre Festival the summer before. My hope, and that of the Public Theatre, was to embrace what was good about the play and change or clarify the rest. This was a rather pretentious mandate for me to harbor. After all, I was about to meet 'America's greatest living playwright'. I felt a little like David meeting Goliath. I just wasn't sure if I'd packed my slingshot. And I had no firm grasp on who Arthur Miller was as a man. I remember thinking to myself, 'Just have the experience. He won't hire you anyway. Just enjoy this.' The excitement and anxiety seemed in equal measure as I knocked on his door. Arthur opened it suddenly, perhaps even dramatically. His firm handshake was accompanied by a warm smile and a clear, confident voice. His manner was familiar and I soon realised that he reminded me of my grandfather – a man I had loved and admired deeply. And even though they were worlds apart they both shared the same straightforward, unpretentious manner. I was struck by his ease and colloquial style of humor. I found myself instantly drawn to him.

And, as Arthur Miller's deep eyes scrutinised me, I remembered why I had come in the first place. I wasn't here to discuss problems in the script. I should be so lucky. I had come because I was first and foremost drawn to this play. I had responded to its bold and unbridled ambition, its non-linear timeline, the difficult central character and its surprising elements of fantasy. It was full of highly theatrical scenes and had an odd but seductive blend of humor and tragedy. *Mount Morgan* had a diversity of style and exuberance that I would have associated with more youthful writers. Had it not been written by Arthur Miller, the play might have been celebrated as a bold, exciting new work with a bright future ahead for its young writer. Perhaps it was this aspect of the project that intrigued me most. Then suddenly, mid-conversation, Arthur looked me square in the eye and said, 'I think you might just be the man for the job!' Then he smiled the wide, goofy smile that was his signature and our meeting was over. I walked out of Arthur's apartment a little dazed, then smiled to myself as I thought of what had transpired. How ironic! I needed to tell someone so I immediately called my mother.

Arthur, then in his mid-eighties, seemed to be boldly exploring new territory in his writing. At one point he told me that, of his contemporaries, he had always felt a closer aesthetic connection to Tennessee Williams than he had to O'Neill. He felt that *Death of a Salesman* had shocked people not just because of its content but by its non-linear storytelling. He believed that he had been defined too rigidly by the academics and was now looking for a kind of liberation from his past – a reinvention of himself. I suspect that Arthur's strong focus on character and his muscular writing style invited realistic interpretations of his work. Perhaps many of his plays would have benefited from a less literal approach, but certainly the writing in *The Ride Down Mount Morgan* seemed to demand it. A fluid production, capable of instantly and effortlessly moving us back and forth in time, was essential. And the occasional but complete departure from reality allowed me the freedom to be visually creative. For example, I imagined an image of a car quietly falling through the snow, then violently exploding and becoming a hospital where, in Lyman's mind, ski patrol rescue units were juxtaposed with nurses who floated through the air, or interns who became giant aggressive crows pulling at his entrails.

None of this seemed to faze Arthur. He was remarkably open to all of these ideas. Perhaps it was because past productions hadn't succeeded in putting the material across to his satisfaction. But I also suspect that this fell into a world of interpretation which he understood to be within the director's purview. It might be another thing for him to accept criticism of his script, especially from someone half his age. I saw this project as an artistic partnership and collaboration. I believed it was necessary to achieve that with Arthur if we were to succeed in improving the play. He truly loved the act of creating theater, taking great delight as ideas were brought to life in front of him. I would try and build on that.

In the first week of rehearsal, sitting with Arthur and actors discussing the play at the table, I started to ask provocative questions hoping to begin a dialogue. I struggled to find my voice in the rehearsal room with Patrick Stewart, Blythe Danner and the 'great man' himself. Arthur had warned me that his presence in rehearsal could be challenging for directors. He said that actors seldom took their clues from anyone but him and that it might be difficult for me. He didn't want to get in the way and was intent on staying away to give me my creative space. I appreciated his respect for my rehearsal process but I needed him there to change things in the play, especially the chronology of events, which needed serious clarification or else we were going to lose the audience as we moved back and forth in time. When I brought up some of these concerns at the table, Arthur's response was to tell a story about Ibsen, which I suspect he had related before. On an opening night in Oslo a hundred years ago, a patron came up to Ibsen after the performance and took issue with a detail in his play. She suggested that it was impossible for his heroine to have had a daughter of such age and that perhaps he had overlooked the facts. According to Arthur, Ibsen replied, 'Madame that is none of your goddamn business!' That was a moment when I had no trouble getting the actors' attention. All eyes were on me.

How was I going to address the larger issues of the play if I couldn't even get Arthur to do simple but necessary clarifications in the timeline? Eventually the solution came from the practical concerns brought up by the clothing. Thankfully, costume design is a world of specifics and we were forced to decide on certain dates so that the events of Lyman's infidelity and Leah's pregnancy could be tracked through the different seasons. As Arthur responded tangibly to all these decisions, he helped us to create a narrative that was far more convincing and therefore could be manipulated as he had intended. The timeline now in hand, I moved my intentions to two scenes which I felt weakened the play. In one, Lyman brings up a complex relationship with his business partner, Raoul. This speech echoed a relationship from *All My Sons* but seemed out of place in this instance. It simply never went anywhere. Patiently we waited for Arthur to cut it. But as we approached previews it seemed destined to stay.

The other was a scene toward the end of the play. It was a flashback in which Leah, the sexy younger wife and career woman, seemed to make a complete reversal in her thinking, capitulating at a critical moment and giving up all of her strong, clear-headed values. During the eighties Arthur Miller had been somewhat out of fashion and was criticised in some circles for his portrayal of women. In many of his plays the women close to the central male character are portrayed as either good, suffering wives or sexually charged home wreckers. In his defense, Arthur has always been interested in large gestures and the nature of his truth relies on certain archetypes recognisable to his audience. I worried that in *The Ride Down Mount Morgan* Arthur had created a very slippery moral landscape, a play about a bigamist with two archetypical wives. I felt that it came down to issues of credibility regarding the motivations and character of these two very different women.

Casting Patrick Stewart in the lead went a long way to help with this issue since he is a charismatic, good-looking man whom one might believe could win the undying love and loyalty of two women. But the character of Leah, the younger wife, and the one Lyman was attracted to because of her strong, modern attitude, lost all credibility when (in this eleventh-hour scene) we see her manipulating Lyman into marrying her by threatening the abortion of his child. This scene not only undermined her but, in my opinion, the moral balance of the play. Lyman's choice to be in two marriages was based on his own coercion and not the result of an 'evil' woman's tricks. Lyman, suddenly, was no longer responsible for his actions. If the scene wasn't cut I felt that the balance in the triangle of the play's relationships would be lost, causing a less provocative conclusion as Lyman tries to choose between the two wives. I knew that Arthur wanted nothing less than the strongest play, but it took much effort to arrive at this change. Perhaps this was generational. I may have been flying in the face of Arthur's personal experience and particular truth, but I felt compelled to make a change that would honor the younger generation of women. The discussion, and Arthur's subsequent decision to remove the scene, became the turning point in our working relationship. It also taught me the level of engagement Arthur was still willing to have with a director. My admiration for him soared. He was not only open but artistically generous.

On the first preview at the Public, having stayed away from all of the technical rehearsals, Arthur sat in the theater watching the production for the first time. I had never been so nervous.

Everything was on the line. At intermission he remained in his seat. What was he thinking? Then he looked around for me and waved me to his side. Both he and his wife Inge seemed thrilled. 'It's terrific!' he said, then brought up the section of the play that the cast and I had been referring to as the 'Raoul scene'. Patrick and I had been secretly wishing it away for weeks. 'We don't need it, do we?' Arthur said with a definitive tone.

'No,' I said simply, trying not to sound too eager.

And then Arthur did something I'll never forget. He said, a little sadly but without sentimentality, 'Poor Raoul.' And that was it. An understated moment of mourning, and a character was gone for ever.

Almost a year later, I found myself back in Arthur's apartment talking about the Broadway transfer of *The Ride Down Mount Morgan*, discussing where we might improve on our successful Public production. It was a beautiful day and Arthur suggested we go to the roof for our meeting. Afterwards, as we started down, the elevator stopped suddenly and we found ourselves stuck between floors. I tried not to panic but I kept thinking of the headlines in the *Post*: ARTHUR MILLER AND UNKNOWN COMPANION DIE IN ELEVATOR ACCIDENT. The elevator phone rang. 'I think the phone's ringing,' I said. Arthur couldn't hear the ring or the voice on the other end of the line, but the voice screaming through the phone assured us that help was on the way. We stepped back into his apartment and related our adventure to Inge. She seemed undaunted and sprinted off to the streets of New York with her camera. Inge was a brilliant photographer and remarkable force of nature. She had met Arthur shooting stills during the filming of *The Misfits* as his life with Marilyn Monroe was ending unhappily. His sense of calm and well-being could easily be attributed to her presence. Learning more about their relationship, I began to understand why he presented the wives in his plays with such dignity. There wasn't the least suggestion of self-pity in Inge. She had the capacity to support both Arthur and her own interests with tireless enthusiasm.

I held on to these insights of Inge as I began to work on the next incarnation of *Mount Morgan*. I didn't know it at the time, but this observation of Inge's character would manifest itself on stage in a simple but profound change in the staging. As Arthur walked me to 'that elevator', he stopped in his tracks and put his hand firmly on my shoulder. Then, with all the excitement and enthusiasm of a twenty-year-old he said, 'There is nothing like a new production!!'

Soon we were back in rehearsal and found ourselves seeking a stronger ending to the play than the one we had at the Public. At one point Patrick and I were discussing the specifics of Lyman's near-fatal accident that lands him in the hospital where his two wives meet. I asked Arthur if the character meant to commit suicide. Was there a dark motivation there? We had already acknowledged that the play had a direct relationship to *Death of a Salesman*. His answer wasn't definitive. It came out almost as a query. He ventured that Lyman wasn't exactly attempting suicide but that a part of him was ready to tempt fate. If he died then he died. Lyman was exhausted by the game he was playing and on some level willing to put his life on the line. As I pressed him further he conjured the memory of Marilyn Monroe. Patrick and I barely breathed. Not wanting to appear insensitive, we had never felt free to bring her up, but now in the context of the play we were discussing some of Arthur's most painful history. 'You see,' he said, 'Marilyn never believed she was going to die. She just kept pushing the boundaries further and further.' Like Lyman, she was testing the limits of her life. 'Of course, I wasn't there when she died,' Arthur acknowledged and then, as if he were reliving it, added, 'But I was all the other times.'

A clearer sense of the play was beginning to emerge and I believe we found some new layers as a result of the openness we were all now sharing. We continued to calibrate the ending. Arthur wrote new material that attempted to address Lyman's ambiguity and I changed the staging leaving Lyman's first wife on longer and intensifying her rejection of him. The gesture gave the character a dignity she had been missing. Looking back, I believe the writing may always have been crafted that way. Perhaps I just hadn't seen it.

As we moved toward our first Broadway preview the anxiety mounted but it never seemed to overwhelm Arthur. He was in his element. This was home. He remained fiercely loyal to the process, refusing to allow any interference from the producers. This sometimes put me in an awkward position politically, but I appreciated it artistically. It was clear to me that very few people dared to take on Arthur Miller and that he provided a unique protection that one seldom experiences working on Broadway.

Arthur often showed this kind of generous spirit and sage

wisdom. He never took things out on the people he was working with, no matter how much personal anxiety he might have felt. And there was plenty, I'm sure. Age, I discovered, was no protection from the forces of criticism and Arthur had experienced enough rejection at key moments of his career to balance out all the acclaim. Each new play and its production was a raw and vulnerable experience for him as for all of us, and seeing that in him gave an insight into a life in the theater. This was part of what made working with him in his last years so deeply rewarding.

Following our Broadway experience, I was invited up to Arthur's farm in Connecticut. It was a picture-perfect summer day and Arthur was enjoying the quiet, simple life. He was transfixed by a small invention of his, a piece of heavy wire he had bent into a shape that could twist and turn as it balanced on the rough table. In the intense sunlight it cast an ever-shifting shadow. Arthur seemed particularly relaxed. He had a profound sense of well-being as he marveled and took delight in this simple device, like a child exploring a new toy. It was only one of many singular moments that had convinced me that Arthur in his late eighties was one of the youngest people I knew. By which I mean that his sense of wonder at the mysteries of life, small or large, and his youthful passion for humanity seemed uncensored and fresh. It was at this farm near Roxbury where Arthur found his greatest peace. He had bought it for Marilyn and some of her possessions remained, like a photograph of Abraham Lincoln which still hung on the wall. But it was with Inge that it had become home. In the center of the property, just down from the house, was a pond, which seemed to have an almost spiritual draw. Inge meditated and swam in it almost daily. Inside was Arthur's hand-crafted furniture, not to everyone's taste, perhaps, but that was not the point. The Connecticut house was in sharp contrast to the apartment in New York, which felt spare with its modest, unremarkable furniture with only some theater posters to give it personality. Up here, on the vast acreage that he had bought before it had economic value to anyone, Arthur had centered his existence.

I spent an afternoon here with Arthur and his lifelong friend, the late Robert Whitehead. Robert intended to produce *Resurrection Blues*, Arthur's next play. He would lovingly and conspiratorially share comments about Arthur whenever we were alone for a moment. These two old friends together reminded me of a commedia sketch. They were always at each other in a warm and familiar way. It was a privilege to be there that day and marvel at their collective experience. I knew that soon it would be over and that I would be holding this piece of history in my memory.

Neither Robert nor Inge would live to see *Resurrection Blues* at the Guthrie later that year. It was difficult for Arthur to move forward. Obviously, their deaths had created an enormous vacuum in his life. It was essential that Arthur work and I think he understood that. Still, I was surprised that he could. My time with Arthur in Minneapolis would turn out to be one of the most special and irreplaceable in my life. The play was still in an early form and under the circumstances many important aspects of the writing had not been attended to. But this time around I was much less concerned about that. I was excited to be back in a rehearsal room with Arthur and grateful to be part of his healing process.

We went into rehearsal with a company of actors and designers so deeply engaged and dedicated to this play that it almost rivaled the spiritual experience that was the subject of the play. Minnesota happened to be the state where I grew up and the Guthrie was where I saw *The Miser*, my first professional play, starring actress Zoe Caldwell (the recently widowed wife of Robert Whitehead).

The rehearsal process at the Guthrie was relaxed and full of joy. The design approach demanded Arthur be even more trusting than he had on *The Ride Down Mount Morgan*. We wanted to start and end with an empty stage. The play was about illusion and we were using shadow play as an element of the production. He was anxious as always about how his work would be received but it was a far cry from our recent past. We had come to Minneapolis to escape the pressures of New York and to remember what we loved about making theater. Arthur used every opportunity to say that. He might have been exploring his spiritual side in this play but he never forgot his political battles. His vigilant fight for progressive politics was always in play but he had his pet peeves as well and one of them was what he believed was an invasive, hostile and manipulative press.

Arthur spent most days in rehearsal watching and enjoying the process, basking in his element. He said that this time he preferred to be in the room and I was happy to have him there. We changed things as needed but with very little angst. We would even do notes as we swam in the pool. That was a first for both of us. It was as full and rich an experience as one could imagine. The warm summer days in Minnesota conjured memories of my childhood and dreams of one day being in the theater. But I had never imagined that there would come a time when I would be sharing all of it with America's greatest living playwright.

On the 4th of July we had a barbecue, then an evening boat ride. When we returned, Arthur said, 'Do you think I should put on my bathing suit?'

I remember saying, 'How many more 4th of Julys are there going to be like this?'

'You're right!' he said with his big, warm grin and off he went to change. The next thing I know he was up to his chest in the outdoor hot tub flanked by at least two beautiful women, a plastic cup of red wine in one hand and a sparkler in the other. He looked boyishly happy. Arthur Miller, Yankee Doodle Dandy, you are for ever young.

Richard Eyre

Director: The Crucible, New York, 2002

A large part of my luck over the past twenty years was getting to know Arthur Miller, so after his death when I heard in interviews – or was asked myself – the question 'Will Arthur Miller be remembered as the man who married Marilyn Monroe?' I felt a mixture of despair and indignation. The motives of the questioners – a mixture of prurience and envy – were, curiously enough, the same as the House Un-American Activities Committee when they summoned Arthur Miller to appear in front of them. I asked Arthur about it some years ago. 'I knew perfectly well why they had subpoenaed me,' he said,

it was because I was engaged to Marilyn Monroe. Had I not been, they'd never have thought of me. They'd been through the writers long before and they'd never touched me. Once I became famous as her possible husband, this was a great possibility for publicity. When I got to Washington, preparing to appear before that committee, my lawyer received a message from the chairman saying that if it could be arranged that he could have a picture, a photograph taken with Marilyn, he would cancel the whole hearing. I mean, the cynicism of this thing was so total, it was asphyxiating.

The question that lurked then – and lurks now – is this: why would the world's most attractive woman want to go out with a *writer*? There are at least four good reasons I can think of:

By 1956, when he married Marilyn Monroe, Arthur Miller had written four of the best plays in the English language, two of them indelible classics that will be performed in a hundred years' time.

He was a figure of great moral and intellectual stature, who was unafraid of taking a stand on political issues and enduring obloquy for doing so.

He was wonderful company – a great, a glorious, raconteur. I asked him once what happened on the first night of *Death of a Salesman* when it opened on the road in Philadelphia. He must have told the story a thousand times but he repeated it, pausing, seeming to search for half-buried details, as if it were the first time:

> The play ended and there was a dead silence and I remember being in the back of the house with Kazan and nothing happened. The people didn't get up either. Then one or two got up and picked up their coats. Some of them sat down again. It was chaos. Then somebody clapped and then the house fell apart and they kept applauding for God knows how long and . . . I remember an old man being helped up the aisle, who turned out to be Bernard Gimbel, who ran one of the biggest department store chains in the United States who was literally unable really to navigate, they were helping him up the aisle. And it turned out that he had been swept away by the play and the next day he issued an order that no one in his stores – I don't know, eight or ten stores all over the United States – was to be fired for being over age!

And with this he laughed, a deep husky bass chortle, shaking his head as if the memory were as fresh as last week.

He was a deeply attractive man: tall, almost hulking, broad-shouldered, square-jawed, with the most beautiful large, strong but tender hands. There was nothing evasive or small-minded about him. As he aged he became both more monumental but more approachable, his great body not so much bent as folded over. And if you were lucky enough to spend time with him and Inge Morath (the Magnum photographer to whom he was married for forty years after his divorce from Marilyn Monroe) you would be capsized by the warmth, wit and humanity of the pair of them.

It has been surprising for me – and sometimes shocking – to discover that my high opinion of Arthur Miller was often not held by those who consider themselves the curators of American theatre. I read a discussion in the *New York Times* a few years ago between three theatre critics about the differences between British and American theatre:

FIRST CRITIC   Arthur Miller is celebrated there.
SECOND CRITIC   It's *Death of a Salesman*, for crying out loud. He's so cynical about American culture and American politics. The English love that.
FIRST CRITIC   Though *Death of a Saleman* was not a smash when it first opened in London.
THIRD CRITIC   It's also his earnestness.

If we continue to admire Arthur Miller, it's because we have the virtuous habit of treating his plays as contemporaneous and find that they speak to us today not because of their 'earnestness' but because they are serious – that's to say they're *about* something. They have energy and poetry and wit, and an ambition to make theatre matter. What's more, they use sinewy and passionate language with unembarrassed enthusiasm, which is always attractive to British actors and audiences weaned on Shakespeare.

In 1950, at a time when British theatre was toying with a phoney poetic drama – the plays of T. S. Eliot and Christopher Fry – there was real poetry on the American stage in the plays of Arthur Miller (and Tennessee Williams) or, to be exact, the poetry of reality: plays about life lived on the streets of Brooklyn and New Orleans by working-class people foundering on the edges of gentility and resonating with metaphors of the American Dream and the American Nightmare – aspiration and desperation.

The Depression of the late twenties provided Arthur's sentimental education: the family business was destroyed and the family was reduced to relative poverty. I talked to him once about it as we walked in the shadow of the pillars of the Brooklyn Bridge looking out over the East River. 'America', he said, 'was promises, and the Crash was a broken promise in the deepest sense. I think the Americans in general live on the edge of a cliff, they're waiting for the other shoe to drop. I don't care who they are. It's part of the vitality of the country, maybe. That they're always working against this disaster that's about to happen.' Then he stopped, looking up at the bridge. 'These are our cathedrals,' he said.

'I thought those were,' I said, pointing across the river to the Business District and the twin towers of the World Trade Center (this was in 1999).

'Oh sure. "The business of America is business", that's what Calvin Coolidge used to say. He was the first president I can remember.' Then he stared at the buildings. 'None of them were here when I lived here. Not one. And in all those windows there'll be somebody counting figures. Piling up money.' Then he smiled ruefully. 'And snorting cocaine, I guess.'

He wrote with heat and heart, and his work was felt in Britain like a distant and disturbing forest fire – a fire that did much to ignite British writers who followed like John Osborne, Harold Pinter and Arnold Wesker; and later Edward Bond, David Storey and Trevor Griffiths; and later still David Edgar, Mike Leigh, David Hare. What they found in Miller was a visceral power, an appeal to the senses beyond and below rational thought, and an ambition to deal with big subjects.

His plays are about the difficulty and the possibility of people – usually men – taking control of their own lives, 'that moment when, in my eyes, a man differentiates himself from every other man, that moment when out of a sky full of stars he fixes on one star'. His heroes – salesmen, dockers, policemen, farmers – all seek a sort of salvation in asserting their singularity, their self, their 'name'. They redeem their dignity, even if it's by suicide. Willy Loman cries out, 'I am not a dime a dozen, I am Willy Loman . . .!' Eddie Carbone in *A View from the Bridge*, broken and destroyed by sexual guilt and public shame, bellows, 'I want my name' and John Proctor in *The Crucible*, in refusing the calumny of condemning his fellow citizens, declaims, 'How may I live without my name? I have given you my soul; leave me my name!' In nothing does Miller show his Americanism more than in the assertion of the right and necessity of the individual to own his own life – and, beyond that, how you reconcile the individual with society. In short, how you live your life.

If there was a touch of the evangelist in his writing, his message was this: there *is* such a thing as society and art ought to be used to change it. Though it's hard to argue that art saves lives, feeds the hungry or sways votes, *Death of a Salesman* comes as close as any writer can get to art as a balm for social concern. When I saw the New York revival five or six years ago I came out of the theatre behind a young girl and her dad, and she said to him, 'It was like looking at the Grand Canyon.'

Three years ago I directed the first production of *The Crucible* on Broadway since its opening nearly fifty years ago. He loved our production and was closely involved with rehearsals. I never got over the joy and pride of sitting beside Arthur as this great play unfolded in front of us while he beamed and muttered, 'It's damned good stuff, this.' We performed it shortly after the Patriot Act had been introduced. Everyone who saw it said it was 'timely'. What did they mean exactly? That it was time*less*.

'There are things which he stretched, but mainly he told the truth,' says Huckleberry Finn of his creator, Mark Twain. And the same could be said of Arthur Miller, which is perhaps why it's not a coincidence that my enthusiasm for his writing came at the same time as my discovery of Mark Twain's genius. And it's not a surprise that what Arthur Miller said of Mark Twain could just as well have been said about him: 'He somehow managed – despite a steady underlying seriousness which few writers have matched – to step round the pit of self-importance and to keep his membership in the ordinary human race in the front of his mind and his writing.'

I had an e-mail shortly before Arthur's death from a mutual friend in New York who had just seen Arthur in hospital, unable to talk after his recent treatment. It read: 'When I saw Arthur Sunday I told him that I had had dinner with you last week in London and he gave a loving smile in return.' I e-mailed him back that I would call Arthur at the weekend when he'd been settled back in Connecticut. I heard of his death that Friday afternoon. When I got home I saw a note to myself on my desk: 'Ring Arthur.'

Robert Falls

Director: **Death of a Salesman**, *Goodman Theatre, Chicago, 1998, Eugene O'Neill Theatre, New York, 1999;* **Finishing the Picture**, *Goodman Theatre, Chicago, 2004*

Arthur Miller was a man who said, 'Gee.'

There's a moment in *Death of a Salesman* when the elder son, Biff Loman, is being pressured by his father to pay a visit to Bill Oliver, his former employer who may or may not be willing to help Biff with a new business venture. Willy, the father, wants to know how much money Biff is going to ask for and Biff responds, 'Gee, I don't know.' To this, Willy snaps back, 'And don't say "Gee". "Gee" is a boy's word.' Interestingly, Willy himself uses the word later in the play, in the dreamlike image that ends Act I: 'Gee, look at the moon moving between the buildings!' It's a small moment, a moment of guile and wonder amidst the towering social and emotional issues that pervade this play. But to me, it's that mixture of guileless innocence and wonder, so pure and so purely *American*, that captures the essence of Arthur Miller.

Arthur Miller was, of course, an icon, one of the true cultural giants of the twentieth century. But working side by side with him, as it was my great pleasure to do last fall on *Finishing the Picture*, he was simply and unpretentiously a writer, rolling up his sleeves and relishing his work, finding as much joy in crafting a play as he did in crafting furniture in his workshop in Connecticut. As we'd watch a rehearsal, he'd lean over to me to say, 'Gee, that's a marvelous scene,' or, 'Gee, that works well.' And I'd see that tremendous satisfaction that comes simply from the act of creating something. Just as Willy Loman was never so happy, as Biff says in the final scene of *Salesman*, as when he was making the stoop or putting on the new porch, Arthur Miller was never so happy as when he was making a play.

I first read *Death of a Salesman* when I was twelve years old. Upon finishing it, I burst into tears, devastated by its emotional and intellectual power; and it made me want to direct plays that had that same force, that power to move. At that age, of course, I identified keenly with the character of Biff, who struggles to create a life for himself amidst his father's inflated expectations. When I directed the fiftieth anniversary revival of *Salesman* many years later, I found that I now connected more personally with the father, Willy, and his heroic and tragic dreams. But decades later, the play still devastates me, still moves me to tears (as it has countless audiences) with its beauty, its power, its craft and its innocence – all created by a man who said, 'Gee.'

Joseph Fiennes

Actor: A View from the Bridge, Bristol Old Vic, 1995

My commitment to acting came at the same time as my introduction to Arthur Miller, by way of witnessing night after night his plays at the Young Vic theatre as an eighteen-year-old usher making ends meet for my studies at drama school. *The Price, Two-Way Mirror* and *The Man Who Had All the Luck* left me giddy with excitement and riveted by his language. I couldn't wait to get the audience seated so I could get on and escape into Miller land, so much so that I rudely told a woman in a dress and heels hovering at the far end of the darkened corridor and holding up the show (also the back stage area as the Young Vic is in the round) to bloody well sit down as the show was about to go up. She replied in a cool and slightly sexy manner, 'I'm about to go on, darling,' and then she did, sharing the two-hander with Bob Peck. Helen Mirren's and Peck's command of the language gave me the sense of the playwright; kind and generous to all his characters, smart and funny, extremely insightful of the human condition to the point of rendering an audience deeply moved and affected (ushers have plenty of time to study their audience).

Just a few years down the line, I found myself on the other side of the Miller looking-glass.

David Thacker, whose staging of the Miller plays I had been so rapt by, asked me to join the company of *A View from the Bridge*. I was amazed how at times the play had struck a chord between comedy and pathos. The play is not wholly a comedy but has elements the audience could laugh at. One night, while doing a scene with Bernard Hill where he teaches me to box (all the while wanting to land a blow to put my lights out), an old lady cannot control her laughter. The tension is too much for her, so much so that Bernard and myself are infected with fits of laughter too. It is moments like these that sum up Miller's ability to strike the balance between menace and humour, although it climaxes to a hugely powerful and tragic end. It deals with obsessive love. The play is as modern as anything around today, focusing on human need and social constraints.

And now here I was, on the inside of his work where it became clear how emotionally powerful, psychologically involving and gripping these narratives were.

My love of film also converged with Miller. The brilliant Sidney Lumet shot his version of *A View from the Bridge* in Brooklyn and Paris, which has to be seen for the great cinematography and most importantly for the juxtaposition between Eddie Carbone and the dockside worker in Kazan's *On the Waterfront*. It shows Miller's courage as a playwright to have his main character denounced by the community. What I love about Miller in this respect is how he allows us to examine the underbelly of the human condition, the demons and pride of Carbone and still feel an utter devastation for him.

Before the curtain fell each night, on the final tragic scene, the silence would leave those in the auditorium in a vacuum of sorrow, almost in an altered state.

To have Miller fly from New York to see his plays in London showed his respect for Thacker (who was the champion of the Miller revival in London), and his dedication to his work abroad. It seemed his audience at home were less inclined to have a mirror held up to reflect American sensibility. In my eyes, the best I could offer to the playing of Rodolfo in front of Miller was never going to reach what the playwright had in mind but, to my surprise, this elegant gentleman, who stood so tall, was extremely complimentary and in the few moments of meeting him it seemed to me that he would give little away other than a charming wry smile and a twinkle from that all-knowing gaze (as if to say, it all takes a lifetime to master). To my mind Miller had the touch of what all geniuses have; the ability to delve into the human psyche and throw a light on it, warts and all, but still emerge with compassion and a deeper understanding. This is what matters about Miller. He is the great modern classic and his language is for everyone.

Gerald Freedman

Director: **Death of a Salesman,** *Great Lakes Theatre Festival, 1994;* **The Crucible,** *Roundabout Theatre, New York, 1990;* **The Creation of the World and Other Business,** *1972; Up from Paradise*

I was fortunate to have taken over the direction of *The Creation of the World and Other Business*, directed a revival of *Death of a Salesman* at Great Lakes Theatre Festival in 1994 with Hal Holbrook and Elizabeth Franz, which went on national tour, a revival of *Up from Paradise*, a musicalisation of *Creation of the World*, and a production of *The Crucible* at the Roundabout Theatre in New York City in 1990. Arthur worked with me and gave me notes or rewrites on each of these ventures.

I grew up in Lorain, Ohio, a small Midwestern steel town hit hard during the Depression years. Lorain had a small Jewish community of which my family were members. I went to Northwestern University in Evanston, Il. Arthur's first wife came from Lakewood, Ohio, a few miles away and his college education was at the University of Michigan. I set down these simple facts because Arthur was the voice of my conscience framed by these reference points – Jewish, Depression, classic American values and a developed social conscience. Years before I met him he eloquently, passionately, spoke to everything I had been taught to value and defend. He never disappointed me. His works and his actions consistently matched each other.

Creation of the World was in trouble in Boston. Robert Whitehead, with the blessing of Harold Clurman, a revered mentor of mine, asked me to take over the direction. Whitehead, the producer of *Creation*, was familiar with my work when I had directed his wife, Zoe Caldwell, off Broadway in *Collette*, with Mildred Dunnock. He confessed they probably had gone into production prematurely. Arthur had written some wonderful scenes with wit, wisdom and humor, retelling the Genesis story. But had he written a play? It was a father-and-son conflict without a resolution. The cast was demoralised as a result of cast changes out of town and there were more to come. There was a feeling that there was no clear sense of what Arthur wanted to say. The production moved to the Kennedy Center in Washington and we continued to work on the play. We agreed that Arthur had addressed some important questions in three episodes of Genesis but some longer issue had not emerged. We spent a week of afternoons trying to pin down a line through but couldn't state it successfully or succinctly. We settled for three questions.

One afternoon I went downstairs to his room in the Watergate Hotel for our usual question-and-search session. Arthur was watching a rerun of *Some Like It Hot* starring his former wife, Marilyn Monroe. We sat on the edge of the bed till the end of the film. The moments following were mellow, good-humored and reflective. We didn't get much work done. It was a matinée day.

Carlos Fuentes

Writer

There exists a photograph of some thousands of Parisians marching along the Rue Soufflot towards the Panthéon on the day of the inauguration of the president of France, François Mitterrand, in May 1981. Among the crowds, a man taller than any of the others stands out. Those who know him can easily identify Arthur Miller, his head uncovered in the stormy afternoon, his raincoat flung over a shoulder, his spectacles firmly placed on that dignified profile so reminiscent of the monumental presidential sculptures of Mount Rushmore. Or as William Styron says, 'Arthur Miller is the Abraham Lincoln of North American Literature.' But Miller's great physical height, I thought to myself walking by his side that May afternoon in Paris – and I come back to this thought on this intensely sad day of his death – is only comparable to his enormous moral, political and literary height. Nothing belittled him. Not personal tragedy. Nor political controversy. Nor intellectual fads.

I grew up in the USA in the 1930s, that 'dark valley' as the British historian Piers Brendon has called it, that cruel decade when ideological conflicts, economic policies and the very condition of being human entered a profound crisis. Between the financial crash of 1929 and the outbreak of world war in 1939, the answers to the crisis were cures worse than the disease: totalitarian regimes, militarism, bloody civil wars, violations of rights and life, apathy and indifference towards democracy . . .

The great exception was the United States of America. President Franklin Delano Roosevelt and the policies of the New Deal didn't have to turn to totalitarian measures, nor to the suppression of liberties, in order to face the challenges of unemployment, the financial crisis, the poverty of millions of citizens and the bankruptcies of thousands of companies. Roosevelt and the New Deal turned to the best of the USA: its social capital, its human dividend. The country was rebuilt with its human and social potential, but also thanks to the impulse given by the arts and, in particular, the theatrical arts. This is the world that shaped Arthur Miller, and his Mount Rushmore profile is also the profile of an era in which the great North American nation placed its trust in the strength of the people's work and acted with the energy and justice that arise when, as then, ideals and practice are united.

Later, or whenever the United States has divorced ideals from practice, when its rulers have said that the United States doesn't have friends but interests, when its leaders have affirmed that the United States 'is the only surviving model of human progress', excluding the rest of humanity – that is to say, all of us – I return to Arthur Miller. I return to Roosevelt, to the New Deal and to Miller's eternal theatre, which expresses the highest artistic representation of an inclusive politics that recognises the other as both different and equal in brotherhood.

Whenever my faith in the great North American nation began to crack, it was enough to turn my gaze to Arthur Miller to renew it. He confronted Senator McCarthy who, under the pretext of combating Communism, duplicated the practices of Stalinism: denunciation, rigged trials, the destruction of lives, families, reputations, careers. He confronted Senators McCarran and Walter who withdrew his passport, as if the practice of criticism were an act of treason against the homeland. The Senators have been forgotten. But their threat must be remembered. The horizon of the twenty-first century opens with dark clouds of racism, xenophobia, ethnic cleansing, extreme nationalism, terrorism with no face and terrorism of the state, arrogant hegemonies, contempt for international law and its institutions, fundamentalism of several kinds . . .

What lies beneath all these dangers? Not the axis of evil but the axis of intolerance and contempt towards that which is different. Be like me, think like me, and, if not, watch out for the consequences. The splendid theatrical work of Arthur Miller, all of it, is a humane, inclusive project, a call to pay attention and reach out a hand to those, precisely, who are not like you or me, to the men and women who, owing to their differences, complete our own identity. To recognise ourselves in him or her who is not like you or me. Perhaps this value, expressed in terms of dramatic conflict, is the common thread that runs through Miller's dramas, *All My Sons, Death of a Salesman, The Crucible, A View from the Bridge, After the Fall.*

Arthur Miller makes us feel that the dilemmas of the men and women of North America are our own, shared by a world to which Miller says: there is an America that, like the rest of us, like all our brothers and sisters, is wounded in its humanity. In *Death of a Salesman,* Willy Loman talks to us tragically from the abyss of a growing separation between being and not being, having and not having, belonging or not belonging, loving and being loved. I say 'tragically' and I allude to Miller in this way not only as the inheritor of the situational theatre of Ibsen but also the cathartic theatre of Sophocles. In reality, the human and social conflicts of Miller's theatre are built upon a revived tragic vision which tells us, let's not deceive ourselves. We don't live in the best of all possible worlds. It is our duty to re-create a humane community, a city worthy of our best possibilities as creatures of God. To know ourselves as fallible is to know ourselves as human and to recognise ourselves as interdependent. The theatre of Arthur Miller possesses the power of tragedy; it turns our experience into destiny and our destiny into freedom. William Styron said that Miller was a Lincoln of letters. I say that he was a Quixote on the world's great stage, showing us, again and again, that windmills are gigantic and that human imagination, if it can't change the world on its own, can – and it always can – imagine a new and, hopefully, a better world. The death of Arthur fills us with great pain, but also with a nostalgic affection for all his friends.

Translated by Hazel Marsh

Michael Gambon

Actor: A Memory of Two Mondays, Unity Theatre, 1961; The Crucible, Old Vic Theatre, 1965; A View from the Bridge, National Theatre, 1987

The first time I met Arthur Miller was in 1965 when I was playing a small part in *The Crucible* for the National at the Old Vic. He was introduced to the cast and I told him that four years earlier I had played a boy in a warehouse in his play *A Memory of Two Mondays* at Unity Theatre. He seemed interested to hear this because he said it was very rarely done; he told me the play was autobiographical. We next met when I was playing Eddie Carbone in *A View from the Bridge* for the NT in 1987, which he came to see a couple of times. He seemed to like it a lot and the fact that he approved was so moving.

One night there was a dinner given in his honour, to which we were all invited. I think all the people there from the literary and arts world were a bit miffed that I was seated next to Arthur and we were chatting away about tables and chairs. That was what we shared, I think: a need to make things with our hands. I love working with metal and he loved working with wood.

He was a wonderful raconteur. I remember him telling a story about his friend Richard Widmark who, as a young actor, had worked with Ronald Reagan and now, in the 1980s, would look in the mirror each morning and remind himself in amazement, out loud, 'Ronnie is President!' And Arthur recounted how, when he had met Reagan at some White House do, the President had told the assembled dignitaries how he liked to meet the Marines because he knew the way to salute them, performing the gesture with great delight.

Miller was one of those legendary people, literary gods (Harold Pinter is another) who, if you had told me when I was starting out that I would ever even meet them, I wouldn't have believed it. Actually to have got to know them a bit is incredible.

Henry Goodman

*Actor: **After the Fall**, Royal National Theatre, 1990; **Broken Glass**, Royal National Theatre and BBC/HBO, 1994*

What Arthur meant to me:

'Man is least himself when he talks in his own person. Give him a mask and he will tell you the truth . . .' said Oscar Wilde. For me, Arthur Miller as a writer not only wore a mask that reveals his true insight into people and politics that provoke us all to action, he also gave us, the actors, a mask so fine that we can only wear it well if we want to accept the challenge to reveal truth. His work makes acting a dignified job. He was also wickedly humorous. As the self-loathing Jew, Phillip Gellburg, in *Broken Glass*, I was about to have a heart attack and near dying in bed having discovered 'there are Chinese Jews' when he said at one rehearsal, 'Ya know, he can laugh before he dies!'

His autobiography is a great testament to his frank insight into the times that shaped him as a young man. But the plays are the place where the struggle in each of us to have the courage to see beyond ourselves is realised. If you keep sanding and polishing the surface of one of his beloved pieces of wood you get smooth, beautiful, fluent, flowing shapes that are the grain soothed over. But if you have the courage, and a really sharp saw, cut a cross-section down through the same honed plank of glowing timber, and you can see the corpuscular tension that keeps the whole thing together. His plays have that exposure of the fibres of everyday life while always tempting us with beguiling surface shapes that try to keep our gaze – success, money, nice homes, nationalism, moral superiority. What are they built on, what is the vein-filling resin that really binds them together? When I act in his plays I feel as if I am inside the timber looking out. I believe he lets the audience see the timber whole and, through the actor/characters, the bits and bonds that made it whole.

Nadine Gordimer

Writer

Arthur Miller, Shaw, Beckett and O'Neill are the playwrights who interpreted and illuminated the twentieth century, not only the events but the effects on the formation of the contemporary human ethos – socio-political, moral and personal. On stage, for the larger stage of our existence, they brought together each in his own way in the essential *disunity* of our times, what we made of ourselves, what we are as we attempt to transform the world in the twenty-first century.

Great works gather relevance as one era passes to another. Arthur Miller's *The Crucible*, harking back to the witch-hunts of Salem to expose those of McCarthy, is a living allegory of the fundamentalist witch-hunts among which we are surrounded in the 'globalised' millennium. Many of his other plays open deep into the ground of sexuality and politics: timeless motivations in human lives.

Arthur Miller's stunning plays mean that he will always be celebrated as a dramatist. But he also wrote a unique autobiography by a twentieth-century man of the arts and from the existential experience of that violent century. *Timebends* is brilliantly written, a statement of a life fully lived, shouldered, along with the destiny of developing a great creative gift, with the circumstances, the stark realities of the world as a writer and as a man; courage without bravado, honesty without self-advertisement.

I had known Arthur through my strong responses to his plays long before I met him for the first time when he was President of International PEN. Often it's best not to meet the writer whose work means much to you; encounters in the flesh rather than through the transformations of creation can be dismaying. I've had some such . . . Arthur's clear-cut self was an immediate exception. And when we met on the unexpected pleasure of his invitation, during my subsequent visits to the USA, we found without need to be explicit that we had much in common. Arthur in his risky and punished opposition to the Un-American Activities Committee and the Vietnam War, I in opposition to apartheid and the banning of my books in my country; both of us in action against racism anywhere. By coincidence my son Hugo Cassirer was one of a team who made a documentary film about Inge Morath and this brought us closer. A decade ago my husband Reinhold Cassirer and I went to the Miller–Morath home in Roxbury over Thanksgiving and I remember with special pleasure the hour spent with Arthur introducing me to his carpentry workshop. Not really a surprise that his skill with words found a material complement in shaping wood.

In 2004 I thought it was time writers did something together to raise awareness of the pandemic of HIV–AIDS and I took the chance of writing to twenty suggesting that if each would give me, without fee, one of what they considered among their best stories, I would compile an anthology to be sold for the benefit of people suffering the disease in Southern Africa, worst afflicted area in the world. I had an enthusiastic response from all twenty, who numbered among the most distinguished internationally. I didn't request a particular choice of story that I was familiar with in their oeuvre, with one exception. I had recently read Arthur's story 'Bulldog' in the *New Yorker* – the most delightful, funny and moving exploration of adolescence, halfway between childhood and burgeoning sexuality. Written by a man in his eighties, what a perfect example of the gift of writers to identify with the mind and emotion of any age, personally long past, or still to be lived! I asked Arthur to choose that story, and he amusedly consented. It is the opening one in the anthology *Telling Tales*, whose contents include tales by five Nobel Literature laureates; Arthur should, if the Nobel Foundation had not been inexplicably remiss, certainly have been the sixth. Fourteen publishers worldwide published the book, taking production costs only, no royalties, and over 90,000 copies have been sold.

I can say with no less than the frankness and honesty Arthur himself kept to, in work and life, how wonderful it was to know him. When Inge and Reinhold died within weeks, four years ago, he wrote to me as only he would know, the right words between us: 'This is to touch hands.' The anthology was launched by the Secretary-General of United Nations, Kofi Annan, in December 2004 and Arthur agreed that he would give a reading of his story in participation with me, Salman Rushdie and John Updike – and then there was the sad call when he told me that he was suffering a second bout of pneumonia and would not be able to be with us. His voice was even more thoughtfully gentle than that I knew; it dropped as he added in the confidence of our friendship, as if another touch of the hands, 'It's cancer.'

Arthur Miller was a whole human being: his outstanding gifts as a writer, his warmth of understanding, his public courage. He stays with me in the steadfast example of his own words from *Timebends* as he refuses to 'kowtow before the state, the century's only truly credible god' and in his knowledge of how one really works as a writer. He says what is as true for me, in the writing of a novel: 'One learns to listen to what a developing play is trying to say.'

Stephen Greif

Actor: Death of a Salesman, National Theatre, 1979–80; A View from the Bridge

Arthur Miller. The name is a mantra to me. Arthur alone is enough. For some, William Shakespeare or just plain Will does the trick. For me it's Arthur, Arthur Miller. I never tire of chanting that name. But why? When I was a kid, my dad, who was a terrific salesman (Austrian-Jewish, the best), used to say to my elder brother, 'Son. Whatever happens, never work for commission only, it's the death of a salesman.' That phrase, meaningless to me then, stuck. Years later, by chance, I saw Rod Steiger on UK TV in a play with that same title and was poleaxed by the similarity in dialogue and attitudes to business and people that pervaded my own family. In the same year I saw Richard Castellano play Eddie Carbone at the Sheridan Playhouse in New York. I had never seen a family drama and acting as real as in that production. I went round to meet Mr Castellano afterwards to tell him so. I had to. I couldn't not. The following year I saw John Neville play Willy on stage in Nottingham (he was a revelation. Willy as a thin man! By now I had seen pictures of Lee Cobb and Paul Muni) and shortly after that Albert Salmi and Harold Gary in *The Price* in London. I went with my dad and we were sat near the front row and at the curtain call Dad looked up at Mr Gary (who was playing Solomon, easily the best I have ever seen) in open-mouthed admiration. I had never seen that look on my father's face. So strong was it that Harold Gary looked down at my dad and smiled and nodded in a kind of mutual understanding.

All these were the works of one man, Arthur Miller, who wrote about families and their conflicts, conflicts that were real and true and, as I have said, in part bore comparison to my own family and background. How could a stranger know about my family and me? Arthur Miller did. Ten years later the National Theatre revived *Salesman* and more than anything I wanted to play Biff. I had to. I met Michael Rudman, whose wonderful Nottingham production I had seen, and read for him and Warren Mitchell who was to play Willy. He and I had played father and son before on television in a play by another Jewish playwright, Bernard Kops. I got the part. I was in Arthur Miller heaven. The man himself came over from Connecticut to work with us for a week. That was Miller heaven times ten, as it must be for anyone who has had the good fortune to work with him. Over the years I have corresponded with my great hero from time to time and once when I had difficulty with a moment in *A View from the Bridge* I wrote and asked him for his advice. He replied by return, clarifying the moment and solving my dilemma.

But it is not just the work. It is the man and his character and his wonderful face. Is there another face to the Miller we have seen over the years on documentaries and in print, championing the cause of writers and injustices? I think not.

What I think I will cherish and remember most is that rascally, almost cheeky, wide-knowing, narrow-eyed grin of his after a knowing remark; that and his hearty open laugh on the photograph commemorating his eightieth birthday, which stands proudly on my desk as I write this and makes me smile every time I look at it.

John Guare

Writer

A vivid memory: an evening in 1951. I've just turned thirteen.

My father: 'Hurry up. Finish your dinner. We're going to the movies.'

A school night?

My mother: 'What movie?'

My father: 'Not you. Just him and me.'

My mother: 'What movie am I not invited to?'

'*Death of a Salesman.*'

'That depressing thing? Include me out. Isn't that by Arthur Miller? Isn't he in your favorite book? And you're going?'

She pointed to the book my father kept by the television/radio console. It was called *Red Channels* and named names in show business, telling you who was a Communist so you could avoid their work when they dared come on the air.

My father had to refer to it a lot in his proud capacity as vice-chairman in charge of Americanism at his American Legion post, Elmjack #298. He was a World War One veteran, had been wounded and took his post with utmost seriousness. I wasn't sure what the responsibilities of that powerful position were, but if, say, Lena Horne was singing on the TV or the radio, Eddie would instantly snap her off.

'Hey, I was listening to Lena Horne.'

'You can't. She's here in *Red Channels*. She's getting her message across.'

'I don't hear any message.'

'Of course you don't hear it. I hear it and I'm not going to have her poison in this house.'

While my father put on his coat, I looked into *Red Channels*. There was Arthur Miller! All his activities! 'American Youth Congress. 1938.' (The year I was born.) 'Speaker' in 1947: 'Abolish America's thought police' reported in the *Daily Worker*. Two and half pages of Communist listings! Why were we going to something written by a Commie out for world domination? Wait! Was my father going to close down *Death of a Salesman* the way Father Mooney a few years before at our church, St Joan of Arc, had organised a protest against the showing of the film *Stromboli* starring the previously saintly Ingrid Bergman when it played at the Boulevard Theater. (Ingrid Bergman, who was happily married, had become pregnant by Roberto Rossellini in defiance of the sacred fact that she had played our very own Joan of Arc on stage and in the movies, thereby defiling and insulting women everywhere but especially the women of our parish. Father Mooney had shut *Stromboli* down.) Was my father about to lead a protest against *Death of a Salesman*? This would be exciting. Or embarrassing.

We walked fast up the street to the Colony Theater. We had to be there when it started. I was stymied. I couldn't ask him anything about this. Talking was not in the range of comfortable tasks for him unless he was in a rage, which was a lot of the time, and then he yelled in an incoherent blather, or else had a lot of drinks under his belt, which was every weekend, making him very merry and not shut up from Friday night to Sunday. Either way he was pretty much unintelligible. My mother blamed it on the tensions of his working in a job he hated in the New York Stock Exchange.

The theater was empty, not packed as it was when a Bob Hope/ Bing Crosby road picture played. The movie began. Frederic March drove around in a car, looking frightened. I didn't like this movie. It jumped around in time. Can we go? My father told me to keep quiet and stared at the screen, transfixed. He even stayed awake, didn't fall asleep the way he always did at every other movie. Willy did something bad in Boston. Willy died. There was a funeral. I hated funerals. As an altar boy I had once fainted at a funeral and was never assigned to funerals again. I wanted to get out. It was over.

We walked home. I was very puzzled.

He said, looking straight ahead, 'I wanted you to see this movie – because – you have to know this.' Oh God, know what? I was adopted? I was being sent away? Divorce? This is what he said: 'I got out of the war. 1919. Left New York. Went to Los Angles. I was a salesman.'

'You lived in Los Angeles?' This was so exciting!

'For Proctor and Gamble.'

'You worked for Ivory soap?'

'It didn't work out.'

'What didn't work out?'

'It. It. It! I wanted you to see this story so I could tell you this.'

'Tell me what?'

'This! What you just saw! It didn't work out. Now you know.'

What had I seen?

Silence.

We got home. Laughter. My mother was watching late-night Jack Paar. 'How was *Death of a Salesman*? Wow. A real laugh fest.' She got up to make a last cup of coffee. Eddie mumbled something and got ready for bed.

I whispered to her, 'Did you know after the war, Eddie lived in Los Angeles and sold Ivory soap?'

My mother stopped scooping coffee into the percolator. 'News to me.' She turned on the flame and went back to the antics of Jack Paar and his guest.

My father never mentioned anything about this again. If I pressed him for details on Los Angeles or his secret time as a salesman, he'd say, 'What are you studying for – the FBI?' In Miller's play they ask, 'What happened in Boston, Willy?' and we find out. But in my life, what happened in Los Angeles, Eddie? What didn't work out? That question never got answered. But what was he trying to tell me that winter night in 1951? What had he thought seeing *Death of a Salesman* explained to me in a way that he could never explain? What was it that so transfixed my father that it compelled this vice-chairman in charge of americanism not only to break his vows of battling the forces of international Communism and see this story by this man in *Red Channels* but also risk taking his kid to it? What was he trying to tell me? What hadn't worked out? What was the unintelligible secret that Willy Loman's story had illuminated so clearly to him? What was he trying to pass on to me?

I went to the library and got a copy of *Death of a Salesman* but it was too hard for this thirteen-year-old to read. I mean, I could read the words, but I was looking for the secret, the line, the moment that had spoken with such clarity to my father. What story had he seen?

I started reading other plays. *The Glass Menagerie. Three Sisters.* Did they have a secret that nailed people to their chairs, that gave a voice to people who didn't have a voice. Would I find a play that spoke to me, for me? A play can do this?

To this day *Death of a Salesman* remains the most mysterious play I've ever seen or read.

A. R. Gurney

Writer, friend and neighbour

Arthur Miller was a protean guy, so it's hard to pick him up by one particular handle. But I'm not sure that enough attention has been paid to his delicious sense of humor. Several of his plays have funny scenes, most notably those with the old furniture dealer in *The Price*, but, for me, Miller's comic instincts showed up most engagingly in real life. Over drinks, at the dinner table, driving down to New York, between sets on the tennis court, his eyes would twinkle and out would come an ironic observation or extended anecdote which would lead to a wry comic pay-off. Miller is often associated with Ibsen for his solid craftsmanship and moral sensibility, and sometimes with Bellow for his ethnic awareness and breadth of vision. Yet as I remember him personally, I'm more often reminded of Mark Twain.

Ronald Harwood

Writer

I first heard of Arthur Miller just after the Second World War when I was still a schoolboy in Cape Town where I was born and educated. His name was inevitably linked with Tennessee Williams. The two playwrights had exploded on the post-war scene and were universally hailed as the outstanding dramatists of the new generation. Having become obsessed by the theatre, I remember longing to see their plays. The chances of doing so were not quite so dim as might be expected in a place several thousand miles from the centre of things.

For a small city Cape Town had, it seems to me now, a flourishing theatrical life. There were occasional visits from British variety stars – George Formby and Tommy Trinder loom large in my memory – and big overseas touring productions of *Oklahoma* and *Annie Get Your Gun*. Alicia Markova, Anton Dolin and an Italian opera company led by Beniamino Gigli and Luigi Infantino thrilled us; we also had a weekly repertory company and there were productions of more serious work by the university drama department. However, some of the more outstanding plays of the time were presented by independent producers and directors among whom Leonard Schach was an outstanding example.

Schach, whom later I knew well, was talented, well-off and well-travelled. In the immediate post-war years he made sorties to England and the United States where he managed to cajole agents and playwrights into selling him the rights of the most acclaimed plays being performed in the West End and on Broadway. It was Leonard Schach who brought *Death of a Salesman* to Cape Town.

For the production he imported an American actor, Jacob Ben-Ami, to play the part of Willy Loman. Ben-Ami hailed from the

Yiddish theatre and was a star both in Europe and the United States. Arthur Miller, I learned later, thought him excellent and referred to him in a lecture as an example of an actor whose impressive technique owed much to Stanislavsky. It would be foolhardy, after more than fifty years, to trust my memory absolutely but I carry an image of an actor with a powerful presence, stocky, with high cheekbones and fierce eyes, a melodious voice capable of lilting inflections that betrayed his Yiddish background. I thought him magnificent.

But it was the play that overwhelmed me. I should explain that my father, who had died shortly before I attended the performance, was himself an unsuccessful salesman – commercial travellers, we called them – who tried to sell plastic hangers and, later, Sir Seymour cigarettes, named after the English actor-manager Sir Seymour Hicks. No more, I think, need be said. I had been moved by other playwrights, carried along by the stories they had to tell, quickened by their use of language, but never before had I felt so personally involved. This was a play about me and my world. I set Arthur Miller on Olympus.

Whenever the opportunity presented itself I saw a Miller play or read it. In England, when still an actor in rep, I appeared in one of them, among his best, *All My Sons*. My admiration for the playwright intensified although I have to admit I was critical of some of the work, which I occasionally found a touch didactic and strained. But *The Crucible* I thought a masterpiece, a brilliant historical metaphor for a contemporary malaise. And I think now he must have influenced me as a writer, for I was much drawn to the way he tackled moral and political dilemmas.

He provided an example of another sort and that was his fortitude, his ability to stand up for his principles when under enormous pressure, as he was during the McCarthy hearings. I also came to admire his strength and persistence to go on writing almost to the day he died.

My personal memories of him are vignettes, random but vivid, and they may be more about me than him, for which I apologise. Nevertheless, I want to set them down because, although I cannot claim to have known him well, my few encounters with him reveal, I believe, something of the endearing warmth of his personality.

More than twenty-five years after I saw *Death of a Salesman* I met him for the first time in New York, where I happened to be for two reasons. I was attending the final rehearsals for my play, *The Dresser*, which was about to have its Broadway première. Conveniently, I had also to interview on film American theatrical luminaries for my BBC 2 history of the theatre, *All the World's a Stage*. Arthur Miller had agreed to take part. We filmed him in my hotel suite. Apart from the BBC crew, my wife Natasha, and one of the producers of the series, Haidee Grainger, were also present. He arrived. The women's knees visibly weakened. He was obviously attractive, even I could see that, but what took me by surprise was how relaxed he was, how loose, how typically New York, how unlike one's imagination of, well, an Olympian playwright.

Interviewing him was a pleasurable experience largely because he wanted the conversation to go well. Afterwards I remember telling him of the effect *Death of a Salesman* had on me as an adolescent. I also told him that my father had been a failed salesman. He gave me the look of a man who had heard such confidences too many times before. I think he regretted that look because immediately afterwards he told me he had just booked seats for *The Dresser*.

Our paths did not cross again for ten years or so when I became President of English PEN, one of the many centres of the world organisation for writers which, among other things, fights for freedom of expression and seeks to help writers who have been oppressed for what they have written. We invited Miller to London to give the English PEN Centre's Writers' Day annual lecture. The evening before, we entertained him and his wife, Inge, to dinner at our home in Chelsea and, at some point during the evening, the subject of literary rows came up. I asked him whether he'd ever been involved in a literary row. He said yes, he had, with Norman Mailer. 'What was that about?' I asked.

He squeezed a smile and said, 'The Marilyn thing.'

On the day of the lecture, panic; he had either forgotten to pack the lecture or it had been lost. He made hurried notes and delivered a splendid talk. I never quite made up my mind whether the lecture had been genuinely mislaid or whether the loss was a ruse to enhance the excitement of the event, which it certainly did.

In 1993 I was elected International President of PEN following in his footsteps; he had held the post in 1965. Because PEN had successfully campaigned for Václav Havel when he was being hounded by the Czech Communist regime, the first week-long

Congress I presided over was held in Prague in November 1994. Havel, by then President of the Czech Republic, was our host. Arthur attended and so did Tom Stoppard. It had been decided that during the week the four of us would hold a public symposium on playwriting in a theatre in Pilsen. Stoppard and I were allotted cars in Havel's motorcade but Arthur and his wife decided to go by train. As I told them afterwards, they missed a sensational ride. Escorted by motorcycle outriders, we sped from Prague along the highway at enormous speeds. When we emerged from our cars, Tom said, 'I could get seriously used to this.'

The pity is I remember very little about what was said at the symposium except that Arthur, Tom and I spoke, of course, in English and Havel in Czech with the aid of an interpreter. What I do remember, however, was Arthur's enjoyment of the event. He said afterwards, in a somewhat surprised voice, 'That was fun. I really enjoyed it.' Later, Inge told a colleague he thought he'd like to do more of the same, talking about his trade with other writers. He was visibly warmed by fellowship.

We met for the last time in New York. He'd come to see my play *Taking Sides* which he said he much admired. But I'd received a rotten review from the *New York Times* and it must have been somehow evident in my demeanour. 'You don't seem too pleased,' he said. No, I told him. I was touched that he liked the play but then explained the reason for my obvious despondency. 'Don't worry about it,' he said. 'You'll find as you get older they'll start giving you nothing but good reviews.'

'Is that what's happened to you?' I asked.

'Not yet,' he said.

Roy Hattersley

Writer, politician: former Deputy Leader of the Labour Party

Arthur Miller was late. The reception began at half past five, but at almost a quarter to seven the guests in the combination room of Saint Catherine's College were still awaiting his arrival. He had, the Master explained, spent longer in London with Isaiah Berlin than his schedule allowed and missed his train to Oxford – clearly an adequate excuse for the long delay. Small talk was impossible. Life was suspended until Arthur Miller arrived.

At first, as he came through the door, I assumed that he had hurried straight to the reception without changing into the suit he was to wear for his inaugural lecture as Visiting Professor. Months later I realised that, on that auspicious night, he was wearing what he always wore – tweed jacket, slacks and open-necked shirt. But at that first meeting – seeing him looking like an Israeli Cabinet minister about to address the Knesset – I was deeply impressed by his ability to remain calm and composed, though late and strangely dressed. My admiration for his poise was to be increased immensely by his demeanour at the end of the lecture.

To be honest, it was not really a lecture. For almost an hour Arthur Miller chatted discursively about his life and work. Life occupied more time than work. But he did describe his growing rage, back in the fifties, against the pogroms of Senator Joe McCarthy and the United States Senate's Un-American Activities Committee. McCarthy, he said, had described General Marshall – Secretary of State to President Roosevelt and the only true begetter of the economic plan which saved Europe from starvation – as a Communist. And Marshall was 'the nearest thing in modern America to George Washington'. Perhaps Miller was doing no more than emphasising how absurd the allegation of treason was. But I suspected that he was also revealing his close connection to old-fashioned patriotism. Arthur Miller was always in search of a better America.

At the end of the lecture, the Master of the College – Professor the Lord Plant of Highfield, distinguished political philosopher – told the audience that Arthur Miller had agreed to answer questions. There was the usual hiatus. Then a man in a loud tweed suit rose and, rather unsteadily, asked for more biographical information. 'Which did you enjoy most, watching the Brooklyn Dodgers, working in the Brooklyn shipyard or sleeping with Marilyn Monroe?' Lord Plant looked as though he was about to suffer a heart attack. Arthur Miller cupped his hand to his ear and in what, I was later assured, was a confession of genuine deafness, asked for a reprise.

The audience was too traumatised to hiss or mutter its disapproval. The questioner, on the other hand, was full of vigour. He repeated his question word for word. I feared that Lord Plant's incipient heart attack would be complicated by a cerebral haemorrhage. Arthur Miller, despite hearing the question at the second time of asking, remained absolutely calm. 'I would', he replied, 'be happy to answer were I convinced that you were genuinely seeking information.' The lecture hall burst into spontaneous applause. Doctors of Literature cheered. Authorities on Anglo-Saxon stamped their feet. Experts in Jacobean poetry clapped wildly. Miller seemed hardly to notice.

I sat next to him at dinner – irresistibly reminded of a Cambridge dinner long ago when the Nawab of Pataudi was so overawed by the proximity of Jack Hobbs that he could not bring himself to speak. Realising, as the coffee cups were cleared away, that he must say something, he blurted out the first thing that came into his mind. '*The Times* says that I'm the best young batsman in England.' When I found words, they were almost as gauche. A couple of months before I had seen *The Last Yankee* and had not enjoyed it. Indeed, I had rather disapproved of the way in which it treated mental illness. Did he, I asked, mind a philistine audience laughing in the wrong places? 'Not at all,' he said. 'One of the objects of the theatre is to bring happiness . . .' Before I could quibble, he added, 'And laughter in the theatre makes box-office managers very happy indeed.' Collapse of stout party.

We moved on to *The Ride Down Mount Morgan,* which I had seen in New York. It had been neither a critical nor a commercial success when it was produced in London and Tom Conti, the star, had told me why that was. He felt too young and too small for the part and found difficulty in making a hero out of a character who 'whines and whinges his way through the first act'. The play was obviously going wrong in rehearsals but he dared not say so. 'He was Arthur Miller and I was just Tom Conti and he's such an obviously good man as well as a genius.'

It must have been difficult to contradict, or even second guess, a man who inspired both awe and affection. And Miller's physical presence, as well as his literary reputation, made him a man with whom it was difficult to disagree – especially on the subject of his own plays. But Patrick Stewart showed the way during the rehearsals for the Broadway *The Ride Down Mount Morgan*. In Miller's rewrite, a character who never appeared on stage was discussed during the first act but then forgotten. The cast agreed that he was surplus to requirements and, after much hesitation, deputed Stewart to say so. Miller asked for a day to think it over. Next morning, his first words were, 'He's gone.' Modesty was, no doubt, a sign of confidence. That night he seemed totally unaware of the reverence in which he was held. He argued with me aggressively. But he argued as if we were equals – which was highly flattering but equally absurd.

We argued about *The Ride Down Mount Morgan*, which he called 'an investigation into the morality of deceit'. I was foolish enough to say that I had always thought of his major plays as being essentially messages of hope. In their darkest moments, they always pointed to something better than the tragedies which were being acted on stage. Miller did not argue, but asked me, 'How much hope is there in *Hamlet*?' We then agreed that hope is where you find it.

Despite my wholly enjoyable evening, when the *Guardian* suggested that I write a profile of Arthur Miller, awe still prevented me from writing directly to him. Lord Plant sent a note to New York preparing the way for what would have been my formal request – had Miller not replied to Plant by return of post with both his agreement and a suggested date. The date was hideously inconvenient but, of course, I accepted at once.

The humble austerity of Miller's flat should not have surprised me. I could not, however, have been expected to anticipate the early drift of our conversation. He had made much of the furniture himself and he was anxious to display and talk about his handiwork. A table was overturned to demonstrate the professional neatness of the joints. Somehow the subject moved from carpentry to Montgomery Clift – an actor whose phenomenal appetite had caused him to raid the Millers' refrigerator, in the middle of the night, and eat the cold chicken which had been prepared for the following day's lunch. I had expected a struggle to keep up as the greatest living playwright considered Ibsen and Chekhov. And for the first half-hour of our meeting we gossiped.

Had he, I asked, ever met General George Marshall? He told me again of the disbelief he felt when 'the closest to George Washington this country has ever come was accused of being a card-carrying Communist'. Warming to the subject he added, 'The country was going crazy, infected by evil. The *New York Times* published this garbage and, when asked why, said it was news. We were over the cliff and up to our neck in water. I could barely breathe. The only way I could survive was by metaphor.' The metaphor was called *The Crucible*.

Some of his closest friends and associates had testified before McCarthy's Un-American Activities Committee and had supplied the names of men and women who, they alleged, had attended meetings of the Communist Writers Association. Among the turncoats who agreed to testify was Elia Kazan, with whom Miller had worked since the first production of *All My Sons*. 'It was black. I was totally disheartened about human beings. It's hard to explain how I felt. It's like trying to talk about toothache. How do you describe toothache? Pain is indescribable. It was all pain.'

In the end, Miller forgave everybody – Kazan included. Lee J. Cobb – Willy Loman in the first production of *Death of a Salesman* – he forgave at once. 'He testified because all he wanted to do was act. He had no connection with anything political. He went through the ritual and said he had been a Communist and named Tom, Dick and Harry so that he could get back on stage.' The forgiveness was mixed with contempt. Political commitment, however displayed, was clearly very important to him. He told me, without a hint of intentional hyperbole, that 'after his bombing of Cambodia, Henry Kissinger should have been tried as a war criminal' and then described with disbelief how the Chicago Police had dispersed a demonstration of anti-war protesters in 1968. 'The police had coils of barbed wire on their jeeps and drove them so near to the protesters that the front row got cut. I could not believe that was happening in the United States.' His innate belief in the fundamental decency of the Great Republic survived attempts to impeach President Clinton, which he attributed to a right-wing conspiracy. Clinton came very close to being his favourite President. 'At least I could talk to him. We had some humanity in common.'

The mention of humanity emboldened me to raise a subject which it was impossible to avoid during any long conversation with Arthur Miller. Did he, or did Joe DiMaggio (her first husband) say that Marilyn Monroe 'needed a blessing'? Instead of answering the question directly, he replied, 'She needed a miracle and none were available'. Marilyn Monroe, he said, 'was a basically serious person who had hopes for herself in that direction but did not have time to develop'. At the press conference to launch the film version of Terence Rattigan's *The Sleeping Prince* (*The Prince and the Show Girl*) she had announced that she hoped to play in a stage version of

The Brothers Karamazov. 'She even knew the part she wanted to play, Grusenka. A journalist asked if she knew how to spell it. They could not believe that sex and seriousness existed in the same woman.'

After lunch Miller suggested that, next evening, I went with him to the Signature Theatre on West 42nd Street, where a ceremony was taking place 'to honour John Guare' – a playwright and screenwriter whose entire canon had been performed at the theatre during the previous year. Miller (apparently wearing the same jacket, shirt and slacks he had worn in Oxford) spoke the first encomium. It included an old joke in which Moss Hart shows George S. Kaufman the fully grown trees which had been planted in his California garden and suggests, 'Imagine what God could have done if he had the money.' It also contained congratulations to Guare on writing the film script for *Atlantic City* and thus achieving the almost impossible task of making Burt Lancaster look human. He then returned to his seat on my left and, leaning across me, waved in the direction of a small, neat, bespectacled man sitting on my right. 'Do you', he asked, 'know Ed Albee?'

At supper that night we talked about politics, not the theatre, but it was difficult for me to think of anything else except that moment in the stalls of the Signature Theatre.

> Say I'm weary, say I'm sad
> Say that health and wealth have missed me
> Say I'm growing old but add
> One night, in a little theatre in New York, I sat
>   between Arthur Miller and Edward Albee.

Václav Havel

Writer, politician: President of the Czech Republic

At the turn of the 1960s, when we in Czechoslovakia were living in profound isolation from the Western world and Miller's plays were first staged here as an enormous rarity and sensation, I had the impression, particularly in view of my youth and relative social exclusion, that this author hovered somewhere in the firmament of world drama; subconsciously I was unable to imagine that he could be a real person with a physical existence, let alone that we might meet one day. Miller visited my country shortly after its occupation by the Warsaw Pact in 1968. At the time I was so utterly taken up with local events that I failed to realise something of great importance.

At that time I met with him in the apartment of my friends, the artist Libor Fára and the photography theorist Aneta Fárová, who happened also to be a friend of Miller's wife and later organised an exhibition of her photographs in Prague. I think we lunched together at the Fáras'. And right after lunch I excused myself because I had to collect my car from the auto-repair centre, and left, as if unaware that I had a chance to speak with this visitor from the heavens and that I was leaving for reasons that must appear trivial or even absurd to him. But I really did urgently need my car for some patriotic task, and the repair centre closed early and it was not possible for them to deliver it to my home – as in capitalism; I had no one to pick it up for me, the weekend was coming and I just had to go for the car. My departure was extremely inappropriate, of course, and I agonised over it afterwards – particularly in jail, when I discovered how Miller was working actively for my release.

That discomfiture lasted at least twenty-one years, i.e. until I started meeting Miller more and more frequently after our revolution, and I discovered that not only had he not been annoyed with me, but that he had no memory at all of my hasty and somewhat shameful departure. I was already President by then and Miller and I met many times, and once he actually prefaced his own speech with my speech about Madeline Albright at a dinner in her honour in New York. Another time, along with other 'celestial beings', we partied at the Styrons' home in Connecticut, and once we discussed theatre together on the stage of the attractive Municipal Theatre in Pilsen during the Theatre Festival there. But that is another chapter of my life and of terrestrial and celestial history.

This year I have used this occasion when we all commemorate Miller's ninetieth birthday, simply to admit for the first time how stupidly I behaved all those years ago, when he descended from the literary and civic heavens before my very eyes and how that recollection tormented me for so long. I am sending this message to him in the real heaven to which he departed not long ago.

Nick Hern

Publisher

'But you can't call it *Timebends*, Arthur. That makes it sound like a science fiction novel!' It was 1985 and we were, of course, discussing Miller's autobiography, which, as drama editor at Methuen, I had commissioned him to write.

'Listen, Nick,' he answered in his implacable drawl. 'No one much liked *Death of a Salesman* as a title either. They said nobody would come to a play with death in the title, and who was interested in salesmen anyway?'

Well, there was no answer to that and the autobiography was duly published – as *Timebends* – on 5 November 1987. Arthur liked hearing that this was – appropriately – Fireworks Day, just as he liked other quirky British-isms. Once, when he and Inge and I were playing hookey from a conference in his honour at the University of East Anglia, we came across a signpost to the Norfolk village of Great Snoring – which provoked Much Grinning. And he would insist on referring to my own place of residence as Chiss-wick, always accompanied by a twinkle in the eye and that grin that would split his face in half. The last time I saw him alive – in November 2003 at the 92nd Street 'Y' in New York, where he had just given a public interview to a packed and (for him) overly reverential audience – the first thing he said to me was, 'Hey, Nick, do you still live in that funny place, what was it?'

'Chiss-wick, Arthur?'

'Yeah, that's it, Chiss-wick!' And that grin again, totally belying his eighty-eight years.

I first met Arthur Miller in the winter of 1983. Chris Bigsby had alerted me to the fact that there were some unpublished plays that pre-dated *All My Sons*, which he, Bigsby, was seeking to persuade Arthur to allow to be published. I put it to the powers that be at Methuen (one of whom was Geoffrey Strachan, also a contributor to this volume) that if they stumped up for Chris and me to go on a transatlantic fishing trip, the catch might be some unpublished Arthur Miller. To their credit, they duly stumped up – and eventually they got their money back. But it wasn't as simple a decision as it must now seem.

The general perception throughout the seventies was that Miller had gone off the boil, had not written anything much since *After the Fall,* and that even that play was badly flawed, being a self-seeking justification of his treatment of Marilyn Monroe. Americans, I think, actually blamed him somehow for her death, however much that ran counter to the facts. In Britain he was admired – and endlessly prescribed on O and A level syllabuses – as the author of *The Crucible* and *Salesman,* but otherwise he was pretty much a blank, past his best, possibly even dead. Far from it, of course. As I got to know Arthur better, it emerged that not only were there the forgotten plays from the thirties, there were also much more recent plays which had had largely unregarded premières in the States in what we would call the provinces – and then slipped from sight. So, back in London and with Arthur's very active co-operation, I was able to publish in 1984 – for the first time anywhere in the world – *The Archbishop's Ceiling,* and a double bill of one-act plays, *Two-Way Mirror,* which brought the Arthur Miller canon up to date and which led eventually to the British premières of these plays at the Bristol Old Vic (1986) and the Young Vic (1989) respectively. Two years later came another double bill, *Danger: Memory!,* published in advance of its world première at the Lincoln Center. It is now difficult to credit a situation where the recent work of a writer of the stature of Arthur Miller could as it were be lying around unpublished and unperformed. But such was the slump in his reputation.

The money Methuen initially lost on these publications – as I've indicated, they weren't exactly snapped up by an eager public – was partly offset by two paperback collections of his work, *Miller Plays One* and *Two.* Miller's London agent, Elaine Greene, who I think was having a bit of a spat with Penguin at the time, alerted me to the fact that paperback anthologies were not specifically covered in Penguin's publication contracts for Miller's plays. It was a loophole I was glad to exploit. Arthur and I discussed what to put on the covers. The series that the volumes were destined for had made a point of finding a correspondence between the writer and a particular painter. The covers of Pinter's plays, for instance, all featured Magritte. For Arthur's work I suggested Van Gogh, whose *Potato Eaters* in particular seemed to capture some of the implicitly campaigning sympathy for ordinary people to be found also in Arthur's plays. 'Too gloomy,' he pronounced. Somewhat floored, I suggested instead the painter he was most close to: his and Inge's

95

daughter, then barely in her twenties. And so it is that these editions carried original artwork by the now distinguished novelist and film-maker, Rebecca Miller – probably her first ever professional commission.

I saw a lot of Arthur throughout the eighties. He would come over to London quite frequently – with or without Inge – to see various productions of his plays. I particularly remember driving him down to Bristol for the British première of his 1944 play, *The Man Who Had All the Luck*. It was a lovely day (we had the roof off the car), and we were ahead of schedule, so I turned off the M4 to show him one of my favourite spots, the stone circle at Avebury. Entranced by its magic, we lost track of time, with the result that we found ourselves careening down the motorway well in excess of the speed limit so as not to miss curtain up. Arthur loved it. He was a man's man when it came to cars and had been emphatic in his approval of my upgrade from a Ford Orion to this BMW convertible. Whenever I turned up at his house in Roxbury, Connecticut, one of his first questions was always: 'What car are you driving now?'

My trips to Roxbury became even more frequent than his to London. He and Inge (and Inge's mother) were generous but unfussy hosts, and I would always stay over, sometimes for more than one night. Often there were dinner parties gathered round the huge oval cherry-wood table that Arthur had fashioned himself from trees grown on his own land. I never quite got used to finding Richard Widmark or Volker Schlöndorff or Martha Clarke also at the table. But informality was the keynote. Inge and her mother did all the cooking themselves, much of it again from produce grown in their garden – though 'garden' doesn't really cover it. The only grandiloquence of which Arthur could ever be accused was his evident pride in the fact that he had gradually bought more and more acreage surrounding his home until he could say, standing on the hill on whose summit sat the rangy timber-built house, that he owned all the land he could see. As a boy from Brooklyn, whose parents had been devastated by the Depression, this provided an enduring sense of security.

Just down the hill was a pool: not the bright blue, purpose-built job of American suburbia, but a natural depression in the hillside filled from an underground spring. It was the freshest water I've ever swum in and I'm sure that regular immersion in it contributed to Arthur's healthful longevity.

He also played a mean game of tennis well into his seventies. An enthusiastic but not very practised latecomer to the game myself, I remember facing up to his serve in a doubles game which happened to feature another playwright, A. R. (Pete) Gurney, as Miller's partner. With his racket an improbable – and surely unfair? – nine feet in the air at the point of impact, Arthur would send the ball across the net at a frankly unreturnable angle and velocity. I wasn't invited to play again.

But my most treasured memory is of the visits made during the writing of the autobiography. We fell into a routine. I would drive up from the city arriving in time for lunch, after which Arthur would produce the pages he'd written since my last trip. I would then retire to his study – which was a log cabin away from the house – and sit on its porch in the sunshine luxuriating in Arthur's rich and multi-layered life story. After I'd finished I'd make my way back to the house and join in with whatever the family and that evening's guests were doing until dinner time. Because the book was to be co-published with Harper and Row in New York and because they were going to employ an editor to work with Arthur on the detail, my role was the blissfully simple one of providing support and encouragement during the actual writing – and discussing the occasional 'big question' of structure or tone. But there was never anything I found problematic: the book seemed to flow from him fully formed. My memory is that what I read, episode by episode on the porch in Roxbury, was, apart from the odd correction of a date or a name, the book that was published as *Timebends.*

My lasting impression of Arthur Miller is of a man of impressive intellect and wisdom who was at the same time a 'regular guy'. A conversation with Arthur was one of the most stimulating experiences life could offer. Because of his droll matter-of-factness combined with wide-ranging erudition, I constantly felt a step or two behind, but the effort to keep up made me a better, wittier, more articulate conversational partner. Or so it seemed at the time. Arthur 'turned me on' more than than anyone else I've met. Plus there was always his only slightly world-weary sense of the ridiculous. His accounts of his and Harold Pinter's trip to Turkey to protest at the torturing of writers or of his ironic jousting in Lithuania with Tankred Golenpolksy (whom he suspected of working for the KGB and whom I had also encountered in Moscow the previous winter) were as full of laughter as of outrage. Everyone knows how seriously he took politics and world affairs, but he enjoyed pricking pomposity and nailing vanity. He had a good joke about Norman Mailer, who was apparently renowned for looking himself up in the indexes of other people's books. Arthur told of one book where, anticipating Mailer's attentions, the relevant entry read simply: 'Mailer, Norman – Hi Norm!'

Though famous, Arthur was not so well-known that he was unable to move around without being recognised. He would and could take public transport when he wanted. He told a story of waiting for the scheduled bus to take him from the airport in New York to upstate Connecticut. He asked the young man at the desk to be sure to tell him when the next bus was ready to depart. The young man went back to his book. Time passed. It became clear the young man had become so engrossed in his book that the bus had come and gone without his noticing. Arthur went to remonstrate and saw the title of the engrossing book: *The Crucible*. 'Isn't that something?' Arthur would say as he came to the punchline. And his face would fall in half with that infectious grin.

Greg Hersov

*Director: **Death of a Salesman**, 1985; **All My Sons**, 1988; **The Crucible**, 1990; **A View from the Bridge**, Royal Exchange Theatre, Manchester, 1992*

When I was a student I saw *Death of a Salesman* and *All My Sons*. Like everyone else I went 'that's my father and that's me' as Willy and Biff fought it out and I remember the total appalled attention that *All My Sons* compelled throughout. This direct connection, the passionate in-the-gut feeling I had and knew everyone there was also having, is something you treasure, as you never have that so purely once you become part of the profession. I always wanted to direct his plays because of those first encounters.

When I started as a director, Miller's stock wasn't that high in the UK. There seemed to be an image of this dry, serious, earnest intellectual who wrote rather ponderous plays that demanded solemn respect and little else. Because the Royal Exchange Theatre is a 750-seat purely in-the-round space, plays can only come alive through an emotional union between the actors and the audience. I knew that Miller's plays had this from my own experience but now I had to discover a way into them.

My inspiration was *Timebends*. If you're working on a Miller play this book is indispensable. He's deliberately left so many clues to the special atmosphere and circumstances in which his plays flower: his adolescent experience of the system crashing during the Depression and the way that fires his awareness of the true cost of business in *Salesman*; the idyllic Midwestern family setting with its secrets that he as an outsider experienced, that grew into the black hole of the Kellers' garden in *All My Sons*; his personal turmoil during which his marriage was ending and he was meeting Marilyn Monroe, and the way that fuels the erratic passions of the triangles of the Proctors and Abigail and the Carbones and Catherine in *The Crucible* and *A View from the Bridge*. This intertwining of his personal state with the history of his country is the great quality of *Timebends*. For me it released the red-hot emotions in the plays that made a nonsense of the abstracted coldness that his critics detected. I'm sure this was the reason Miller has been reclaimed and treasured in this country. The big ideas and issues make his work universal but it's the humanity of his characters and their personal stories that make his plays last.

I gave *Timebends* to an American writer, Alex Finlayson, whose play I had just directed because I think it can give great encouragement and help to any budding writer. She was galvanised by the great passage about *The Misfits* and decided to write a play about the events on the set of that strange, haunted film that brought together such an extraordinary group of disparate, talented egos. Suddenly Arthur Miller had become a character in another writer's imagination. The play *Misfits* was critical of him in some ways and that felt strange but I believed in it and continued my journey of understanding Miller through *Timebends*. The fascinating thing when you're reading the book is how the language and syntax of the writing starts to crack and fragment as he describes what he was going through as a writer and a husband up to and during the filming of *The Misfits*. I do think that *The Misfits* was a huge turning point in both his life and his art. It does seem extremely fitting that his last play, *Finishing the Picture*, returns to that time and place in his life.

I always carry in my head something Miller said about what theatre can do for us. 'It can make us feel less alone.' Whether you're an actor, director or audience member that's what his work does for you. Whatever your struggles, secrets, vulnerabilities, it's OK, you're with everyone else, just part of the human race.

Dustin Hoffman

Actor: **Death of a Salesman**, *New York, 1984*

The first time I met him was when I stage-managed *A View from the Bridge*. I thought I was going to faint when he came in to see the cast. He was my hero. He was so articulate. He was this great storyteller. He sounded like a New York cab driver. He was so unpretentious and earthy, and yet you're laughing at one minute, then you're thinking the next, then you're touched the next, because he is a storyteller. He's hitting those colors on the canvas.

My brother gave me a collection of plays when I was sixteen years old, before I ever thought of being an actor. I don't know why he bought me plays. It was the Gassner edition of the Best American Plays. I had never read a play and I had a small breakdown for about two weeks afterwards. I would walk around suddenly bursting into tears once in a while.

When I was up in Connecticut Arthur Miller asked me what I was going to do now and I said I think I'm going to do a play. I've been going through plays. And he said, 'Why don't you do *Salesman*?'

And I said, 'I can't do that part.'

And he said, 'Sure you can.'

We had a series of informal meetings just sitting on the grass for about two months. He knows his play like no one knows *Salesman*. It was like sitting on the lawn with Shakespeare and asking him how Richard III should be played. When we were rehearsing, if there was a new thought or idea he would say, 'Go ahead. Try it.' We would try it and he would say, 'Gee, I never saw that done before. Gee, that's kind of interesting.' He was always open to it or if he didn't agree he never said no. He said, 'I'll tell you why that doesn't work.' It was a very logical thing. It was as if he had never done the play before.

When he directed it in China, Inge told me, they wondered how it would go because this is about how capitalism can ruin a human being and they didn't have capitalism in China so what relevance would it have there. But it went off so well. A woman came up to her after the play and she was in tears. Inge said to her, 'Was your dad like Willy Loman?' and the woman said, 'No, my mother was like Willy Loman.' And that's the answer. It doesn't matter if your father or you mother is like Willy Loman, or if you are Chinese. It transcends.

I think you can tell from his plays whether a writer loves actors. Arthur gives you tap dances. He gives you arias.

He is what I look up to as a kid does to his father. He was my artistic father.

James Houghton

Artistic Director and founder of New York's Signature Theatre Company whose 1997–8 season featured Arthur Miller as a Playwright-in-Residence.

In early 2001 I was asked by the National Endowment for the Humanities to write a piece about the unique relationship that developed between me and Arthur Miller for an edition of their magazine, *Humanities*, celebrating Arthur on the occasion of his Jefferson Lecture.

Today, after making many attempts to write something new in honor of Arthur in recognition of our great, collective loss, I kept coming back to this piece for some reason . . . maybe because I'm still not ready to write about him in the past tense.

Here it is with a few thoughts to follow:

Sitting atop a Manhattan apartment building in a community garden lush with flowers marked the beginning of a relationship with Arthur Miller that opened my eyes and heart to a vista of possibilities I had not imagined.

Now, we all know that Arthur Miller has had an extraordinary life. You can pick up any one of his many plays, essays, or short stories, or perhaps his autobiography. We also understand that Arthur is highly regarded for his intellectual, cultural, and political contributions to our country and beyond. Some might recognize his good taste or know a bit about his carpentry skills and his passion for making practical furniture. Perhaps it is his relentless activism that strikes a chord with you. Maybe you have heard a thing or two about his travels around the world and his relationship with various leaders across the globe. Friends might note his family, his laps in his pond, or the grandchild that tickles him. Maybe it is the sweet ditty he wrote, 'Sittin' Aroun', from *The American Clock*, one of my favorites.

I suspect you have an inkling of the remarkable decades of experiences he has lived through and affected. The Great Depression comes to mind or, say, the McCarthy era, the civil rights struggle or the too frequent assassinations. Maybe it is the great jazz or big band era or the golden ages of radio, television, film, and, some would say, theater. Perhaps it is Watergate, Cuba, the Berlin Wall. It could be World War Two, Korea, Vietnam, or the Holocaust. You get the idea.

The whirlwind of history through which Arthur has passed is nothing less than tremendous, but what distinguishes him from others is that his passions have insistently pushed him to note time. He has been compelled to remember our past and, by not forgetting, to inform our future. What strikes me most about him, however, is his absolute insistence on living life in the present tense.

Living is something that Arthur does extremely well. Through each decade of his astonishing life, he has managed to be deeply touched and to have deeply touched many. His intellect is extraordinary, his wisdom cup full, his heart swollen to capacity, and his spirit is that of a shy, six-year-old kid trying not to let on.

One of my great pleasures in recent years has been to nudge Arthur about that deep well of optimism I know lies within him. I usually get a good laugh out of him when I warn him that he might be in danger of exposing that neatly covered reservoir. You see, I believe Arthur Miller is a dreamer and seeker of truth – the truth that lies within the mystery of human existence. He seeks the truth and dares to ask the big questions: 'Why am I here? How can I make a difference? Who am I? What am I?' By merely asking these questions – let alone pursuing cogent answers – Arthur reveals the optimist living within him. No one makes it through the last eighty-five years standing without a pillar of optimism to hold him up in the face of disappointment. Arthur Miller, not only are you an optimist, but a cheery one at that. Sorry, Arthur. Your cover is blown.

Perhaps most profound for me is Arthur's willingness to embrace his own fear. Fear is the common denominator for all of us. If there is a single gift that my friendship with Arthur has bestowed, it has been the demystification of fear.

Let me go back for a minute to that rooftop in Manhattan. I remember sitting across from Arthur that breezy spring day. We were there to talk about working together at my theater, Signature Theatre Company, where each year we have the pleasure of dedicating a season to a living writer. Arthur and I started by discussing each and every one of his plays and the various experiences associated with his canon. The work began to tell us what might be a meaningful season, as it always does when it's good. We talked not of his works known by many but, rather, the plays that held a special place in Arthur's heart. Some cried out for mending, some just for another chance, but all fed the spirit of discovery in both of us. As we talked, that kid inside Arthur surfaced. His eyes lit up as the ideas percolated.

We talked of putting together a season that would address those 'I wish I could reinvent' or 'If I had to do it over again' moments we have in our lives. It was quite a joy to give birth to the renewed potential in each play and, in doing so, to present a broader, deeper experience and appreciation of Arthur's work with Arthur involved in every step of the discovery.

Our conversation ultimately resulted in a 1997–98 season that included a reworking of *The American Clock*, *The Last Yankee* with *I Can't Remember Anything*, and the world première of *Mr. Peters' Connections*. In addition, the season presented a live broadcast of a radio play from the late thirties, *The Pussycat and Expert Plumber Who Was a Man*; and a reading by Arthur of his children's story, *Jane's Blanket*, which he read to a crowd of children and his now grown daughter Jane.

That season I had the pleasure of seeing Arthur at work – an artist who is completely in tune with his craft and, most important, who is understanding and respectful of his collaborators. He was always available and ready to expose the mystery of the creative moment, either by his willingness to accept newly discovered subtext, or by acknowledging the wonder of the creative process itself. No pretense . . . no bull . . . straight out. He gave life to his work by allowing it to breathe and evolve through respectful collaboration.

There was a fun moment when we were in rehearsal for *The American Clock*, a Depression-era tale that confronts the impact and toll of the time. It is a bit of a monster with fifteen actors playing some fifty roles and over thirty songs from the period to be performed. It's a big one. We were in the first week of rehearsal, breaking down the text and trying to get all the circumstances of the play in place, organising the facts. I remember one of the actors had pointed out a discrepancy in the text to Arthur – two facts that could not have occurred simultaneously. The room fell silent as Arthur contemplated this discovery. He turned to the actor and, with great authority and a devilish grin said, 'Mind your own business.' He was caught . . . and so were we all, by his honesty and good humor. It seems a simple thing, I suppose, to witness someone 'fessing up', but somehow the stakes seem higher when you are sitting in the room with one of the finest writers and minds of the twentieth century.

Toward the end of our season I sat with Arthur at the opening of his new play, *Mr. Peters' Connections*. We sat out in the lobby, both having opted to enjoy the peace of an empty room over the tension of an audience surely judging our every move. He turned to me and said, referring to our audience, 'Where do they come from? Who are they? Why do they come?' There was a sort of puzzlement, or anxiety – or could it be fear – that ran across Arthur's face in that moment, a revealing reflection of my own state of mind.

Those questions got me thinking and ultimately I realized that if we are to learn anything about ourselves, we must be willing to be afraid, to step forward into the abyss of uncertainty. Arthur's willingness to expose his own doubts and fears was an invitation for me to forgive my own. Surely, I thought, he has been at this a long time and doesn't feel what I feel. But of course he must. Arthur, by example, provided me with a great gift that day, liberating me from expectation and the grip of fear.

I realized in my time with Arthur that experience informs the present, but does not provide answers. Although we all hope for a clear path to take us wherever we think it should, remarkably, we finally realize there is no such thing. Here is Arthur Miller, playwright, intellectual, activist, etc. He must have it figured out, right? Wrong. What he has is the willingness to say 'I don't know', and to muster up enough courage to proceed, one foot in front of the other. He confronts his fear every day and runs straight at it, full speed ahead. Time has told him that there is no other choice worth pursuing if you are to live in the present tense. The final punch is that while our past informs our present, both are irrelevant unless we have the courage to 'know' nothing – to approach the present as if it were the first time. After all, isn't it?

Fear is a powerful tool when someone teaches you how to use it. Courage is contagious when you see the good it does and how it liberates you. Both, together, open your eyes and heart to a vista of possibilities previously unimagined. The 'kid' that is present in Arthur is the fear itself. It is his wonder at humanity and his astonishment that we ever connect to one another at all. He has managed, for all his years, to hold on to wonder, embrace fear, and challenge himself and a few others along the way.

That is some remarkable kid.

Shortly after I wrote this piece I worked with Arthur again on *Mr. Peters' Connection*, directing the first regional production in the United States at the Guthrie Theater in Minneapolis, under the artistic direction of Joe Dowling.

Again, Arthur inspired us all as he reimagined his play for this production. By infusing the rehearsal room with his life force, he refused to let his work or himself be treated as relics. He continued to put himself out there by challenging himself and inspiring others with his work.

We had many personal moments that even now continue to feed my soul: the phone calls, his recent letters of support for the company in our effort to build a Performing Arts Center at Ground Zero, the lunch here or dinner there, all burned into the memory of my dear friend.

As I write this and acknowledge the passing of Arthur, I feel the contradiction that our relationship even now continues to grow. So fierce was Arthur's lust for life that I feel him present, always present with me, continuing his legacy of living in the present tense.

Corey Johnson

Actor: **Death of a Salesman,** *Royal National Theatre, 1996; A View from the Bridge, 2003*

I came to Arthur Miller late. I was twenty-four. Of course, I knew who he was; after all, I was an American actor. And every American knew him as our greatest playwright. I just never had the opportunity to act in any of his work, even though, to this day, *The Crucible* is the single most performed piece of theater in the American educational system. And I came to him not from within America, but from outside of it, at the Central School, my drama college in London.

There was a reason I'd come to London. Every actor I knew thought that the Method, as taught by Lee Strasberg, was the be-all and end-all of what an actor should be. But I wasn't sure, and so I was looking for something . . . else. After six years studying acting in the States, I felt I'd cracked 'the emotional thing', as I thought of the visceral side of acting, and needed 'some technique'. Precisely what I meant by *that* remains a mystery to me, but I felt that one thing theater should do is tell a great story. And I remember having an inkling that acting, great acting, should be like an infernal machine: indefatigable, relentless, awesome to watch, yet fearful to behold.

And so I found myself in London, in a small room in Swiss Cottage, with about seven other people, reading various passages of dramatic literature, which on this day included the last act of *The Crucible*. If you asked me right now, I probably couldn't tell you exactly what took place. I only remember a line of John Proctor's – '. . . because it is my name . . .' – remember it because Arthur wrote it, or a variation of it, about half a dozen times in that scene. The effect of the repetition was electrifying – dramatic, theatrical and, above all, emotionally honest. It was the first time I can recall having a sense of something happening that was bigger than I could understand, but at the same time I found that his writing was available to me, open and accessible. This man Proctor was laying himself bare, almost painfully so, fragile yet fighting, and ennobled by his struggle.

Arthur, I think, was impressed and inspired by humanity, by the human condition. In his writing, he manages to find the best in people and bring it out, even when they are sometimes doing the worst things. I recall him saying, with regard to Marilyn Monroe: '. . . The great thing about her to me was that [her] struggle was valiant. She was a very courageous human being. And she didn't give up . . .' I'm sure he wasn't under the illusion that their union was perfect; but in hindsight, he was able to see her with compassion and insight. He brought the same abilities to his work and used them to illuminate the darker aspects of our natures without flinching, but with sensitivity and grace.

Arthur's ability to mine his life in order to show us a version of our own is not without precedent, but rarely has any playwright written with such a simple and subtle poetry, which nevertheless carries an enormous emotional impact. He accomplished this in a style that was at once lean and compact, yet complete; there was never anything unfinished about what he wrote. In his preface to *A View from the Bridge*, Arthur recalled hearing for the first time the story of Eddie Carbone, the longshoreman who loves too well; from the opening sentence he knew exactly how it would end, but also saw that he felt compelled to hear the tale in spite of knowing it. I believe the linearity of Eddie's journey led Arthur to experiment with *View* . . . like no other play he wrote. It was written first as a one-act play, and in verse. In another draft Eddie was openly in love with Catherine in the play's finale; later he was reconciled with his wife Beatrice as he died. It has also been made into an opera. In yet another version Eddie even committed suicide. But one single idea Arthur carried through was that it be told dispassionately, and so he honed and shaped this already spare story until it moved with an inevitability that was Greek in its purity, absolute and terrifying. Unlike his narrator Alfieri, he never settled for half and his work was all the better for it.

In 1996 I was fortunate enough to be cast as Happy in *Death of a Salesman*, at the Royal National Theatre by David Thacker, who knew Arthur from having directed his plays in the UK. At that time both he and Arthur had been asked to attend an international theater conference in Schloss Leopoldskron, Salzburg, and David seized the opportunity and wangled a 'working week' for the Loman family at the conference. We would attend as guests of the festival, participate in workshops with other attendees, and have the chance to sit and work on one of the greatest plays of the twentieth century with the man who wrote it.

We climbed the stairs in the Schloss to his apartment, where he was staying for the duration of the festival with his wife, the photographer Inge Morath. After we'd knocked on the door, a few seconds passed before it was opened . . . and all the light in the air seemed to vanish. When my eyes adjusted, I found myself standing in front of Arthur Miller himself, who ushered us into his rooms. He was a huge man – well over six feet tall and broad-shouldered. But he behaved without artifice or grandeur, in spite of the plush surroundings. After all, we were in the very Schloss made famous by Julie Andrews and Christopher Plummer in *The Sound of Music*. I think I must have been awestruck and shaking with excitement and anticipation. Arthur made some incidental small talk – so as to put us at ease, I'm sure – and then settled us down to go to work.

And as I recall, 'Uncle Arthur' worked as hard as any of us. We discussed the play. He discussed the play. He told anecdotes. When we asked him to, he read the very lines we would be saying as the people in his play. It is an indescribable thing to hear a man reading his own words, to hear characters from his head, on his pages, now made flesh from the author's lips. I could have sat there for hours, soaking up the atmosphere he created, both with his work and his generosity of spirit. When he played Willy's mistress, he had such an offhand way of informing her femininity you could easily see this giant of a man growing softer and sweeter as the minutes passed. And when he laughed – what a shock! It was not the hearty guffaw of a Brooklyn longshoreman, but the wistful, coy cackle of an eighty-year-old teenager about to be kissed again for the first time!

Then he moved on to Willy. For Arthur, this must have been like recalling a long-dead friend to people he'd just met, and he seemed to speak slower and in a more measured way, as if he wanted us to understand this man without having to explain him to us. And it is one of the mysteries and majesties of his art that, in allowing his words to do the work for us, what *we* do becomes transparent and, out of nowhere, his story becomes titanic. He was reading a scene where Willy is talking to Howard, the son of the company's founder, about his father, who had hired Willy all those years ago. And Howard hasn't the time for Willy's stories today, and attempts to hustle him out of the office. Suddenly, in the mood of the scene, Arthur drew lightning from his skies, and thundered, 'I am talking about your father!' and I froze at the sheer power unleashed in those six words. Here was a man, struggling not against some great wrong perpetrated against nameless, faceless multitudes, but for his own simple human dignity; in fact, for the dignity of all mankind. I was struck dumb; we'd been reading the play for weeks; I thought I'd heard every line in it. And no matter how many more times I see it, or am lucky enough to be in it, I shall never forget hearing those words on that afternoon in Salzburg.

I could see how he might get bored of this kind of thing, of us asking the same questions he'd heard over and over in the past, but he never did. He answered everything with eagerness, a sense that he was rediscovering this play, these people, all over again. Hearing first-hand from Arthur about Biff's longing, about Linda's loneliness and strength, and exploring with him the logic and reasoning behind Willy's insanity was education itself. It fed my hunger for the story and my curiosity for its elemental truths.

Hours passed like minutes as we read the play. We queried it, analysed it and read it again, until deep into the afternoon. I looked at Arthur then, and saw that he had his eyes closed and wore a pained expression on his face. At first, I thought he was trying to stay concentrated, but Inge told us earlier he was suffering from a cold, and after all, he was an eighty-year-old man. I remember looking at David Thacker, then toward Arthur; Thacker saw too, took the hint and called time on our rehearsal for that day.

As I left and made my way back to the seminar, something Arthur had said to Alun Armstrong, who was playing Willy Loman, stuck in my mind. We were trying to figure out something about the quality of the memories Willy was having, whether they were accurate, or fanciful, or complete untruth. Arthur wanted us to understand that these memories were ongoing in Willy's present, but had to come from somewhere in the past to get to where Willy is now. I'll never forget it – he said, 'They are torn . . . from the web of forgetting . . .' and then he added quickly, '. . . piece by piece . . .' It is such a simple phrase, yet it manages to evoke a sense of the necessity of recollection, twinned with a feeling of the loss that's involved. It is perfect as an example of the exquisiteness that is unique within humanity. He was a poet, but he didn't write poetry. He wrote to the poet in us.

One more thing: after dinner that night, David Thacker walked up to me. I had only met him a few weeks before, and didn't know him very well, so I was a bit uncomfortable when he put his hands on my shoulders, looked at me and said, 'He's great, your Hap . . .' I absolutely buried my instinct to blurt, 'My Biff would be even better!' Instead, I swallowed my arrogance and thanked him for being so nice. Before I could turn away, he gave me a squeeze, squared me up in front of him and told me simply, 'Arthur said that.'

Like I said, a poet for us all. I'll take that particular poem to my grave. And thanks, Arthur.

Gemma Jones

*Actor: **The Ride Down Mount Morgan**, Royal National Theatre, London, 1991*

I was thrilled and honoured to be cast to play Theo in the first production of *The Ride Down Mount Morgan*. My initial shyness at meeting Arthur Miller was very soon dispelled by the rehearsal process. He was a wonderfully attentive presence in the rehearsal room but also diplomatic in his contributions, which he always filtered through our director, Michael Blakemore. We soon relaxed in his presence and there was a lot of laughter in the room too. He was quite inscrutable in response to the inevitable struggles of the rehearsal process. I hugely admired his patience and tolerance and good humour as we wrestled with his 'baby' and felt very privileged to be with him. Although he was always 'behind the desk', and I never had intimate conversations with him, I felt his sympathy and developed a great affection as well as admiration for him. I cycled to work at that time and more than once Arthur carried my bicycle up the steps to the rehearsal room for me – and he was in his seventies then!

Stacy Keach

*Actor: **The Crucible**, LA Theatre Works radio production; **Incident at Vichy**, Williamstown; **Finishing the Picture**, Goodman Theatre, 2004*

Yes, it was a sad day when Arthur Miller passed away. Even though few of us will ever be able to measure fully the scope of his extraordinary life and his contribution to theater worldwide, with all humility I feel extremely fortunate to have known him and to have spent some time with him.

Arthur Miller was a legend, and I count myself among the blessed to have had the privilege and honor to work with him and to have embodied a few of his wonderful creations. My first encounter with one of Arthur's characters was playing the Prince in a Williamstown production of *Incident at Vichy*. Little did I know at the time that I would be directing the same play for national television some years later, which was a great thrill for me. Arthur graciously acknowledged that production in his autobiography, *Timebends*, calling it the most expressive production of that play he had seen up to that point. How proud I was to have received such a good review from the author himself.

Some years later, I had the opportunity to play John Proctor in an LA Theatre Works radio production of *The Crucible*, with a wonderful cast that included Richard Dreyfuss, Michael York and Fionnula Flannigan. I was once again struck by the power of that play and the brilliance of the writing. However, there is little question that my recent experience with Arthur, doing the world première of *Finishing the Picture* at Chicago's Goodman Theatre under the direction of Robert Falls, creating the role of Phil Ochsner, trucker-turned-producer, was one of the absolute highlights of my theatrical career.

The entire cast, wonderful actors all, were enthralled by Arthur's presence during the rehearsal process. Frances Fisher, Linda Lavin, Harris Yulin, Stephen Lang, Matthew Modine, Scott Glenn and Heather Prete were each a delight to work with and play with. Although Arthur was not in the best of health during the run of the production, his spirit was more than alive and well; his enthusiasm for the play and the production were a constant source of inspiration for all of us. I shall always remember the smile on his face on opening night in Chicago when we came to take our bows after the final curtain.

Now that the final curtain has fallen on Arthur's extraordinary life, I feel that the applause for his work will go on for ever, and he will continue to thrill audiences the world over for centuries to come. Arthur gave us so many priceless treasures and we are so grateful to have known him, to have worked with him, and to

receive the inspiration and strength he gave us by his amazing
energy. Thank you, Arthur. We will cherish your memory, always.

Charlotte Keatley

Writer and journalist

The first time I met Arthur Miller we talked about buses; in an
empty bar, on a November afternoon in Manchester. Downstairs at
the front door there was a mob of fans come to see Arthur, to touch
him, speak to him, get him to sign bits of paper they were waving,
possibly ask him about Marilyn. It was the promotional tour for
Timebends, and Nick Hern, who had just published it at Methuen,
was on crowd control. Nick saw me sidling up in my anorak and said
to me with slight desperation, 'I'm in charge of the greatest living
playwright here . . .' And then he sent me and Arthur upstairs, with
the line, 'Arthur, this is Charlotte, another of our writers.'

So I'm standing in the bar with the very tallest of playwrights in
the world. He has that straight back that seems to come to some men
in old age, and the quiet but steady gaze that makes me want to say
nothing but the truth. He doesn't start the conversation, he waits.
At this moment I feel I understand the real meaning of the word
'humility', which is not soft and cowed as I'd vaguely thought, but
upright: a human who has nothing to prove, who has no need to
speak unless there is something relevant to say.

I am very short and very young. I am on the dole, living in a nasty
damp old terraced house, as writers must do for a while. I've written
a play that has only been performed for nine nights at Contact
Theatre, down the road; but Nick Hern has already published it.
For two years the play had been rejected by various important
theatres, for having a structure where time is jumbled, and for being
about ordinary women. Over years to come the play travels the
world, but right now it still needs me to carry it along and believe in
it. And Nick Hern has connected me by a thread to this world of
giant, great playwrights. Here I am with Arthur Miller. I wouldn't
be surprised if Ibsen and Chekhov appeared round the bar and
joined in the conversation.

'How did you come here?' asks Arthur. I take it he doesn't mean artistically. Writers don't usually talk about writing.

'On the bus,' I reply. We look down across the street, at the raggle-taggle queue of people – with their shopping bags, briefcases, pushchairs, or spiky pink hair, as the bus heaves to a stop and they pile on. Then we talk, easily, about getting the bus. How buses are the cheapest way to get about, which is something important to theatre writers, since one rarely earns a living wage. More importantly, how one is immersed in a certain pace of life: of waiting in the street, then jostling for a seat, standing when you are tired after work, listening to people talk about their worries and concerns, watching the different shapes and quirks of humans, being assailed by the drunk on the last night bus who has the best stories, the best lies.

Arthur Miller's plays made ordinary people into heroes. I wanted to say to him, that's what I'm trying to do, too: tell the stories of the unnoticed people, who have little power; write their dramas with the greatness of Greek tragedy; create recognition in the audience, and out of this, hopefully, generate a new understanding of fellow beings that stays with those who experience the play, for the rest of their lives.

I was too shy to say any of that. On that November afternoon I stood talking with Arthur Miller who has proved how a theatre play (*Death of a Salesman*) can make a difference in society; and the fact that he was talking to me simply gave me the affirmation: keep going.

The last time I spoke to Arthur Miller was at his eighty-fifth birthday party, in Norwich.

FIRST SCENE (*afternoon*)   An ancient medieval timbered room, with high arched beams and heraldic emblems on old plaster walls and men in black gowns and floppy hats, with gold chains and badges. The few of us civilians in the pews are sitting quietly, in case we make the wrong noise and one of the City Fathers points his stave at us. Then Arthur Miller and Inge Morath mount the platform and are presented with the keys to the city of Norwich. Arthur and Inge have been given black robes too, with a trimming of fur round the neck. The event is like a surreal epilogue to *The Crucible*.

Arthur is still very upright but his face is paler, slightly transparent; he misses his step as he climbs on to the dais. Then he speaks, without notes, from the lectern where others have shuffled their papers to make their speeches. The sun slants in on the dust motes and on his large, bony hands. They are hands that rest with the fingers slightly curled in, as if about to pick up a lathe; hands that like to build. We stand and process out: into the Saturday afternoon market square, where people with shopping bags and pushchairs and spiky pink hair are haggling over stalls of cheap knickers, local apples, or bargain CDs.

SECOND SCENE (*which takes place in the morning*)   I'm on the train, because Manchester to Norwich is too far by bus. On the journey I've made friends with a woman who offered me hankies because I was so relieved to catch the train that I burst into tears – I am now a divorced single parent, of a lively four-year-old, living a hectic life. Arthur Miller is still the greatest playwright in the world. Eileen on the train is awed and amazed that he has come to Britain to celebrate his eighty-fifth birthday; Eileen is not a theatre person but to her Arthur Miller is a star, he is a voice across decades, who has stood up for principles of freedom of expression at times of political corruption.

THIRD SCENE (*evening*)   The elegant dinner, hosted by Christopher Bigsby. A waterfall of silver and gold fireworks outside the vast windows. I wander among the famous and wait for a moment to go over to Arthur with my small present.

What do you take as a eighty-fifth birthday present for Arthur Miller? A few years before I was walking in Crete and went at dusk to the site of, reputedly, the oldest theatre in the world. The light was fading, the sea was near, the site was grass and dusty stones. I picked up a piece of terracotta stone. I took it home. I felt very guilty, until now. I realised I had not so much stolen it as borrowed it to pass on to a hero of our age. So amidst the glittering celebration of the party, I went over to Arthur. He was sitting in a chair being entertained with an anecdote by a famous actor. Arthur turned to me and his eyes looked extra searching, magnified by his large glasses. I gave him the stone and explained where it was from. He took it, silently, and turned it over in his large hands, then looked up at me. 'Thank you. I shall put it on the table where I write.'

After that, Miller's voice kept on coming across the Atlantic; I remember his searing article in a British newspaper dismantling the dubious victory of Bush in 2001 and the American election system; then there were new plays – more that needed to be said, right up to the end of his life. He reminded me – us – that you never give up, if there are things that need to be said – in the media, on the stage. His voice never sounded old, it sounded urgent.

What I remember most is that Miller never wrote about himself. In the individualistic times we live in, it has been encouraged and accepted that a play or piece of journalism is also about the writer. With Miller, we got down to the subject and that was all. Even *Timebends* is constructed so that Miller says look past me, look over there at what I was witnessing or struggling to be part of.

Just after Arthur Miller's death, I was reading my new play to my boyfriend in a café, and when I read the very last line, he said, 'That's like the end of *All My Sons*.' Rats, I thought. Some critic or director is going to spin all sorts of theories out of the reference to Miller, when it's simply a line I arrived at out of the progression of the play and the characters. For four years I've been writing and rewriting this huge war play called *All the Daughters of War*, and suddenly I realised this is also quite naturally the very last line spoken by a woman to a girl whose parents have been killed. I stared at the line and wondered if I should change it. But I've left it. If it is some echo of Miller, well, it's a way to keep the conversation going.

Sara Kestelman

Actor: The Crucible, Manchester Royal Exchange, 1966; The American Clock, National Theatre, 1986; The Price, Watford Palace Theatre, 1988

In 1988 I was preparing to do *The Price* at Watford. In March of that year Arthur was in London writing a screenplay with Karel Reisz and overseeing his new play *Danger: Memory!* in which Karel's wife Betsy Blair was starring and which Jack Gold was directing at the Hampstead Theatre.

I had first met Arthur in 1986 at the National Theatre when I was playing Rose in Peter Wood's production of *The American Clock*, staged first in the Cottesloe Theatre and later transferred into the

Olivier in 1987. Arthur and Inge had come to a performance in the Cottesloe shortly after we opened. Completely thrilled by Peter's production, he was also most generous and touching to me about the interpretation of Rose, which he said was uncannily like his mother on whom, of course, the character is based. Naturally I was overjoyed. Photographs were taken when the cast met him on stage over a glass of wine after the performance and I particularly treasured two of them. We were all still in costume and one picture was of Arthur alone with me as Rose and the second had Inge in the photograph as well.

It was Easter 1988 and Arthur was staying at Browns Hotel. An American friend of mine suggested that I contact him to ask if we could possibly meet and have a little chat about *The Price*. At first I needed some persuading but eventually, taking my courage in my hands, I called the hotel and asked to speak to Arthur and to my surprise was put through immediately. He greeted me sweetly and apologised, explaining that as he had deadlines to meet he thought it unlikely we would be able to meet up for a chat. I said that I completely understood, of course, and then, on a whim, asked if I might drop by the hotel with my much loved hardback copy of his autobiography, *Timebends*, and leave it at reception for him to sign at his leisure – and I mentioned the photos too. He said that would be fine and that he'd be delighted and that I should call on Easter Monday afternoon.

So on Easter Sunday I drove down to Browns Hotel and left a large envelope with the book and the photos, and a little note thanking him and asking him to choose which of the two pictures he preferred to sign. On Monday afternoon, as agreed, I returned. The front desk put me through to Arthur's room and he apologised again for not having the time to meet, wished me good luck with *The Price* and told me the book was waiting for me at reception. I thanked him, wished him good luck too and said goodbye. In eager anticipation I opened the envelope and then saw with dismay that the precious photographs were not there with the book! Anxiously I went back to the front desk to see if perhaps the pictures had slipped out. They searched and searched but found nothing, and then, before I knew it, they called Arthur's room and passed the phone to me! Stuttering with embarrassment I shyly asked about the photographs. There was a hair's breadth pause before he asked if I could possibly wait for a few minutes. Yes, yes, sure, I said, of course! So I sat and waited in reception, now feeling a tad uneasy. Then I heard the guy at reception pick up the phone. 'Yes, Mr Miller,' I heard him say, then he lowered his voice and put the phone down. He glanced over at me, picked up the phone again and made a call, turning away so I couldn't hear him. He followed that with another call and I heard him address 'Mr Miller' again. I had absolutely no idea what was going on but I sat there for about twenty minutes before it was explained to me that Arthur was checking out the next day and so had been clearing his desk after his long stay, and that housekeeping had been called to collect all the waste paper needing to be thrown away.

And that's when I realised that there had been an awful misunderstanding over the photos, which apparently Arthur had mistakenly thought I was giving him, and as he didn't really want them had added them to the paper collection to be chucked out! Poor man! But good fortune and serendipity came to the rescue and in the nick of time everything was found just moments before being condemned to the incinerator, and sure enough there were the photos safe and sound. Arthur brought them to reception himself. He handed them to me and sat down. We made no reference to them. He knew that I knew, and I knew that he knew that I knew! I felt dreadful. He was gracious and charming. And we did talk a little about *The Price* after all, which was wonderful except that I was in such a state by then that I didn't take much in! Finally I thanked him again and left. I couldn't bring myself to ask him to autograph the pictures! I was exhausted. I expect he was too.

It was a very fine production of *The Price* at Watford and for a while there was talk of a possible West End transfer, which sadly didn't come to pass.

The last time I saw Arthur was in a restaurant in New York. He beamed at me and shook my hand warmly. How very nice to see you, he said. His eyes twinkled. Did I imagine it or did the great man wink at me?

He was a giant in every way and with his death a huge light has gone out.

Tony Kushner

Writer

Arthur Miller died on Bertolt Brecht's birthday. There are two ways
in which this means nothing at all: I'm sure Arthur didn't plan it,
and the two playwrights, apart from being universally described,
and self-identified, as 'political writers', don't have all that much in
common. But their difference is interesting. Arthur Miller's was a
great voice, one of the principal voices raised in opposition, calling
for resistance, offering critical scrutiny and lamentation – in other
words he was politically progressive, as politically progressive is best
defined in these dark times. He demanded that we must be able to
answer, on behalf of our plays, our endeavors, our lives, a really
tough question, one that Arthur wrote was the chief and, in a sense,
only reason for writing and speaking: 'What is its relevancy', he
asks, 'to the survival of the race? Not', he stipulates, 'the American
race, or the Jewish race, or the German race, but the human race.'
He demanded that our work and our lives have some relevance to
human survival. The question implies anxiety about that survival, a
refusal of complacency, an acknowledgment that there is a human
community for which each of us bears responsibility, and a warning
that we are in danger. Miller tells us that what we do, the things we
choose to struggle with in art and elsewhere, can have some effect
on the outcome. There is, in other words, reason to hope, and
change is possible. Arthur was a grieving pessimist, but what truly
progressive person isn't?

He was one of those political people who refused an identification
with a specific race or nation or movement or party. He certainly
wasn't a Communist and he wasn't a Socialist. During the
Depression his grandfather, whom Arthur described as 'a
Republican all his life . . . [with] bags under his eyes like von
Hindenburg', shocked the family by turning to his unemployed
grandson one night after dinner and saying, 'You know what you
ought to do? You ought to go to Russia.'

> The silence that fell [in the dining room, Arthur wrote], is
> better described as a vacuum so powerful it threatened to suck
> the walls in. Even my father woke up on the couch. I asked [my
> grandfather] why I should go to Russia.

'Because [he answered] in Russia they haven't got anything. Here they got too much. You can't sell anything any more. You go to Russia and open a chain of clothing stores; you could do a big business. That's a new country, Russia.'

'But', I said, 'you can't do that there.'

'Why not?' he said, disbelieving.

'The government owns the stores there.'

His face would have put fears into Karl Marx himself.

'Them bastards,' he said, and went back to his paper.

The grandson was a great believer in democracy and self-reliance and in anything conducive to and supportive of individual human dignity and integrity. His drama was the drama of individual integrity, individual wholeness or completeness or repleteness, versus unaccountable power – or perhaps one could say of the individual versus history. And one way in which Arthur Miller's theater and politics differ from a writer like Brecht's is that Arthur focused his critical gaze, and located his sense of political struggle, within the arena of an individual consciousness, in an important sense his own individual consciousness. Would it be correct to say that he was not a joiner of parties or group identities because, a loyalist only to the human race, he manifested that loyalty by being true to himself? Though he was clearly interested in history, he was uncomfortable writing about it. *The Crucible* and *Incident at Vichy* are not, finally, historical plays. Each sets its scene in the midst of a historical crime in progress, but soon the great dramatist that Arthur Miller was has turned his unsparing, unblinking, loving intelligence away from the grand-scale horror to demand of a single human being: *Never mind all that out there, as overwhelming as it is. Even in the face of horror you must still ask yourself, and hard as it is, you are capable of asking it: What do you mean to yourself, what do you know yourself to be? What, in other words, is your relevance to the survival of the race?*

He wasn't interested in the examination of history as the opportunity to illuminate meta-theories about the ultimate direction the human community was taking. Arthur Miller was one of those very rare people whose politics were inseparable from the drama of his own personal integrity. He was his own proving ground; he felt his successes and his failures as a human being were consequential to something greater than himself, and so they were publicly examined and, in a sense, the only thing worth talking about. He wasn't certain that a single individual has relevance to our collective survival, but he saw no other question worth pursuing.

He once wrote that he stopped studying economics as an undergraduate because economics, as it was and is taught, can 'measure the giant's footsteps but not look into his eyes'. His observation reflects both his indebtedness to left political analysis – a central tenet of which is the critical consideration of the human, ethical and political meanings of money, rather than the mere prognostication of its tides and currents – and also it reflects his conviction, or perhaps predilection, or natural inclination, even when considering the giant, to look for truth by looking in his eyes, the windows of the soul. Arthur Miller had the curse of empathy, even for the enemy. Humans justify themselves to themselves, even bad humans, and Arthur the playwright always wanted to know how and why. *Look into his eyes.*

He made it clear in his plays and his essays that his critical thinking and social consciousness had their genesis in the red politics that were pervasive when he was growing up, a politics catalysed by the suffering he witnessed and experienced in the Great Depression, a politics shaped in response to the toxic, obnoxious valorisation of greed always, always re-emerging in American history as a bedrock tenet of the political Right. Although he refused the mechanical determinism of the unthinking Marxist Left, he created, in his greatest play, a drama in which it is impossible to avoid thinking about economics – money – in any attempt to render coherent the human tragedy unfolding before you.

Consider the Lomans: What has brought darkness down upon this family? Their flaws are part of their tragedy, but only a part – every flaw is magnified, distorted, made fatal by, well, alienation, by the market, where the pressure is inhuman and the human is expendable. Consider the moment when the Nothing of tragedy is enunciated, and annunciated, in *Salesman*, Biff and Willy's final fight ('Pop, I'm nothing! I'm nothing, Pop! Can't you understand that? There's no spite in it any more. I'm just what I am, that's all. Will you let me go, for Christ's sake'). It's a tragic negation, vast and shatteringly intimate; everything is annihilated, and at the same time something new is being born. It's the 'nothing' of the tragedies of Euripides and Shakespeare, and in Miller's post-war, market-place masterpiece, one hears an echo of another 'nothing', tragic but also political – namely, 'you have nothing to lose but your chains'.

If Arthur's Emersonian temperament saved him from the terrible mistakes of the doctrinaire Left of his time, if his habits of scrupulousness and independence carried him into a healthy, immensely vital skepticism, if he refused partisanship, he also never ceased reminding us of his indebtedness, indeed his affinity, with the Left, with progressive thought. He never became a cynic, or a nihilist, or an ego-anarchist, or a despoiler of humanist Utopian dreams, or a neo-con. His great personal courage, and his graceful confidence in his stature and talents, made it unnecessary for him to cuddle up to power elites, allowed him to retain his sympathy, his affinity for the disinherited, the marginal and the powerless. He never wanted us to forget that without economic justice, the concept of social justice is an absurdity and, worse, a lie.

I first saw Arthur Miller in person at the 1994 Tony Awards, when I sat behind him, too unnerved to introduce myself; for the whole evening I stared at the back of his head, which was far, far more interesting to me than anything transpiring on stage. Inside this impressive cranium, inside this dome, I thought to myself, Willy Loman was conceived – for an American playwright, a place comparable in sacrosanctity to the Ark of the Covenant or the Bhodi Tree or the Manger in Bethlehem. I wanted to touch the head, but I worried its owner might object. The ceremonies ended and I'd missed my opportunity to make contact with the quarry whence came one of the post-war pillars upon which the stature of serious American playwriting rests.

Thanks to my friend Oskar Eustis I got to meet Arthur several years later, in Providence Rhode Island, when I presented him with an award. On that occasion I had the chance to thank him personally. I said,

Mr Miller, yours is a career and a body of work every playwright envies and wishes were her or his own; yours is the difficult standard against which we are measured and measure ourselves. For many sleepless nights and days of despair, I want to say thanks a lot; and for making my heart break, and burst into flames, time and time again, since the night, when I was six years old, I saw my mother play Linda Loman in a Louisiana community theater production of *Salesman*, and I think at that moment secretly deciding I wanted to be a playwright. Seeing *Incident at Vichy* on TV a few years later, I admitted to myself the decision I'd made. Watching splendid recent revivals of *A View from the Bridge*, *Salesman*, *The Crucible*, I have gone home, chastened, to requestion all my assumptions about what playwriting is and how one ought to do it. And for always being there, on my bookshelf, when people say that real art can't be political, or that a real artist can't also a political activist, your life and work are there to remind me what preposterous canards those are – for all this, I want to say thanks a lot.

For American playwrights who come after Arthur Miller, there is of course an unpayable debt. Those of us who seek mastery of dramatic realist narrative have his plays to try to emulate. Scene after scene they are perhaps our best constructed plays, works of a master carpenter-builder. Those of us who seek not mastery but new ways of making theater have to emulate his refusal to sit comfortably where *Salesman* enthroned him. Arthur once praised Tennessee Williams for a 'restless inconsolability with his solutions which is inevitable in a genuine writer', for making 'an assault upon his own viewpoint in an attempt to break it up and reform it on a wider circumference'.

American playwrights have most to learn from the sound of Arthur Miller's voice: humility, decency, generosity are its trademarks. Turn down the braying of ego, it says to us, turn down the chatter of entertainment, the whine of pornographic sensuality and prurience, abandon the practice of rendering judgment as an expression of isolation, superstition and terror, and reach for a deeper judgment, the kind of judgment that pulls a person beyond his expected reach towards something more than any single human animal ought to be capable of – towards something shared, communal, maybe even towards something universal, maybe even towards God. It's a path to knowing that is the birthright of dramatists, and 'genuine writers'. It seems to me difficult because it's a lonely path, and Jewish in its demanding interiority. It's Jewish also in its faith that words have an awesome almost sacred power, force, weight. God, or the world, is listening, Arthur Miller reminds us, and when you speak, when you write, God, or the world, is also speaking and writing. 'A great drama is a great jurisprudence,' Arthur wrote.

Balance is all. It will evade us until we can once again see man as a whole, until sensitivity and power, justice and necessity are utterly face to face, until authority's justifications and rebellion's too are tracked even to those heights where the breath fails, where – because the largest point of view as well as the smaller has spoken – truly, the rest is silence.

Michael Kustow

Writer (biographer of Peter Brook) and producer

Arthur Miller was sometimes reproached for his earnestness, even by his friends. 'He has a rabbinical righteousness,' said the Broadway producer Robert Whitehead, who frequently presented his plays. 'In his work there is almost a conscious need to be a light unto the world.' The phrase, recalling the injunction to the Jews to be a light unto the nations, could be a cue to pay homage to Miller's Jewishness. And yet this bony, angular, handsome writer whose plays connected to the public and personal dilemmas of his time, cannot be co-opted by anyone. Jewish, Marxist, Freudian – he was all and none of these.

To those who thought his work was too self-consciously tragic, Miller even told a story against himself. In 1967, having just completed *The Price*, he was taking a holiday in the Caribbean and recognised a man paddling. It turned out to be Mel Brooks, Miller's polar opposite as an artist. When Brooks asked him what his new play was about, Miller (according to David Gates in *Newsweek*) began, 'Well, there are these two brothers –'

'Stop!' yelled Brooks. 'I'm crying.'

The Price is a pivotal play in his career, and a rich, layered one. Built upon a gut-wrenching, Cain-and-Abel encounter between two brothers who have come to dispose of their deceased father's furniture, it throws a painful light on the dysfunctions and disruptions of their lives and times, just as *Death of a Salesman* did. But with the arrival of the furniture appraiser, Gregory Solomon, a new note of impish humour overlays the heartache.

'Enter Gregory Solomon', Miller's stage direction begins, becoming almost Dickensian in his portrait of the wily, wise old man. 'In brief, a phenomenon: a man nearly ninety, but still straight-backed and the air of his massiveness still with him.' (Almost a description of Miller himself in his eighties.) 'He has perfected a way', concludes Miller, 'of leaning on his cane without appearing weak.'

Warren Mitchell's enchanting performance in the play's revival at the Tricycle Theatre and in the West End (2003–4) was the epitome of an essential Miller quality, his charm, as well as a rendering of the Russian-Yiddish idiom of an immigrant from the old country. Asked whether he wants a glass of water after trudging up stairs to the top of the house, he replies, 'Water I don't need; a little blood I could use.' Miller's acute ear – for Brooklyn Italians, seventeenth-century Puritans, Connecticut WASPS – was matched by his capacity to distil observation into theatre poetry, and by a carpenter's mastery of dramatic structure. He was proud of his handmade furniture, which he produced in a barn on his Connecticut estate. Working with wood was both a respite from working with words and a model for getting the material of a play into durable shape.

The Price was the last time he had a critical and commercial success on Broadway. The attacks had begun early. 'The world has made this author important before he has made himself great,' wrote the *New Republic* of *The Crucible* in 1953. Of the many put-downs he endured, the then *New York Times* critic Frank Rich penned one of the sharpest when he dismissed *Danger: Memory!* in 1987 as 'an evening in which the pontificator wins out over the playwright'. Another critic who did not welcome his later plays, Robert Brustein of the *New Republic*, more shrewdly noted that where America had consigned Miller to the wilderness, Britain had given his later work première productions and revived his early classics. Alan Ayckbourn, Richard Eyre, Nicholas Hytner and David Thacker kept Miller alive as a theatrical presence. 'It shows,' wrote Brustein, paraphrasing Bernard Shaw, 'that Britain and America are two countries divided by a common playwright.'

For the new generation of British playwrights, Miller was like a gale sweeping in off the Atlantic. 'I sense that the British theatre is hermetically sealed against the way society moves,' Miller said at a symposium at the Royal Court Theatre in November 1956, six months after John Osborne's *Look Back in Anger* had begun to crack open those seals with a passionate play, encouraged by the example of Miller, Tennessee Williams and the new American drama.

As a young man, Miller never hung out with the New York crowd of Jewish writers – novelists like Malamud, Bellow or Roth, critics like Alfred Kazin and Irving Howe. After the Depression he connected his native insights to American experience by working in the Brooklyn shipyards and for radio. Writing for radio and reading the Book of Genesis taught him to let nothing get in the way of the story. 'You read about the Creation and in about a page and a half you've got the human race,' he's said. 'That is the way to tell a story, and a story that never dies. It is the imprint of a hot iron on the soul.' That biblical lilt, that poetry of the pulpit, lifts his plays into the unique sphere they occupy in world drama, making poetry out of everyday realism. Small wonder that so many British playwrights, from John Arden to John Osborne to Arnold Wesker, have learned from Miller's pulse and rhythms to lift off from naturalism.

In 1956 Miller, the son of a wealthy manufacturer who lost everything in the Depression, moved in on the London theatre and the British class system when Peter Brook directed *A View from the Bridge*. In his autobiography *Timebends*, Miller recalls the auditions, held in a rehearsal room near the Covent Garden fruit and vegetable market. Watching well-spoken young actors painfully pick their way through speeches he'd written for Brooklyn Italians, and seeing the vitality of Covent Garden outside, he asked Brook why he didn't audition some of the Cockney hawkers for the parts.

'Doesn't a grocer's son ever think of becoming an actor?' I asked. 'These are all grocers' sons,' Peter replied, indicating the group of young gentlemen awaiting their turns, 'but they have trained themselves into this class language. Almost all the plays are written in that language and are about those kinds of people.'

On the Sunday before opening, Brook invited the families of the stage crew in to see how the elaborate set was put in and operated. 'The families oohed and aahed,' wrote Miller. 'In New York I had never had interest of this kind on the part of the back-stage people, and the realization was saddening. With us it was all pure bucks.'

Miller felt the absence of a non-profit American theatre. He could be irascible about the snobby New York elite and its tax-deductible benevolence for opera and ballet, whereas every production on

Broadway had to turn a profit. 'If the thing is gonna be regarded the same as the fish business,' he growled, 'it ain't gonna work. In the whole entertainment enterprise, the theater has become a fifth wheel. People only take parts hoping it will lead to the movies.'

But Miller stuck to his abiding loyalty to the wounded of American society, the underdogs of capitalism like Willy Loman, crying out 'A man is not a piece of fruit' or the glamorous victims of celebrity culture like Maggie in *After the Fall*. After he had surmounted the end of his marriage to Marilyn Monroe and found Inge Morath, his gaze became wider, more European. He was drawn to deal with the ultimate expression of human hatred, the Holocaust, which surfaces in *After the Fall*, *Incident at Vichy* and most memorably in his dramatisation for television of *Playing for Time*, Fania Fenelon's book about surviving as a classical musician in Auschwitz.

It is utterly characteristic of this incorruptible artist that, taking on the most painful subject for any Jew, he should have refused to give way to organised pressure from Jewish groups to sack Vanessa Redgrave from playing the lead because of her support for the Palestinians. Miller belonged to no one but himself. He was a titanic figure and, in a great Jewish tradition, a universal man. Like Heine or Spinoza, he is a resistant spirit, standing inside and outside the fold. But that is where some of the most creative Jews have stood.

Joanne Leedom-Ackerman

Writer and journalist: International Secretary, International PEN. Chair of International PEN's Writers in Prison Committee 1993–7; President of PEN Center USA West, 1989–9

I met Arthur Miller only a few times, once sitting with him at a dinner in New York and another time at English PEN's Writers' Day in London, where he arrived having forgotten his talk and improvised a brilliant presentation. He was one of the grand writers in PEN. I was of a younger generation, inspired by his work and leadership, but not personally connected to him, except that we were both Americans.

When, as Chair of International PEN's Writers in Prison

Committee in the mid-1990s, I asked him for a video message for a Freedom of Expression conference on behalf of imprisoned writers in Turkey, he obliged quickly. A decade earlier he and Harold Pinter had travelled to Turkey for International PEN, and that trip still resonated with writers and officials there.

Arthur Miller served as President of International PEN from 1965 to 1969 in the years of the Cold War and incipient détente. His imagination quickly grasped the possibilities of this worldwide association of writers dedicated to the free transmission of ideas and literature among nations. His imagination helped shape those possibilities. Miller knew little about the organisation when PEN's General Secretary David Carver first visited him in Paris in 1965 to propose he take on the presidency at a time when PEN was straining under the ideological schisms of the Cold War. Because Miller was a writer of international reputation and because he'd taken a stand in the face of the US House Un-American Activities Committee, refusing to confirm names of writers suspected of ties to the Communist Party, Miller would have the support of writers from both the West and the East, Carver said. In 1965 PEN had centres in Poland, East Germany, Czechoslovakia, Bulgaria, Hungary and Yugoslavia as well as in most of Western Europe and in the Americas, Asia and Africa.

Carver told Miller that PEN was trying to save lives, sending telegrams and letters on behalf of writers persecuted for their political views at a time when Amnesty and other human rights organisations were just beginning. In 1937 PEN had won the release of novelist Arthur Koestler who faced execution in Spain, and in 1956 PEN had been successful in getting the Hungarian government to release and allow a number of imprisoned writers to leave the country after the Russians invaded. PEN was now collecting information and publicising cases of other writers, particularly those behind the Iron Curtain.

Miller himself would send a letter the following year to Nigeria on behalf of a playwright whose name he barely knew. Wole Soyinka was slated for immediate execution by General Gowon during the civil war with Biafra, but when Gowon received Miller's letter, hand-carried by a businessman, he is said to have asked if Miller was the man who'd married Marilyn Monroe and, when assured that he was, Gowon released Soyinka, who left the country, went on writing and subsequently won the Nobel Prize for Literature.

Years later Miller observed in a talk at an American PEN dinner,

I've never been able to imagine how realistic an idea PEN was
to the writers who started it after World War I. These
founding fathers were greatly famous writers like George
Bernard Shaw, Henri Barbusse, Romain Rolland, who had no
need of an organisation to protect them; they were known and
revered wherever books were read. But successful as they were,
they were also moved by the millions of squandered lives in the
recent war, and resolved to do what they could to prevent a
repetition. The idea was to try to unite the intellectuals of
Europe in an organisation, a fellowship is probably a better
word, around the demand for unfettered communication and
publishing, so that super-nationalism might be stopped in its
tracks by criticism from abroad. The Bolsheviks were already
winning in Russia, and hardly more than a decade later Hitler
was in power in Germany, and that was that.

But like his idealistic predecessors, Miller saw the possibility that
dialogue and exchanges among writers might break through
isolation, especially for Soviet writers. At the International PEN
Congress in Bled, Yugoslavia, in 1965, the Soviets sent observers for
the first time. By the end of that Congress, presided over by Miller,
the Soviet writers wanted to engage with PEN. 'Almost despite
myself I began feeling a certain enthusiasm for the idea of
international solidarity among writers, feeble as its present
expression seemed,' Miller wrote in his autobiography *Timebends*
'. . . I knew that PEN could be far more than a mere gesture of
goodwill.'

Thirty years later, in a letter to a Belgrade journalist whose
friends and newspaper were under constant assault by the regime of
Slobodan Milosevic in Yugoslavia, Miller recalled that it was the
murder of writers and journalists that most affected him since these
were the eyes and ears of the people, and democracy depended on a
well-informed citizenry. He felt particular sympathy for those who
tried to function in the face of nationalism and tribalism in the
Balkans, and insisted on the need for the writer to resist those who
saw art as serving only political and partisan ends.

The path towards this goal, and certainly the goal of détente in
the mid-1960s was not a straight one, however, for Miller or for

PEN. At the International PEN Congress in New York in 1966, the Soviet Writers' Union had intended to send observers, but cancelled at the last minute, most likely because of criticism over recent imprisonments of writers in the Soviet Union and the presence of Soviet dissidents at the Congress. Writers from the other Eastern bloc countries did attend.

At that New York Congress Arthur Miller, the first (and to date only) American president of International PEN, presided over more than 500 writers, the largest gathering ever of American and foreign writers. 'The Writer as Independent Spirit' set the theme of the Congress as writers from a wide political spectrum, especially throughout Latin America, gathered in official and unofficial forums. Members of the American Center had managed to get the US ban on 'political undesirables' lowered, thus allowing writers like Pablo Neruda, the poet and Chilean Communist, into the United States.

In his opening address Miller said, 'None of us comes here as a representative of his country. None of us is obliged to speak here as an apologist for his culture or his political system.' PEN is 'a neutral ground, a kind of sanctuary', where reality isn't defined by politics and its divisiveness but by 'the stubborn, underlying sameness of the human spirit whatever the variety of forms in which it is expressed'.

Miller recalled in his autobiography that he felt uplifted by the New York Congress where 'with amazing unanimity writers of the most conflicting political commitments refused to reduce to polemics what turned out to be really informative discussions about the conditions of writers'. By the end of the 1966 Congress Miller was convinced that PEN had to be the conscience of the world writing community. In his closing speech he called on the delegates to seek out what was similar among them and to isolate what separated them, to resolve their differences and to set aside what they couldn't resolve. At the Congress he said Soviet writers were welcome to join PEN as soon as they were prepared to conform to its rules, which insisted upon freedom of expression and publication. In response, the Union of Soviet Writers asserted, 'Attempts to speak to Soviet writers in such a tone and to confront Soviet writers with one-sided conditions are foolish and fruitless.'

Thus the stage was set. In 1967 Arthur Miller travelled to Moscow to meet with the head of the Union of Soviet Writers. By that time he had sent many wires and letters protesting the arrests of writers in Russia and the Balkans; he'd managed to get exit visas for a few writers, and he understood the distance between the practices of the Soviet government and the demands of PEN's charter. From his friendship with other Soviet writers, however, he also understood that PEN provided them with an opening to the West, the possibility of translation and also of protection for freedom of expression.

In Moscow he met with Alexi Surkov, the head of the Writers' Union, whom he had met earlier at the Bled Congress. He recounts the meeting in his autobiography:

> At last Surkov said flatly, 'Soviet writers want to join PEN' . . .
> 'I couldn't be happier,' I said. 'We would welcome you in PEN.'
> 'We have one problem,' Surkov said, 'but it can be resolved easily.'
> 'What is the problem?'
> 'The PEN Constitution . . .'

The exchange continued but it soon became clear that the Charter of PEN – which obliged its members to commit to the principles of freedom of expression and to oppose censorship at home and abroad – was not going to fold easily into nor paper over the gulf between systems, at least not for this group of writers at this time. It would take twenty more years before the first Russian centre was admitted into PEN in 1988. In those intervening years PEN members maintained contact with Soviet writers, however, both as literary colleagues and also as advocates on their behalf when they were imprisoned.

Arthur Miller presided over two more PEN Congresses in the Ivory Coast in 1967 and in Menton, France, in 1969. He extended PEN's work in Africa and Latin America, but the main watch of his presidency remained on the frontier for which David Carver recruited him, pacing along the wall between the East and West of Europe, a lone American, who had himself once been attracted to the ideas of Socialism and Communism as his colleagues in Czechoslovakia and other countries had been, but who had rejected the totalitarian grip. As an artist Arthur Miller was committed to the freedom of the individual conscience and as an American he was moved by 'the miraculous rationalism of the American Bill of Rights'.

'So this was my function,' he reflected years later in his autobiography,

> to be fair, to keep the peace, and to persist in apolitically advancing the political concepts of liberty of expression and the independent author. The great thing was that these were the unspoken longings of most of those present, no matter where they came from. . . . Maybe my very remoteness as an American was my value here . . . I was a stranger to their old feuds. They were first to grasp this, but I caught on at last.

Since Arthur Miller's presidency the Berlin Wall has fallen, the Iron Curtain has lifted, debate and discussion have opened around the globe, and PEN has grown in every region, almost doubling in size, now with 141 centres in 99 countries. At a dinner in New York in April 2001, Arthur Miller told an audience of writers:

> That it [PEN] is still around after three quarters of a century when it has no army, no navy or air force, no political rewards or threats of punishment, is possibly a triumph of illusion over reality, the illusion that hope is rational in this world . . . [W]ith all its flounderings and failings and mistaken acts, it is still, I think, a fellowship moved by the hope that one day the work it tries and often manages to do will no longer be necessary. Needless to add, we shall need extraordinarily long lives to see that noble day. Meanwhile we have PEN, this fellowship bequeathed to us by several generations of writers for whom their own success and fame were simply not enough.

Margot Leicester

Actor: The Last Yankee, Young Vic, 1992–3; Broken Glass, Royal National Theatre, 1994

One of the best sentences I've ever read is a line by Arthur Miller in an essay on writing for the theatre: 'It [the play] becomes beautiful to me because it promises to remove some of my helplessness before the chaos of experience.' That line is such a blessing for an actor to read because if actors know about anything it is feeling helpless in the face of chaotic experiences. We think we're the world's experts at feeling vulnerable in the face of random events and it is a comfort and surprise to think that a writer as great as Arthur Miller could experience similar feelings.

Most actors begin their working lives with a hope of great things. Not simply for their own careers but because they genuinely believe theatre can do some good in the world. It is probably why they became an actor in the first place. They got that wonderful feeling of connection to the world through seeing, or better still being part of, some event on a stage. Doesn't matter where the stage is – a school hall or the Palladium – that feeling is to do with transformation, that things will change of course but the hope or trust is that things can perhaps be changed for the better, if not in a directly political way, then through emotional recognition. However fragile and unarticulated these feelings and however dashed by disillusioning experiences, they do prevail.

I think that is why actors always feel blessed and lucky when they are in an Arthur Miller play. Whatever the kind of theatre or the size of part or the sort of company, they know they can be guaranteed an experience that will require serious and heartfelt engagement from the whole of their selves. From their deepest sense of self. But with that comes a huge responsibility. The stakes are very high. If that evening's performance offers you, the actors, and the audience the possibilities of transforming and miraculous changes of emotional recognition through speech and gesture then you don't want to mess it up. The production and your performance have got to measure up to what the play offers. Even more do you feel the need to get it right if you're involved in the first outing of one of his plays. That is why I and several other actors were shuddering with fear in the corridor outside a rehearsal room at the National Theatre before we began a run-through of the play *Broken Glass*. It had begun its performing life in America earlier in the year, but this would be its première in the UK in the summer of 1994. We had been rehearsing it for three weeks but now Arthur and Inge had joined us for the home stretch and while that was a wonderful thought – to have Arthur Miller in the rehearsal room on a daily basis – it was also a terrifying one. Arthur Miller was a hero to us all and to greet him as a working colleague was beyond our reach. We were no longer actors, just a bunch of awestruck fans.

Impossible not to say more about Inge here, whose presence in these situations was like sunlight coming into the room. A very necessary warmth and reassurance as it turned out for us all, as it was clear that not just us but even Arthur, especially Arthur, were feeling the strain at the prospect of seeing his work moved around for the first time. At least in England. Although charm and kindness itself, he was at pains to point out that he was slightly deaf and would we all be sure to sing it out loud and clear. After hearty reassurance on that point we did the usual frantic last-minute pointless checking of rehearsal props and shuffled off to the corridor outside. All eye contact was avoided as we continued to mutter lines to ourselves in a quiet and desperate way. But we were all thinking the same thing. Speak up. Project. When we were all at that stage of truthful conversational mumble at each other, how could we suddenly start bellowing these precious conversations? Oh God.

Inge kindly reassured us later that he only ever worried about hearing stuff because he felt nervous too. I think we thought then how come you're worried? You're ARTHUR MILLER for God's sake . . . Anyway, I'm not sure about the others but I'd guess we all prayed a bit or at least did those kinds of deals actors do with Fate or God and ask him to make this performance wonderful and then they will never ask anything ever again.

I can't, of course, remember a thing about the run-through except it must have been fine because Arthur was happy with it and over the remaining rehearsal time actually did become a working colleague who'd share insights and advice and jokes and cups of coffee with us – a treasured and wonderful resource to have in the rehearsal room.

But I'm going to miss Arthur Miller like everyone else whether they met him or not. At the news of his death I felt as though some sane and necessary goodness had left the world. It is in short supply at the moment and probably always is, and we'll all feel the loss of it. I know I'll feel the same when Nelson Mandela dies even though I've never met him. It's a loss of goodness to us all. But the plays remain and there will always be those lucky blessed actors ready to stand on stages all over the world, trembling and amazed and happy, and ready to measure up and speak out loud the words full of truth and sense and hope and love written by Arthur Miller.

Romulus Linney

Writer

He came to a class I was teaching at Columbia University in 1971. He spoke plainly, directly, more like an intelligent Brooklyn taxi driver talking about streets than a great author saying wonderful things about life and art. In the years that followed I often saw him do exactly that, no matter how big, how small, the situation. As one of the greatest playwrights America will ever produce, that honest directness and the plain eloquence, as well as his immense achievements, will always most honor him and his country.

Tony Lo Bianco

Actor: Incident at Vichy, Lincoln Center, 1965; A View from the Bridge, Long Wharf, 1981, Ambassador Theatre, New York, 1982

When I was going to acting school in 1954, Arthur Miller came to be a guest speaker at the Dramatic Workshop on Broadway across from the Winter Garden Theatre. He was speaking to us, a group of young kids, this great playwright. I remember thinking of how in awe I was. As a demonstration, they put on a short scene from *A View from the Bridge*. Needless to say, I was immediately taken aback by that, loved the part of Eddie, loved the play instantly. I distinctly remember saying to myself, 'Wow, that's a good part for me.'

Well, years passed and I went ahead as an actor and did a production of it in summer stock playing Eddie. It was very effective and every fiber of my being told me that one day I would do this on Broadway. When the next production came in the 1960s, *A View from the Bridge*, which originally was done in 1955 as a one-act play on Broadway, had never been done as a full-length play on Broadway. It was first done as a two-act play in America off-Broadway. I went up to see Arthur Miller and wanted to play Eddie. He thought I was too young, but I assured him I was not. He thought I should play Marco and I told him I didn't want to play Marco, I wanted to play Eddie. Well, that production was done off-

Broadway without me. Arvin Brown, director of the Long Wharf Theatre, came to me in 1980. He asked me what I wanted to do at the Long Wharf Theatre. I said, 'I've always wanted to do *A View from the Bridge*,' and he said, 'OK, let's do it.' So we did a production at the Long Wharf and it was extremely successful; Arthur was there and quite a few other people including Paul Newman, Dustin Hoffman and so on. A year later, in 1982, we brought it to Broadway, at the Ambassador Theatre.

This was the first time *View* was done on Broadway as a full-length play. There it was, twenty-eight years in the making, since I first saw the play. It was interesting to meet Arthur Miller again. I remember him saying to me, 'All right, Tony, are you ready to fall on the knife?' He didn't literally mean that, although that is what happens in the play; he meant, was I ready for the commitment. As far as I am concerned I am always ready for the commitment. I like to be the last man standing. We went ahead and I was the winner of the Outer Critics Circle Award and received a Tony nomination as Best Actor for my interpretation of Eddie Carbone. I remember Arthur and me walking down the street after having dinner. We looked up at our names on the marquee and I said to him, 'Look at that, not so bad for two guys from Brooklyn.'

He laughed and said, 'Yeah, not so bad.'

We were talking about the scene in Alfieri's office in which Eddie tells Alfieri why Catherine and Rodolpho should not marry. Eddie gives a whole bunch of reasons why she shouldn't marry an illegal submarine: he just wants his papers, he's just using you, he's a blond kid who sings, maybe he's gay, and so on and so forth, but the most important thing, I said to Arthur, is that they are first cousins. He then said to me, 'Oh, you're right, we'll put it in the script. Tell the stage manager to put it in the script.' He then gave me permission to write that in *A View from the Bridge*, mind you, a classic. Doing *View*, I felt, as every actor should, that the play was my property, that I wrote it, they were my lines – that was *A View from the Bridge* for me. The lines are inevitable – that's how well the play is written. That is how much in tune I was with Eddie, understanding, as I did, the period of the play in the forties and what it was like to be in Brooklyn at that time, how men and women related to each other in that particular neighborhood where the ships would come in, Red Hook, what doilies are on the couch, what the linoleum and the tablecloths look like. There is a certain feeling, understanding and delivery of the vernacular of the forties which was quite different in the fifties, sixties, seventies and so on and so forth. Language and rhythms are different. This is the essence of the greatness of Arthur Miller, his ability to create characters so unequivocally based and living in reality and the ease in which he presents this reality to his audience.

I took Arvin Brown to Brooklyn, to visit some of my uncles and family, and gave him a real taste of Brooklyn life. That was exciting. Arthur attended a couple of rehearsals. I remember at one rehearsal this play was so personal to me that there was a scene in the play that I just fell to pieces, it just got to me and I started crying so much so we had to take a break. It was very touching, personal, and it was that reality which made the performance what it was. During the run of the play, Arthur was quoted in the newspapers as saying I was 'his Eddie Carbone.' He was always very complimentary. *A View from the Bridge* was and remains the absolute highlight of my career. Having the honor of being 'Arthur Miller's Eddie Carbone' is one of my life's greatest accomplishments.

Prior to this I worked with him in *Incident at Vichy*, with director Harold Clurman, at the original Lincoln Center. I remember at the start of rehearsal he read the play to the actors and director, giving us an indication of interpretation. I was told that was his way of doing things. I recall when they were doing *After the Fall* and Arthur Miller had just consented to working with Elia Kazan. This was most interesting because the play was about blacklisting. This was something that Miller had not forgiven Kazan for – co-operating with the blacklisting committee. Even more fascinating was that the play was about Marilyn Monroe, played in this production by none other than Barbara Loden, the girlfriend of Kazan. I remember Miller and Kazan sitting in the theater. They had come together to do this play. Talent I guess? The dedication that Arthur had to his work overcame whatever hostile feelings he had toward Kazan.

I also went with Arthur Miller to attend a special event celebrating his life. We went to a theater in Houston. They were running a production of *All My Sons*. It was a testament to his great writing. The cast of this production was not particularly good, average performers, no name actors and I realised why Arthur reads his plays to the cast. It is to capture the clarity of the play. Interestingly enough, this particular production came through as clear as day. This was a great lesson to me. The characters in *All My Sons* are simple, ordinary people and these actors were just doing *his* script. That's the brilliance of Arthur Miller.

Frank McCourt

Writer

When I moved into Tophet Road in Roxbury, Connecticut, I did not know that my next-door neighbors would be Arthur Miller and his wife, Inge. Indeed, a spring-fed pond of his fed a stream that flowed into our pond. I called that stream 'Miller High Life'.

About the time we moved in I met Arthur at a party in Manhattan. 'So,' he said, 'I heard we are going to be neighbors.'

'That's right, Arthur. By the way, I read an interview you did a few years ago where you said your great pleasure is cabinetmaking and carpentry?'

'That's right. I love it.'

'I'm thinking of taking up carpentry myself,' I said.

'Really? And what would you do with it?'

'Well, now I've learned we're neighbors, I'm going to build a big fence.'

We had hardly moved in when we found a note on the door from Inge to call them. We did and invited them to the first of many dinners. Then my wife, Ellen, with the help of New York friends Mike and Cynthia Gibbons, organised a croquet tournament on our grass. (I suppose I should call it a lawn but it was too rough for that. A croquet purist would have sniffed.) We played in pairs, about eight of them. Arthur was teemed up with Ellen and Mia Farrow played with me. Mia and I were going strong and it looked as if we had a chance. As far as I know, Arthur had never played before but he went into the lead with a magnificent jump shot, one ball over another right there in the hoop. Mia and I still had a chance to at least pull even but she blew a particularly easy shot. She looked apologetic and I asked what had happened. 'Oh, I was looking at Arthur and thinking how handsome he is.'

His biographers, delving into obscure corners of Arthur's life, ought to know that the croquet champion of Tophet Road had his picture in the official magazine of the American Croquet Association (with my wife Ellen, of course).

He was a boon companion and there was a characteristic in his personality I haven't heard mentioned before: his impishness. He is usually cast as a strong – no, towering – figure, right up there with O'Neill, both artists of high seriousness. But there was that other side that I loved. Before the United States attacked Iraq, Arthur speculated on the damage to come on that country's environment. 'Just consider the effects on Iraq of two hundred and fifty thousand Americans shitting all over that country. I think of the millions of rolls of toilet paper required. We don't hear about this and we want to hear about it.' He'd let go with that marvellous impish laugh and I often wished that impishness could seep into his plays.

A week before he died, I saw him for the last time at his sister Joan's, in Manhattan. The cancer treatment had weakened and reduced him, and his voice was all but gone. I was glad to hear he decided he wanted to slip away in his own house in Roxbury. The imp had dignity.

This year we'll revive the croquet tournament. Maybe I'll team up with Mia again and we might have a chance of winning the Arthur Miller Roxbury Connecticut Croquet Trophy. Unless, of course, Mia is distracted by his memory.

Doreen Mantle

Actor: **Death of a Salesman,** *National Theatre, 1979*

Arthur Miller came to tea with our company in our rehearsal room at the NT. This was August 1979. We were previewing *Death of a Salesman* and still working on the play during the day while performing in the evening. He had already met a few of us informally and had seen a performance, but this was our first get together. I kept a diary at that time and noted that we had been well below our best when he saw the play. Michael Rudman, our director, had had some criticism for us. So we were extremely nervous when we sat down to tea. However, Arthur Miller wisely avoided any reference to our production and spoke in general terms about the play.

He told us how the first tour was picketed by the American Legion as 'Communist inspired'; that the first tour to Boston had an Irish-American cast and Boston had hailed it as a play about Irish-American immigrants, but really it was a play about any immigrant community that had a toehold on society. He said he was more interested in people than in ideas, and started from the premise that every action is a political action. Then he went on to tell us about China where he had been to help with the production of *Salesman* there and where his wife had been eager to take photographs. Going on from the play, he touched on China's economy. Its biggest problem was food. 'A farmer in China can only plough half as much because of his nutrition . . . The last stable community in China was feudal.' It was all fascinating. I was enthralled. I forgot that he might have hated my performance as Linda; that he might have been disappointed in Warren Mitchell's Willy, the very core of the play. It was enough to hear this charismatic man share some ideas with us.

I need not have worried about his reaction to our performances – he told Rudman we were 'terrific'. (I've never known if this was true about me, though I am certain about Warren.) And later I heard that he had tried to arrange for Warren and me to repeat our roles in the States.

I first saw *Death of a Salesman* when Paul Muni played it in London in 1950. It was sold out and I had to stand at the back of the stalls. I was swept up in a great surge of emotion such as I had never nor have ever experienced in the theatre. So when I was given the opportunity to play the role of Linda Loman at the National Theatre it was the happiest moment of my theatrical life.

Julian May

BBC Producer, Miller's Tales, 1995

Death of a Salesman began not with a typewriter and a ream of paper but carpenter's tools and a pile of timber. 'I wanted to build the building to write the play in,' Arthur Miller told me. 'It was my first one. I used four by two under the floor, so it bounced when you walked in. I didn't know any better.' Still, like the play more than half a century later, Arthur's writing shed remains sound. We were in his workshop just below his house in Roxbury when he told me this. The darkness was richly fragrant with baulks and planks of magnificent wood, some of it, he confided, 'older than the United States'.

Willy Loman was a success – but as a carpenter and builder rather than a salesman. 'All the cement, the lumber, the reconstruction I put in this house!' Loman says. 'There ain't a crack to be found in it anymore.' The words reflect not only the playwright's values, but also his nature. Willy was never happier than when he built the porch of his house. Arthur Miller shared with him the satisfaction, the consolation found in practical work. 'It stops you from getting totally depressed,' he said. 'You're feeling depressed? That's the time to go and make something out of wood. If you can't make it out of concepts or feelings.'

We walked back up the slope to his wooden house, surrounded by trees full of birds. I had come here with Christopher Bigsby to record a radio interview for broadcast close to Miller's eightieth birthday in October 1995. Chris and I thought we would never come this way again and were quietly ambitious, eager to cover the writer's entire life and work, and his reflections on the century he had lived through. When we arrived Arthur was busy, but not preparing his thoughts on the politics and culture of the twentieth century. No, Arthur was putting the finishing touches to a bench he had designed and built for the porch where, as the weather was fine, we decided to record.

Chris asked questions and Arthur talked. His wife, the photographer Inge Morath, took pictures and cooked delicious meals. Arthur talked. We went swimming in the big pond full of frogs. We walked among the trees he had planted, planning to sell them to the New York administration to line the streets (which he forgot to do until they were too big). The interview lasted a whole weekend and became *Miller's Tales*, a series of four half-hour programmes for BBC Radio 4.

After we'd covered World War Two and *All My Sons*, in the break before we embarked on McCarthyism and *The Crucible*, I mentioned that I too enjoyed making things out of wood: some small tables, a rough garden bench. How over the last year what friends had taken for a 'novelty bookcase' in our living room was actually a small boat I was building; how I had to remove the window sashes to get it out and that, though I never admitted it, I was never sure it would fit through. Arthur put down his cup, drew himself up and invited me into his workshop.

Arthur's seat was a solid, rather than elegant, bench made from a blond timber that I did not recognise. 'Sassafras. Very easy to cut and light for a strong wood. It's like cherry to work.' Arthur, warming to his subject, engaged like a salesman: 'They use it for fence posts because it doesn't rot easily. This is for the porch, out in the open, so I thought I'd use it.' It was ingenious, economic and strong, the legs and support for the back cut from just two pieces of wood. 'I improvised the design, one thing led to another – a bit like improvising a play to tell you the truth . . . something I enjoy doing.'

Then Arthur pointed out a hefty piece of pale raw timber. It came from an apple tree, which had stood behind the Roxbury house since he first moved there in 1956, and which was already old then. A swing for Rebecca, his daughter with Inge, was strung from it. But it had blown down the previous year. Arthur wanted to make something from it, could not decide what and was not to be rushed. 'I'm waiting for the moment. It hasn't arrived yet.' He ran his palm along the grain. 'It's waiting for the human hand to turn it into something useful, or beautiful. It's exciting if you think of it like that. It's like the beginning of the world, before it was shaped. It's like a blank piece of paper you could make into something boring – or significant. That piece of wood is a challenge. If you want to accept it.'

We went back to the porch and, as the crickets sawed and hummingbirds like flamboyant missionaries called persistently on the flowers, Arthur recounted his life with Marilyn, relived his appearance before the House Un-American Activities Committee and puzzled over Vietnam. Inge cooked salmon and after we'd eaten Arthur went off looking for something. He returned with a smooth elliptical pebble of bronze. It was a shape devised by a Danish engineer that had the largest possible circumference for a given area. It was used to control traffic, Arthur explained – the basis of the shape of Danish roundabouts. He took me into the dining room where there was a table built of beautiful cherry boards, almost but not quite the shape of the bronze casting. 'A circle's no good,' Arthur declared, 'the centre's too far away. I adapted this shape. You can get fourteen people round this and everyone's together, not separated into couples, who happen to be seated next to one another.

And everyone can reach the pickle.' He chuckled. 'I'm amused by the idea – a design for the traffic in Denmark and it's in my living room. We've had twenty-five years of dinners here and it works beautifully.'

Arthur had made the chairs, too, using chestnut beams from a barn built before independence. 'See, this little patch,' he said, jabbing a finger at a square that didn't match the rest of the surface. 'It's sunk into the other wood because it was splintering there.' I felt like a medieval apprentice recently bound to a venerable master. 'This is called a Dutchman.' Arthur loved the wood itself, the working of it, but also the language of carpentry. 'This is the breadboard design,' he said, pointing out how he had grooved a piece with the grain going in a different direction into the end of a board in the bedroom, to keep it from splaying in all directions.

He had remarked that he improvised at his bench in the same way he would a play, but the connection between the way Miller worked in wood, words and images is more complex and fundamental than this suggests. At school he could never do algebra, but loved geometry because it suggested the real, tangible planes and forms. In the bench and in the plays one idea flows into another. But these are then jointed together so the whole becomes solid. Recently, while making a programme about Willy Loman, I have been struck by the way several actors and directors used the language of woodwork to describe Miller's *Death of a Salesman*: themes fit to create a dramatic framework that is perfectly jointed, the drama is finely planed, the play solid so it doesn't wobble.

'I've always visualised things in concrete masses,' Arthur told me, as he picked up a weighty wooden bookend. 'Look at these. They're just chunks of wood. But they're beautiful. The wood is. I didn't try to fuss with it. And they hold the books real well. I get great satisfaction creating something out of nothing. Which is really what a writer is doing anyway.'

But despite all this truthful concision, Arthur Miller enjoyed the dramatic gesture and theatrical trickery, even in the making of furniture. Some of his beloved chestnut had 'had company'. 'See those wormholes. Chestnut's always wormy. In fact, in Italy when they fake old chestnut they fire a shotgun at it . . . Course, then it's full of bits of lead.'

As well as his bench, the dining-room table, the chairs, shelves and bookends, Arthur Miller built the bed on which he and Inge Morath slept all their married life. 'My wife, every time she goes to sleep, says "I love this bed." Nothing's going to happen. It'll be there as long as anybody wants to use it.' He paused for a moment, a man of eighty considering the bed he had fashioned a quarter of a century before from chestnuts felled more than two centuries earlier. 'There's something immortal in that bed, if you want to look at it that way.'

I came to Roxbury to record a man who closely observed the forces that shaped the century through which he lived. I listened enthralled: out of his experience he created works full of wisdom and wit that are finely weighed, beautifully put together and will last for ever. And they're not all plays.

Warren Mitchell

Actor: **Death of a Salesman,** *National Theatre, 1979;* **The Price,** *Tricycle Theatre and in the West End, 2003–4*

I think all the best things I have ever done have been easy and so when I read this script the first time I knew I could do it, I knew it was going to be easy. My father was a salesman and he was very ill once, and I took his bag of samples around to a few of the West End stores, never sold a thing, so that was pretty good training for Willy. I never drove all that distance but I knew something about the idea of selling and the disappointment of not selling. That is the magic of Miller, of course, it is easy. You just read it straight off the page and it is there.

My father, like many fathers, wanted me to be successful. He would probably have said, no, I want you to be happy. They all say that. They don't really mean it. I remember when I saw the play first in London the guy who played Biff was magic. The idea of the rebellion against a parent – I was Biff's age and I really sympathised, I understood because I had lived in a house I wasn't happy with. When I first said to my father I was going to be an actor he said, 'Are you mad? How are you going to earn a living doing that? I have got a little business here. Who is going to take it over?'

I said, 'Dad, I can't sell china and glass. It is not me.' When the name was up there in lights a bit he changed his tune. My son the actor.

What drives Willy is the American Dream, which today has been inculcated into us. Every paper is full of ads about how to get rich and we are going down that path, whether we like it or not, and I don't like it. I think that is what made Willy the way he was with outside pressures. The salesman is of noble calling but I am sure Willy was a lonely man. That is why he goes with a woman in the hotel room. But his wife is strong.

Mike Rudman, the director, had a whistle he used to blow if he caught Linda smiling and being nice. He would blow his whistle and say, 'Doris Day just walked in. Get her out of here.' Doris Day and Doreen Mantle took it very well and produced a prize-winning performance as Linda, a lot of it because Michael insisted on the fact that she was a tough, hard woman. There was a hint of steel underneath. When she sees the sons after they have left their father in the restaurant she gives them hell. This man has to have respect and she was a very loyal woman. Marriage was for better, for worse.

When Michael Rudman first decided to do the play we were playing tennis and I had just done the play in a very hurried production in Western Australia, in Perth, and I came back and Michael and I were hitting up and I said, 'Want to see my notice of Willy Loman?'

He said, 'No, thank you. You played Willy?'

I said, 'Yes.'

He said, 'I am thinking of doing it at the National,' hitting the ball backwards and forwards.

I said, 'Really?'

He said, 'Yes, I didn't think of you, Warren.'

I said, 'You are a good friend, Michael.'

He said, 'I wanted to cast it Jewish. I thought of all sorts of Jewish actors, but you better come and audition for him.'

I said, 'Audition? I know the part, I don't need to read it. I know it. I have just finished playing it.' So I went and auditioned. It was a very lengthy process because I know that he was fighting a lot of the establishment of the National who would dismiss me as a television comedian and not as an actor who could play the part of Willy. I think a lot of establishment actors were up in line ahead of me but I think Michael fought for me and he won, luckily for me.

I will tell you what is Jewish about it. Arthur said to us that

Thomas Mitchell played Willy Loman on the first tour and the Irish-American community in Boston said, 'At last a play about an Irish-American family.' Then there was a black cast and it was suddenly a play about black Americans. He said, 'I wrote a play and you can play it how you like.' He said to Michael, 'You can play it, you can cast it Jewish, but I don't want any menoras, or anything that says to the audience this is a Jewish family. It is a family.' There was nothing specifically Jewish, I think, in the writing. It is every family. I think Arthur knew about families. (I played in *The Price*, which is also about a family.)

I asked Arthur, 'What am I carrying on in those cases when I arrive on stage?'

He said, 'Dreams, Warren, dreams.' And I understood then that this was a man who didn't exist in the real world. They were dreams that Willy was carrying in those cases, dreams of success, dreams of being liked and dreams for his children, for his two sons. That was the most important thing that Arthur ever said to me.

The first time I did it was a nightmare because we had roughly ten days of rehearsal and I didn't know it well enough, and I remember the first night, the first preview. I came in for my first entrance and I said, 'Linda, I came back. I did . . . did . . . Biff say anything after I went this morning?' and I couldn't remember a word, a line, and I said, 'I will go and get some milk and crackers' and I went out the door and I stood outside the bedroom door and I thought, I have left out half the play. So I went back in again and said, 'Linda, I was driving along and suddenly the car was going off the road . . . I better go down and get some milk and crackers.' Three or four times I went out the door and came back, trying to remember the plot of the play.

Afterwards the director came round and he said, 'Boy, that was some performance. I have to tell you, Warren, there was a woman came up to me and said, you know when Mr Mitchell stood outside that door dithering like that, I knew the character, I thought that is the most brilliant piece of acting. This man who could not make up his mind, he was so indecisive.' Little did she know I was desperately thinking what are the lines. The longest dry I have ever had.

Willy Loman is the number one part for any actor. I even place it above Lear because you don't have to fight to understand it. It is so blindingly apparent and that is what people love about the play, I guess. You understand it from the moment Willy comes in the door and then you hear the two boys in the bedroom.

Some can't even move at the end of that play. I remember at the National people would say to the ushers after that funeral scene, 'Can we sit here a little while, we can't really face the world.'

When we were playing it in Perth there was a line which we changed. I was supposed to say that people called me Walrus and I thought that was wrong for me so I changed it to shrimp. It had to be something insulting and Michael Rudman said, 'We don't change his words. We have to ask the author.' So he rang Arthur and Arthur said, 'That is funny, because I wrote shrimp but we changed it to walrus because the first Willy was Lee J. Cobb who was a big man.' He said, 'Warren is the first little Willy we have ever had. So he is right to call it shrimp and not walrus.'

Honor Moore

Writer and friend

When asked to contribute to this volume, I considered writing something new, but decided instead to abridge a piece I'd written for a Connecticut newspaper in 1994, which is still an authentic portrait of the years of my friendship with the Millers.

On one of those crystalline days in October 1994 I sat with Arthur Miller on the lawn behind his house in Roxbury, Connecticut. We got settled – in two beat-up old chairs – in a gold dollop of sun on the extremely saturated green grass and began to talk about our shoes. He remarked in fun that mine, cotton high-heeled high-tops, would do well in the rain and began to complain that his pale-blue Nike running shoes had worn out much too quickly. 'I should have known,' he said.

'Then why did you buy them?' His favorite shoes are a pair of L. L. Bean boots the company rebuilt for him a few years ago.

'They were just so *light*,' he said, lifting one of his large feet.

The task that had brought me to Arthur Miller's broad sweep of lawn was a story, this story: to write about our long friendship, to discover – if I could – what it had meant to have a deep and sustaining connection to a writer who is a world figure and a friend. A close friend, and a living example of the passion and commitment that inform the life of a writer.

Suddenly, Inge Morath, Arthur's wife of thirty-two years, emerged from her photography studio in the barn down the hill, gesturing wildly. 'A phone call!' she motioned. Arthur ran to get the cordless. Hollywood was calling about Kenneth Branagh's planned movie of his 1953 play *The Crucible*. Before clicking off the phone, he responded to the caller's birthday greetings.

'Well,' I said, as he clicked off the phone, 'you must have had many calls of praise today . . .'

'And some criticism', he finished, with his mischievous smile, 'from those who are sorry I'm still alive.'

Very much alive, his seventy-nine years hardly show on his strapping six foot four frame, and he says he's learning to live with the arthritis in his back, the waking at 5 a.m. He remains politically active, most recently in efforts to get a retrial for Richard Lapointe of Manchester, Connecticut, accused of murder and convicted on the basis of a nine-hour police interrogation and only slight evidence. 'I feel doubly obligated', Arthur said, 'to speak when I think silence would mean some kind of complicity on my part.' And he writes every day: 'Work is like breathing for me,' he says, 'I don't know who I am without it.'

If you were not to recognise his face, by now an icon of American culture, Arthur Miller would look to you more like a farmer or carpenter than a writer. Last spring he had a new vegetable garden cleared near the large rambling red barn and he was very pleased with the results. 'It's such fertile soil,' he said in August with a farmer's pride, pointing to a bunch of fat red beets on the kitchen counter. Inside the barn, there is a fully equipped carpentry shop. 'Every once in a while I have to lay my hands on something material or I get uneasy.'

As a carpenter, Arthur is no mere amateur – at large dinners we sit around the big oval table he designed and built from five planks of cherry milled from an old log he found in the barn. 'I wanted a table that would seat fourteen,' Inge said. 'I wanted everyone to be able to see one another.' The Millers' entertaining reflects her embracing spirit. Inge is the kind of cook who can taste a dish at a restaurant and reinvent it at home. She'll roast a capon from the farmer in the next town or make a venison stew from deer shot on their land by hunter neighbors. All summer the large salad bowl is abundant with home-grown lettuce, and in the dead of winter pasta is dressed with tomatoes she puts up at the end of summer. It is a source of amazement to her friends that Inge, a world-class photographer with a distinguished and ongoing career, has time to concoct chutney from her own quinces and bake the occasional perfect tart.

Dinners at the Millers' have the feel and informality of family gatherings, and often there is family present, but it has always seemed to me that once brought into their circle by friendship or through work, you become related to an ever expanding family of friends. At the Millers' table I've sat with neighbors like the novelist William Styron and his wife, the poet and activist Rose Styron; the writer Francine duPlessix Gray and her husband, the painter Cleve Gray; the theater director John Tillinger; the literary critic Alfred Kazin and his wife Judith; the actor Richard Widmark and his wife Jean; Vivian Lu, the Yale professor who taught Inge Chinese. I painted eggs there one Easter with John Malkovich (Biff in the Dustin Hoffman *Death of a Salesman*) and pitched horseshoes across the lawn with the German director Volker Schlöndorff.

Often at their table, I'm reminded that Arthur's and Inge's lives as a couple and as artists are international. It was at the Millers' in 1985 that I heard the Russian poet Andrei Voznesensky express cautious optimism that Mikhail Gorbachev, then unknown, might bring change to Russia. Days after the massacre at Tiananmen Square, the Chinese novelist Chang Jie, her daughter translating, spoke of her anguish for her country and her fear that she might never be able to return to her home in Beijing.

Over the years, hearing about a day's mail from Istanbul or Tokyo, Jerusalem or Berlin, the forty productions of his plays in Germany just this year, I have become aware of the extent to which his home country underappreciates Arthur Miller. Though there are scores of American productions of his plays and he is enormously famous and rewarded here, his celebrity seems the consequence of barely a fraction of his output and of his marriage to Marilyn Monroe.

'Those who are sorry I'm still alive' do not acknowledge either the depth of his achievement or its dimension – twenty plays, all in print that sell in the hundreds of thousands a year; an autobiography, *Timebends*; two novels, books of essays and short stories, countless occasional pieces. In light of his productivity and importance, the ongoing diffidence in most of the American critical response to his work is incomprehensible to me. Occasionally I bring this up with Arthur and we discuss, again, the absurdity of the American literary establishment's antipathy to work with social content – 'Imagine if I'd left Willy Loman's job out of *Death of a Salesman*,' he says and goes on to remind me that a writer must think, while writing, of readers and not of reviewers. Always when we talk about his work or the condition of the theater, he comes back to the audience, his passion to reach us in that darkened room.

Because I want to situate Arthur in his life as I've come to know it, and to take a sounding of his thinking in the first days of his eightieth year, I have decided to interview him. When I arrive, the house is tranquil and empty, and I continue up to the tiny studio which he built with his own hands when he and Marilyn Monroe moved into this, his second Connecticut house, in 1956.

As the dogs – my Belgian sheepdog and his big Alsatian, Lola – bang against the screen door, I can't help remembering the passage in *Timebends* in which Arthur describes building a studio at his first Roxbury house before writing, in a white heat, *Death of a Salesman*, the play which half a century later receives seventy productions a year in the United States, has been translated into thirty languages and which, when he directed it in Beijing in 1983, spoke even to the Chinese.

There in the dark sits its author in battered blue jeans, a plaid flannel shirt and a faded denim jacket, bent over a bright computer screen. 'I'm writing to the National Theatre,' he turns to explain. The National Theatre of Great Britain is one of the most avid producers of Arthur's work, having mounted, in the last decade, productions of *A View from the Bridge*, *The Crucible*, *After the Fall*, and, most recently, his 1994 play, *Broken Glass*, which opened there in August and will move at the beginning of February to the West End, London's Broadway. In provincial theaters across Britain, a new Arthur Miller play or revival is a frequent season staple, and at the National only Shakespeare has had more productions. 'They want to celebrate my eightieth birthday, next year,' he tells me. The plan is to invite a group of actors to perform scenes from all his plays. His enthusiastic letter back, big white letters on a royal blue computer screen, illuminates his happy response. 'I've said, just go right ahead.'

I met the Millers in the summer of 1983. I was invited to supper by the choreographer and director Martha Clarke, a Connecticut friend and neighbor. Arthur and Inge would be there, she said. It was as if she'd invited two of the Egyptian pyramids. I spent summers in Kent and knew Arthur Miller lived half an hour away, but I never expected to meet him. Martha put me next to him at dinner. He was not carved from stone like the Sphinx, but he was so tall he dwarfed his small chair, and he talked like a New Yorker, which surprised me. I was tongue-tied and at dessert got raspberry juice on my new white suit. Martha talked to Arthur as if he were a friend, not Mount Rushmore. I thought Inge was beautiful. I was terribly shy. I remember Arthur, in tandem with Inge, describing their flight, on the last plane out of Cambodia before the American bombing in 1971. It was not to be the last time I learned history from the Millers.

They also talked of rebuilding their house, damaged by fire when they'd been in Beijing with *Salesman* the previous winter. I'd written a poem about the burning of my brother's loft and Inge asked me to send it. To my astonishment, I received a letter back from Arthur. He responded not to my account of the fire, but to the poem's real subject, my estrangement from a younger brother – particularly compelling to him, I realise now, given his own treatment in plays of relationships between brothers. It became my secret wish to talk with him about the writer's life. How do you do it? How do you do it your life long?

A year later I moved to Kent full time and my first Connecticut New Year's Eve I was taken to the Millers'. They had gathered friends for dinner, a group that spilled over to a second table, and afterward, while a concert pianist friend played Chopin on the grand piano, we sat on big cushions on the floor in front of a wood-burning stove, on a big down sofa, and on the Biedermeier couch, one of the few things Inge has from her Austrian childhood. That evening Inge said she'd like to photograph me. I was terrifically flattered and, a month after I sat for her, dropped by to pick up a print. With her customary warmth, she invited me to stay for tea and we all sat down – Arthur, Inge, their daughter Rebecca (then twenty-one and a painter; now also a film director) and Inge's mother, then in her late eighties. Arthur began to ask me questions, about poetry, about why I'd moved to the country and finally about politics. I sat upright on a chair, shy, awkward, nervous, aware that the four other people in the room were watching me intently, like curious animals.

'What happened,' I remember him asking, 'what happened to your generation?' This was 1985 and, having been an activist most of his life, he was concerned with the apathy, now that the sixties had passed, of those of us born after World War Two.

I hesitated and then began to speak. 'It was the assassinations,' I said. 'We grew up so admiring certain heroes – Kennedy, Martin Luther King, Malcolm X – and they were all killed. Their deaths took something away from us.'

I remember him nodding and my shyness dissolving. As the conversation unfolded, I felt the quality of his attention. This was a conversation in which politics and ethics were linked to the spiritual and moral struggles of ordinary people. It made sense to me that the writer who had so sensitively drawn the thwarted idealism of Biff, Willy Loman's rebellious son, would understand how the death of a president might break the heart of a generation and batter its spirit.

We talked all afternoon and when the light began to fail, Inge darted into the kitchen. When she returned moments later, she smiled. 'Would you like to stay for supper?' That evening was the first of many around the Millers' kitchen table. The fluorescent ceiling light is always on and the candles are always lit. Always, after Arthur takes his first bite, he says, 'Inge! This is delicious!' then looks at me and says, 'Isn't this delicious?'

My clearest memory of that first summer is of midsummer night. It was ten o'clock and still light, and I remember Arthur and Inge and me leaping around on the lawn, which that evening seemed to slope off the edge of the planet. 'Isn't it wonderful,' Arthur kept saying with a child's delight as the light stayed and stayed. It happened that was the summer I was beginning to grapple with my first prose book, a biography of my grandmother, the American painter Margarett Sargent. I'd written poems, had a play produced on Broadway, edited an anthology of plays by women and written for magazines, but this was my first effort at an extended narrative.

I found the task daunting – how to pull what I was learning in interviews and books into a dramatic telling of the story that had always stood between me and the belief that I could endure as a writer. My grandmother was a vital and fascinating woman who, at the height of a successful career as a painter, turned from her art – a choice that had dire and painful consequences. As summer turned to fall, I often gazed at the computer screen blankly. I didn't let on to the Millers how hard the writing was, complained instead about the bleakness of the winter. Arthur had a gruff New England response. 'It builds character,' he said. Eventually, I left a draft of a chapter for Inge to read and, to my surprise, got a response from Arthur. It was tough to hear but in the end very useful. 'Who's the expert if not you?' he said. 'Throw away the research and write it like a novel.'

He was working on *Timebends*, his autobiography. Having seen his scribbled-over typewritten pages, I had encouraged him to switch to a computer and that had changed our relationship – we now also talked about *his* writing. One day, as if to acknowledge our friendship's new dimension, he gave me the first half of *Timebends* in manuscript. I began reading one Saturday morning, and was immediately plunged deep into a writer's telling of a life:

> The view from the floor is of a pair of pointy black calf-height shoes, one of them twitching restlessly, and just above them the plum-colored skirt rising from the ankles to the blouse, and higher still the young round face and her ever-changing tones of voice as she gossips into the wall telephone with one of her two sisters, something she would go on doing the rest of her life until one by one they peeled off the wire and vanished into the sky . . .

I was enthralled by that child's eye description and surprised by the book's narrative freedom – the aunts dissolving into thin air. Arthur didn't have the trouble I did moving between intimate description and historical telling, and stories seemed to rush from his typewriter unbidden. My excitement built as I read through the Depression childhood, his discovery of writing at the University of Michigan, his decision not to go to Spain to fight and the failure of *The Man Who Had All the Luck*, his first play (about a young man and a mink farm).

I read of the life-changing success of *Death of a Salesman*, an account of his heartbreaking marriage to Marilyn Monroe, the woman who moved him from the theater pages to the gossip columns. In his telling, the 'sex symbol' comes across as a fragile and suffering person of intelligence and dignity whom Arthur sincerely loved and whose decline and death he mourned. This would have surprised me had I not heard her treated with the same respect once when her name came up at supper. And I had seen the poignant portrait of her, taken on the set of *The Misfits*, that Inge considers one of her best.

Timebends manifested my sense of Arthur's contradictions, of which marriage to Marilyn Monroe was just one – an elegant intelligence residing in an oddly graceful, large and awkward body; a stern sense of justice alongside great compassion for people; a startling candor about his own vulnerability to human passions some might describe as weaknesses. I was encountering the history of our century in the language of a storyteller who never failed to enchant me at the dinner table – his youthful career as a radio crooner accompanied by a blind pianist who promised he'd be 'the young Al Jolson'; how, as a boy he'd learned to sew in his father's coat factory; his encounter with Lucky Luciano on a post-war trip to Italy. I read deep into the night and began again the following morning. At about noon the telephone rang.

'Are you going anywhere?' said a truckdriver voice I immediately recognised as Arthur's.

'Why?'

'Well, you have the only copy of my book, and I thought you might go somewhere and lose it.'

'I'm not going anywhere and it's riveting,' I said.

'Riveting?'

I could hear his pleasure. I was the first outside reader, he told me, and he had no sense of what he was doing. How could he be nervous? As nervous as me about sharing his writing? Also, I was amazed he'd given me his only copy.

After *Timebends* was published (in seventeen languages), Arthur went back to *The Ride Down Mount Morgan* (his eighteenth play, first produced in London in 1991, about a man whose two wives meet in the hospital room where he lies in a body cast after an automobile crash). He had been working on it for ten years. By then I'd worked on the biography for eight; what impressed me was that Arthur worked on other things too. He seemed always to have finished a short story or just mailed a piece in to the *New York Times* Op Ed page. I said how I admired that and he got a faraway look in his eyes. He didn't feel he was writing, he said, unless he was writing for the theater. I was struck by how deeply what first engaged him had held him all his life. He told me he wasn't sure he'd ever finish *Mount Morgan*, and that if he did, he thought it would be his last full-length play.

He did finish *The Ride Down Mount Morgan* and it was not his last full-length play. One night the winter after it opened in London, I went to Roxbury for supper, and afterward Arthur read aloud to Inge and me *The Last Yankee*, a new one-act about two men visiting their wives in a state mental hospital. A few months later, *Yankee* had a second act and, before I knew it, New York and London productions were scheduled.

Some time later when I arrived one evening, Arthur was nowhere to be found. 'He's finishing the play,' Inge said.

'I thought it *was* finished,' I said, thinking she meant *The Last Yankee*.

'No,' she said, 'there's another one!' When Arthur came down from the studio, he had finished *Broken Glass* which he'd begun just weeks before. An image, which had returned from time to time for almost fifty years, had inexplicably taken hold and he'd been writing intensely for three weeks.

The idea for a play usually arrives almost lackadaisically, he told me; a memory or an incident starts to occupy him and, some time later, at his desk, he begins to think of characters in a situation and to write scene after scene 'to see if I've got anything'. I'd seen the fruits of that process one day in his studio, an eight-inch stack of paper, pages and pages of dialogue, only a tenth of which eventually found its way into *The Ride Down Mount Morgan*. But the process had been different with *Broken Glass*; the subject had taken him with something like the force of *Death of a Salesman*, whose first act he'd written in 'barely a night and a day'. Sylvia, a vital woman in early middle age, wakes one morning in November 1938, unable to walk. There is no medical explanation. As the play unfolds, it becomes clear that she has been paralysed by her anxiety and rage over the treatment of Jews in Germany, the recent occurrence of Kristallnacht – the breaking of windows of Jewish shops, the rounding up of Jews, the spectacle of old Jewish men forced to clean the sidewalks with toothbrushes. Her husband, in order to prosper, has denied his own Jewishness, and along with it, her reality. *Broken Glass* is a new variation on a great Miller theme: how certain of our personal choices have painful consequences for others, how we refuse that responsibility at our peril.

At the Good News Café in Woodbury, over a rack of wild boar

and red cabbage, Arthur and I began to talk about how he came to write plays. At first he recalled going to Temple as a very young child with his grandfather and great-grandfather, both leaders of the congregation, and how the forceful language of the Old Testament gripped his imagination. Then he told me about a powerful experience he'd had in theater just as he was beginning to write. The play was *Waiting for Lefty* and Arthur had found himself on his feet with the rest of the audience shouting 'Strike! Strike!' along with the aggrieved taxi drivers playwright Clifford Odets had put on the stage. 'It was a revelation,' Arthur said, not of the play's politics but of its boldness. 'He tore down the barrier between audience and actors – we began to respond as if the play's events were reality.' Arthur has never written that way, but that evening instilled a faith 'that the theater could be part of our lives rather than some place you go to waste two hours'.

From his response to an overtly political drama like *Lefty*, you might draw the conclusion many of his detractors have, that Arthur Miller's intention is to write social realism, but you would be wrong. If you pay attention, you grasp immediately that the purpose of his theater is to connect its audience to a deeper reality. 'The dream is the exemplar,' he said that night at the restaurant. His aim is to write so that his plays emerge with the power and economy of a dream.

Ironically, what gave rise to Arthur's vision of the theater were not dreams but the profound social tumult in which he grew up – his father's enormous business success broken overnight by the stock market crash, the move from Harlem luxury to a simple life deep in Brooklyn, his mother's torment at her dispossession, his early and continuous experiences with anti-Semitism. For a sensitive adolescent boy, these dislocations had emotional consequences which lodged themselves deep in his psyche, later to become the sources of his extraordinary art.

It was with a non-conformist's skepticism that the young Arthur Miller looked at the surrounding social landscape – the Depression, the New Deal, the efforts of President Roosevelt, whom he still believes was an absolutely extraordinary leader. Three Democratic administrations had failed to solve unemployment. 'It was the greatest social problem of the twentieth century,' he remembered. 'It had brought Hitler to power in Germany and had radicalised Americans to the left and the right. We all believed we lived in the shadow of a coming battle of some kind, and it was in that shadow that I wrote my early plays. I was trying to pluck the audience from believing in the virtues of doom, to show the way to some human hope.'

'Self-consciously?'

'Oh yes,' he said.

'But', I said, 'how, in a tragic play, do you turn audiences away from doom?'

Arthur began to talk about one of the most famous characters in American literature, a character he created. In *Death of a Salesman*, Biff, Willy Loman's oldest son, is his father's hope for the future, but he is torn between his own desires and his father's expectations. He comes home to make a new start but, in the course of the play, steals an expensive pen from a man he hopes will employ him. His last speech destroys the illusions the Lomans have carefully constructed to keep hope alive – that Willy still has a career and that Biff has a great future ahead of him. 'What am I doing in an office making a contemptuous, begging fool of myself,' Biff cries in a fury at his father, 'when all I want is out there, waiting for me that minute I say I know who I am!'

Watching a video of the Dustin Hoffman production, I understood for the first time that Biff's rage was not merely a son's argument with a father, but a plea for survival. In Willy's refusal to see him as he is, Biff feels the spiritual death anyone denied his or her reality is bound to feel. The artist is a person who, finally, cannot live with that lie. Though *Death of a Salesman* is not an autobiographical play, in his truth-telling Biff is an autobiographical character.

'In order to exist,' Arthur said that day on the lawn, 'one part of us has to deny another part. We all do it.' The subject of as early a play as *Death of a Salesman* and as late a play as *Broken Glass* is the shattering of that denial and the efforts we then make toward wholeness. At those times the spiritual and the political come together.

'That's what I intend,' Arthur said.

The other night, Arthur gave me a play called *Elegy for a Lady*, a one-act he wrote in the late eighties. 'I have a special feeling for it,' he told me, 'because I dared to do it,' he said, explaining that for him writing a play in which two people encounter one another outside any social context was a risk.

As a writer, the most valuable gift I have from Arthur Miller is the example of that daring. At almost eighty, he continues to confound my sense of what an old man looks like, of what happens to a famous American writer in the last decades of his life.

One day a few weeks ago, I called him.

'I'm afraid.' He paused. 'Afraid I'm writing a play.'

'That's wonderful,' I said.

'But you see, dear, it's a dying art,' he said, as if saying, in the face of all the evidence to the contrary, that he himself were about to die.

Just this afternoon I went over to Roxbury and, on the spur of the moment, off the blue computer screen, he read me thirty pages of a new play.

'It's wild, isn't it?'

It seemed wonderfully wild to me as I listened to two old men settle scores, their talk twisting and turning, jabbing and exploding, never letting on where it might lead.

'Just keep at it,' I said.

'I don't know what I'm doing,' he said, with glee.

'But *it* seems to know,' I said.

As I drove away, leaves off the trees now, I remembered what Arthur had said about this new play that afternoon we talked about sneakers on the lawn. 'I'm going further than ever now,' he said, 'following the streams below the story.'

Sheridan Morley

Reviewer, biographer

Without Arthur Miller there would, it goes without saying, have been no Willy Loman. What is more surprising is that there would also have been no Archie Rice. What happened was that in 1956 Arthur was over here accompanying his then wife Marilyn Monroe on the troubled set of *The Prince and the Showgirl*, a movie she was making at that time with Laurence Olivier. Olivier had, he told Miller one morning, just been to see *Look Back in Anger* and thought it rubbish. Miller replied that it was the most important play since the war, including his own, and that if Larry would go back to the Court and give it a second chance he, Arthur, would talk him through it.

Larry agreed, changed his mind thanks to Arthur's tutorial in contemporary theatre, and meeting Osborne afterwards begged him to write him a play. Osborne duly wrote *The Entertainer* and the rest is theatrical history – except that it would never have happened without Arthur.

Miller was the greatest of all the writers I have been lucky enough to interview in print and on the air, and when I think of him now it is first of the size of the man – moral, artistic, physical. Arthur was a carpenter who built his plays the way he built his tables and chairs – to last. You don't somehow think of Tennessee Williams or Noël Coward crafting their own furniture from hunks of oak, but that sense of the builder was central and essential to Miller's work. So too was a vivid sense of the moral and political history of his nation: when I first interviewed him early in the 1960s, when he was over here for the National Theatre production of *The Crucible* (Olivier had repaid his Osborne debt by making it the first play by an American dramatist to be staged at the National), it was already abundantly clear that here was not just a playwright but a historian eager to teach the march of time.

Yet what defines his genius is the realisation that each of us, even Arthur himself, ends up feeling kind of temporary about ourselves to use yet another of the lines from *Death of a Salesman* that has become part of the language. In the way that he told his own life story through his plays, including the very last, and in the way that he took as the title of his autobiography the *Timebends* that a diver feels when he comes too fast to the surface, Miller had a unique understanding of the tricks of time and memory. I can think of no other dramatist who was so centrally plugged in to the public life of his time, from Monroe to McCarthy, nor one who so well understood its treacheries as well as its triumphs.

What you invariably got, if you were lucky enough to interview Arthur as often as I did, was an expert tutorial: in the giant's presence you might have come prepared to discuss a single play, but what you ended up with was a Miller masterclass on the state of the American nation past and present.

I was always amazed that America never made him its president; but then again perhaps he just called the shots on his beloved nation too clearly for that, or perhaps it could never quite come to terms with the fact that he saw its faults more clearly than most; *Death of a Salesman* is not just the greatest play of its time and of ours, it is also the one which maps most clearly the borderline at which the American dream shades over into the American nightmare.

Peter Nichols

Writer

A number of us joined Arthur Miller and his wife Inge at the American Embassy in London for a reception to mark the opening of the Arthur Miller Centre for American Studies at the University of East Anglia. I'd wondered if anyone would ever open a Peter Nichols Centre, even a Perimeter but the prospect of meeting Miller overcame my doubts.

An hour later we boarded the bus for our ride to Norwich. Miller sat in the front seat, tirelessly (at seventy-four) giving a series of audiences to the entire company, led forward one by one by Christopher Bigsby, organiser of the event. My turn came as we were passing through the suburbs of Norwich. To sit chatting with this admirable man would once have seemed more than any boy from north Bristol had a right to expect. We deplored Reagan together and he said Jimmy Carter had failed through his Christian weakness in a country that admires only chutzpah.

Dan Sullivan of the *LA Times* stood in for Michael Billington, who'd been laid low with a kidney stone. He put a view that caused few ripples, though I did challenge his claim that the *New York Times* critic's word was law, that if he praised a play it was away to the races. I reported that *A Day in the Death of Joe Egg* had closed within weeks. This in turn prompted an eloquent ten-minute sermon by Miller on the grim state of Broadway. It was odd how our English voices – fast and gossipy – were stilled by his cryptic, deliberate address, with never a hesitation, delivered in the croaky, deadpan way that comes from having been listened to for fifty years with mute respect. Was this a plea to us not to imperil our state theatres or we would end with nothing, 'like New York, a theatre city that never puts on plays, hasn't done an original play in fifteen years'?

He was the most eminent survivor of the last generation that could speak with such certitude. For us, for more than thirty years, there's been irony, mockery and scepticism of the kind that asks what plays are, how they're made and why, a postmodern attitude that seemed to him to border on the facetious or at best unnecessary.

Only thirteen years his junior, struck sideways by *Salesman* when young, I'm now caught between admiration and the need to lift the prophet's robe and show the feet of clay. That's the cliché, of course, that Mount Rushmore figure. Close to, he's funnier, friendlier, altogether more dry and gnomic.

Benedict Nightingale

Reviewer: The Times

I first met Arthur Miller in the late 1980s at the University of Michigan, where I was teaching drama and he was an alumnus who had, I was told, given a great deal of time and money to his alma mater. I arranged for him to meet my students for a question-and-answer session and, uptight Englishman that I was, told them in advance not to raise the subject of Marilyn Monroe, since it might embarrass him. But barely had he met them than he himself started to talk in his calm and affable way about his second wife, giving her credit for the seriousness with which she approached her acting and the effect she had had on him as a writer 'in spite of the troubles you know about'.

At least I think that's what he said. I was feeling too foolish to jot down his exact words. Whatever the truth, he and I talked afterwards and he was clearly refreshed by undergraduates who, he said, seemed a lot more enthusiastic and less go-getting than their counterparts in earlier times. It was as if, just for a moment, he had become a little optimistic about the future of America and its culture.

That wasn't the impression he gave when I got the chance to talk to him again, first at a theatre conference in Salzburg and then, back in the summer of 2000, at his house in Connecticut. On both occasions, but especially the second, he took a wry yet grim view of a world, and especially of an America, that was rushing fecklessly towards some awful 'denouement', even an 'abyss'. He seemed a man very much at ease in his own skin and very little at ease in his own society. Call him a positive fatalist, a resilient pessimist – and, no, you wouldn't quite have caught that mix of geniality, hopefulness and profound scepticism that characterised him.

Some disdained him and his work for their supposed moral earnestness. That was particularly the case in the America of the 1980s, when drama became alarmingly cut off from the problems of its own society, focusing instead on the nuances of family relationships; but it was a complaint heard in Britain too. Indeed, I myself once thought of him as the elder brother of those British dramatists who, back in the 1960s and 1970s, were so in thrall to their social and political agendas that their work became off-puttingly preachy, substituting attitudes for characters and, at worst, polemic for life.

As I was to learn, that wasn't remotely fair. Miller the man never spoke *de haut en bas*, combined a gentle humour with a due humility and laughed at least as often as the protagonist of his *Mr. Peters' Connections*, whose view was 'who can hit a man when he's chuckling, right?' And Miller the dramatist combined civic responsibility with a passionate concern for the individual. When Clare Higgins, playing Willy Loman's wife Linda in the 2005 West End revival of *Death of a Salesman*, came out with the famous cry 'Attention, attention must finally be paid to such a person', her words obviously could and should have been taken as a moral reproach to the socially selfish. But primarily they were a gut-wrenching expression of personal pain and love. How could Willy's sons, whom he adored beyond measure, neglect the father she, Linda, adored even more?

Miller was described by both well-meaning and ill-meaning people as an intellectual – the great American brain that was once married to the great American body – but you couldn't meet him or experience his plays without seeing how inadequate that was. When we met in Connecticut we sat outside on chairs he himself had made, watched squirrels hopping across a lawn that stretched into a forest, which itself reached to Canada, and relished the quiet and the peace. 'I wish the rest of the world was like this,' he said – and, after a little prodding by me, began to speak about the rest of the world.

At the time he was polishing *Resurrection Blues*, a play set in a poor South American country where the regime is discouraging dissent by staging a public crucifixion which, it emerges, a New York company is keen to televise. So I wasn't surprised to find that his comments on America – and this before George W. Bush had been elected – were decidedly tart. 'Once a day,' he said, 'I think the country is becoming true chaos, in the profoundest sense. It's drifting towards the rocks. There's no one upstairs at all.'

In his view, private avarice ruled. He had turned on the TV the other day, he said, and seen the chief mechanic of an airline company declare that the reason a crash had killed scores of Americans might have been that his persistent complaints about bad maintenance had been ignored: 'What Joe Keller did in *All My Sons* was a joke beside that.' And all around he saw people like the Connecticut neighbour who could not bring himself to make prudent savings, yet lived in dread of the arrival of the Cadillac containing the mogul who would instantly close the diaper factory where he worked: 'Society seems to be an area where you're fighting the lion every day. You kill him or he eats you. There's anxiety everywhere and people are living from sensation to sensation.'

Impatience, restlessness, a sort of sensationalism, have always been American traits, and ones that in many ways explain the nation's drive and success; but in Miller's opinion they had become pathological. He spoke of the speed with which people tossed aside a book or turned off the television if their attention wasn't grabbed at once. He spoke of fidgety friends of his own and of America's increasing obsession with tourism: 'The major preoccupation of Western civilisation seems to be to go to someplace else. Travel should be adding to people's life experience but I wonder if they aren't simply fleeing from experience. Some of them are literally in flight from consideration of anything that means anything. Especially for wealthy people, every moment has to be occupied with not being where they are.'

What, I asked, had happened to the American work ethic, that spirit of get-up-and-go which led Miller himself to take menial jobs after his family's ruin and earn the money to put himself through Michigan? He didn't see much of that any more. When he'd visited Florida, he said, he'd been appalled to find vigorous people in their early fifties doing nothing – 'and looking forward to continuing to do absolutely nothing when they're all going to live until they're ninety'.

Miller himself continued to do absolutely everything, from

cabinetmaking to writing plays and essays, until his death just short of ninety. Everybody will have his or her view about what his main legacy is; but I find that, even more than the moral passion that underpinned them I value the emotional power of his characterisation and the opportunities for actors that this gave them. I'm thinking of Julie Walters as Keller's wife in Howard Davies's fine revival of *All My Sons* in 2000: hunched, bunched, arms doggedly crossed, mouth tight, head forever nodding in emphasis and, by the time she was left sobbing and wailing in agony on the back porch, an unforgettable portrait of maternal fixation. Or Josette Simon as Maggie in *After the Fall* in 1990, a grown-up child with a bottomless need for reassurance, a Monroe figure who gave us guileless trust, wonder, love, pettiness, greed, malevolence and a drunken, drugged confusion that came with an ugly, hacking mix of hiss, sigh, dribble and croak. Or Tom Wilkinson's mulish, defiant Proctor in the same year, the kind of farmer you might find growling over the weather or his cattle today and yet possessed of a deep but unpretentious integrity.

Above all, I recall the Lomans I've seen. There was Warren Mitchell in 1979, expressing all the salesman's exhaustion with his slumped shoulders and creased, pumice-grey cheeks, yet somehow allowing you to sense Willy in his feisty heyday, winking at the shopgirls, swapping wisecracks with the buyers, living on and off his wits. There was Alun Armstrong in 1996: edgy, anxious or bouncy, depending on whether he was beached in the present or mentally revisiting the past, but most effective in the angry, elated, bewildered or awkwardly adoring scenes he shared with Mark Strong's excellent Biff. And in 2005 there was Brian Dennehy: at first a great ox sagging under the weight of a frame it was too exhausted to carry; by the end, a giant bear tormented by dogs he could not see, let alone defeat; and, in between, a baffled man whose big dreamy smiles constantly drooped into a rictus of dismay.

All the performances I've mentioned, except Dennehy's Loman, were given at the National which, with the Young Vic during David Thacker's tenure as artistic director, has been in the forefront of establishing or re-establishing Miller's reputation in England as a major dramatist. Yet the performance I think I will remember most vividly occurred not in London, but in New York in 1984 – and not only because of its star actor.

Unsurprisingly, because the director in each case was Michael

Rudman, Dustin Hoffman had something in common with Warren Mitchell. This small, dumpy figure began by half-waddling, half-trudging on stage, his shoulders slumped as they held a sample case so huge you might think he was selling tree trunks. But, as with Mitchell, resilience in adversity was the dominant note of a Willy who, even in his declining years, cackled loudly and often, clapped his hands for emphasis, amiably tweaked Linda's breast on the line 'you're my foundation and support', did a little dance with her and exuberantly brandished his rump in her direction before leaving the room.

Again, you could see the able hustler Loman once was and still half-believes he is. Hoffman even made his last fateful exit, not with the 'gasp of fear' a stage direction requires, but with a smile, a skip and bounce of the feet, and that trademark clap of the hands. He believes his 'accidental' death by car crash will bring his son Biff $20,000 in insurance money, enough to transform his fortunes, and so, salesman to the last, he exuded a strange, paradoxical glee as he scampered off to clinch his last big deal.

It's hard to present suicide, the ultimate manifestation of despair, as an act of optimism and, lacking any compensating hint of dread or sorrow, Hoffman didn't quite bring off the idea. And perhaps he was more of the cocky vulgarian and less of the doomed drudge than he should have been. But he did suggest that, self-deceiver though his Willy always was, he was aware of his declining powers and fortunes. The smiles became more forced as the play progressed. The slick silver hair above the trim suit – this Willy was walking testimony to the value he placed on appearance and appearances – seemed to lose some of its shine. And suddenly he was wildly blustering at his uncaring boss and hammering at his desk, or tearfully clutching and pummelling at his old friend Charley, or down on all fours, thumping the floor in an ecstasy of frustration and impotent resentment.

But there was one moment which, on the evening I saw the production, seemed to me not just striking but exceptional. That came when John Malkovich's sobbing Biff and Hoffman's Willy, alienated from each other for years, manage a stricken, fumbling, forgiving embrace. There was, it was clear, a repressed intensity of devotion in the son and, on the face of the father cradling him for longer than you would have dreamed possible, the kind of disbelieving tenderness you get from men when they pick up their children for the first time. Hoffman blushed, gulped and inarticulately gurgled in total surrender to a relationship that itself seemed newborn.

Actually, I'd rate that one of the two or three most magic, moving moments of my theatrical life: which was and remains testimony to the dramatist who created it. Miller was writing, as he often did, about the power and, here, the beauty of love in a society where so much was so badly askew. And yet that revival was only revived on Broadway because Hoffman and Malkovich had agreed to appear in an acknowledged classic. As Miller repeated to me in Connecticut, the likes of *Death of a Salesman* or *The Crucible* would not get their premières there today. They would be too weird and risky, too expensive to stage, too lacking in the feel-good factor – and of course not musicals.

For Miller, the old sense of community had left Broadway, plays had become commodities, and the last thing that mattered to theatre owners or impresarios was fostering talent or nurturing art. 'The sole criterion of success is whether you make a fortune,' he said. 'All other values have receded into the background. Broadway is run by real-estate lawyers. It has become a microcosm for America itself.'

Yet, as I say, he kept writing, even though he took a sceptical view of his work's usefulness. As he said in Salzburg, all he could do was shed what light he could on dark places and hope for the best. As he said in Connecticut, he still felt he had something to say about the human psyche, still had 'this impulse to figure out this crazy machine to which we're attached – how does it operate?' But if people didn't want to listen, that was their right and their business. He saw as little point in getting too upset by failure as getting too excited by success.

'Who do I complain to?' he asked. 'Who do I go to? The mayor? The governor? The president?' And Arthur Miller chuckled, a playwright ruefully relaxed in a world he deeply distrusted.

Marsha Norman

Writer

Remarks made in conferring the Dramatists Guild of America
Lifetime Achievement Award.

The Dramatists Guild of America had never given a Lifetime
Achievement Award before. Not that our members had not had
both lifetimes . . . and achievements, but no American playwright
had had a whole lifetime of achievement like Arthur Miller.

While other groups had honored his achievements, giving him his
Pulitzer, his Tony, his Olivier, his Emmy, his Drama Critics Circle,
his Kennedy Center Honor, and all his other truly countless awards,
his fellow dramatists wanted to thank him for his lifetime. We
wanted to honor his courageous life in the theater and his
incomparable presence as a theatrical force in the world at large.

He had been our ambassador abroad, fighting for the freedom of
imprisoned writers all over the world. And he had been our
champion at home, fighting for the existence of serious work in a
theater whose increasing commercialisation threatens the survival of
every writer in this room.

Arthur Miller was the only American dramatist whose first play
on Broadway opened in 1944 and whose last play opened in 2004.
Among his plays are some of the most revered works in the
American dramatic canon: *All My Sons, After the Fall, The Crucible,
The Price, The American Clock, A View from the Bridge, The Ride
Down Mount Morgan*, and that masterpiece of dramatic literature,
Death of a Salesman.

We thanked him not only for writing these plays, but for writing
these kinds of plays, tragedies about Americans, about little men, as
Mr Miller's heroes were called when they first appeared. But he did
not back down in the face of this criticism. He did not even back off.
He went back to his typewriter again and again, and proved beyond
a doubt that these so-called little men do indeed suffer tragic losses
and that, to regain their dignity, they will lay down their lives as
nobly as any king ever did. In writing about Willy Loman, Arthur
Miller wrote about all of us, about our indestructible will to achieve
our humanity, about our fear of being torn away from what and who
we are in this world, about our fear of being displaced and forgotten.

And today, he says, this fear is as strong as it ever was in the days of the kings, perhaps stronger.

Playwrights know about the fear of being displaced, of being torn away from the world where we belong. Every morning, this fear stands between us and the computer screen. But Arthur Miller's life makes it seem possible to go on writing, and that possibility may be all you need a lot of mornings. Arthur Miller proved beyond a doubt that you can work fifty years in the American theater and come out with your reputation secure and your dignity intact. Like some valiant literary war hero, he led us on to the beachhead and dared us to follow.

Arthur Miller stood up to the toughest forces on the American scene and triumphed. He stared down fame and fortune and success and failure and politics and personality and war and peace and time itself. The culture threw everything it had at Arthur Miller and he remained standing. For the vision he had maintained, for the victory he claimed, the Dramatists Guild of America presented its Lifetime Achievement Award to Arthur Miller.

Alibe Parsons

Actor: The Crucible, After the Fall, Royal National Theatre, 1990; Mr. Peters' Connections

It was in London where I was appearing in the Royal National Theatre's production of *After the Fall* that I first met Arthur Miller. His initial appearance at rehearsals was anxiously anticipated. Speaking the words of an eminent playwright in his presence is a daunting experience. A hush preceded him as he walked into the rehearsal hall. Every woman present turned as one to face him, a tall imposing figure. There was no doubt about it, even in his late seventies, he still had 'it': a charismatic presence laced with sex appeal.

My second encounter with Mr Miller was the production of *Mr. Peters' Connections* at the Almeida Theatre in London. He must then have been in his early eighties. His lovely wife Inge was in attendance, as always, 'translating' for him as he had become a little deaf. She was a beautiful spirit. On both occasions he gave us his blessings. He was very down to earth, genuinely in touch with 'everyman'. They both enriched us with their presence.

Ronald Pickup

Actor: **The Golden Years,** *BBC Radio, 1987*

Twenty years ago I had one day in the presence of Arthur Miller. The occasion was the opening of the Arthur Miller Centre for American Studies at the University of East Anglia in 1989. The day was devoted to a forum and talks, culminating in a gala performance in the evening of selected scenes from his plays.

My qualification for being part of this memorable day was that we had done a radio production of *The Golden Years* – a play Miller had kept in a desk drawer for nearly fifty years. It is the story of Cortes's invasion of Mexico and the defeat of Montezuma. John Shrapnel was an ideal Cortes, and I played Montezuma, not ideal casting but made plausible by the magic of radio.

Without in any way wishing to do a critical assessment, it is worth saying just a little about the play at this point. It is, in Miller's own assessment, 'juvenilia'. But aside from a powerful political theme that you might expect, more importantly there is a relish of language, an unashamed joy in flexing the language muscles that Miller honed and hewed at for the rest of his life. This man who caught the tragedy of the 'ordinary' people in a suburban house, nonetheless at an early age was rooting himself in 'great language', the language which in the greatest play, *Salesman*, emerges as the 'emergency speech', as Miller calls it, of a kind of 'superconsciousness . . . not crabbed by pretexts of the natural' (*Timebends*).

And, academic assessment aside, the scenes are rich, fruity, thrilling to speak. Indeed, I suppose Miller left the play in a drawer because he had moved on from what he perhaps thought was mere 'relish'. But the joy at the afternoon rehearsal, very brief because we all had many different scenes to get through, was to feel Miller's genuine pleasure and even surprise that the scene played with a kind of intensity and feeling that he, perhaps, had forgotten as it lay there, silent, in the desk drawer.

After we had finished, a slight pause, then the gravel voice with the rich New York street accent: 'Umm . . . not so bad, is it?' And what was thrilling was to feel that he loved the sheer size of the scene, the kind of size that he never used quite again in the 'rhetorical' sense, but which for ever informed the pressure of the language of his masterworks, his 'emergency speech'.

He made, concisely and quickly, one or two suggestions absolutely in the spirit of the scene, as if instinctively aware of the possibilities. In this respect John and I were lucky – there were no previous productions hovering above our shoulders. But with all the actors, throughout the afternoon, doing some of the most famous scenes in the Miller canon, he was as if hearing and seeing them for the first time.

And it is that extraordinary freshness and ever-evolving sense of discovery that moved me – I think all of us – most during that day. He was only incidentally aware of being 'honoured'. Not ungrateful – he had too much angular grace and generosity to be that – clearly (and this is said as a compliment to us actors, all actors everywhere) he was truly happy in the afternoon simply getting on with the job of doing plays with actors – work in progress, rediscovery.

Even in the evening performance, as he sat on stage for the question-and-answer sessions between each scene, you felt that his real pleasure lay in simply watching these wonderful glimpses at the full range of his work, rather than talk about them – although he was brilliant at that too.

The evening was a great success. So was the dinner afterwards with Miller giving the funniest speech.

Even after such a tiring, if rewarding, day Miller still had time to give to all of us who had taken part some individual time. It was impossible for him to gush, be fulsome. His desire to have a word with each one of us was thanks enough. Graceful, even surprisingly, slightly shy. He asked me what I was doing next. It was to be a TV film about Goebbels's propaganda machine. 'Who are you playing?'

'Oh, I've never heard of him before,' I said. 'Er – Putzi Hanfstaengl.'

'Oh yeah, I knew him, Putzi, yeah!' Amazing. Inadvertently I had happened on an inside picture of someone very few people knew anything about. I received a brief, vivid portrait of this strange, eccentric pianist who had supported Hitler in the early days but survived, and whom Miller met in New York. Interestingly, no judgemental observations, just a succinct, spare, vivid sketch – of incomparable and treasured value to me.

So I knew Arthur Miller for a day, proudly, as an actor. I cannot therefore say I 'knew' him. But, purely as an actor, what I learned, what I felt from him that day, was his profound respect, admiration and, the word has to be used, love for actors. Not saccharine love. A grave, almost austere, tenderness, with humour lurking always. Never soft, always true. I am cheating by quoting something he writes in *Timebends* but his feeling for us is put incomparably.

There is a passage about some of the many models he encountered for Willy Loman, struggling, often failing, but always having 'intrepid valor that withstood the inevitable putdowns, the scoreless attempts to sell. In a sense, these men lived like artists, like actors whose product is first of all themselves, forever imagining triumphs in a world that either ignores them or denies their presence altogether. But just often enough to keep the game going one of them makes it and swings to the moon on a thread of dreams unwinding out of himself.'

Harold Pinter

Writer

Arthur and I went to Turkey under the auspices of PEN International to find out what was happening to writers. We soon discovered that some were in prison and a certain number had been tortured. This we confirmed.

The American Ambassador decided to give a dinner for Arthur and they had to accept me along with him. I was so impressed with Arthur that night because, as he later said, I was the artillery and he was the cool one. I went as an observer, never having dined in an American embassy before.

It started with a woman who was an editor of a newspaper. Neither of us took to her. She was very provocative and more or less accused me of coming to Turkey in order to get copy to write. She was very insulting. So I responded in kind.

Then the American Minister joined in and denied there was any torture in Turkey at all. We knew nothing about it, he said. I said that was preposterous because we had established that without any question there was. Then the Ambassador tapped his spoon and said, 'Welcome to Mr Miller. How nice it is to have you here.' Then he glanced down to the end of the table where I was, maybe thirty feet away, and said, 'As you see, we have democracy here.' I wondered whether he meant at the table or in Turkey itself. Then he said a few nice words about Arthur and then Arthur stood up.

Where he was wonderful was that he said, 'Mr Ambassador, thank you very much for your kind welcome but when you say you have democracy here how is it that the United States makes a habit of supporting dictatorial regimes?' A frozen silence fell. Arthur went on to try to define the word 'democracy', in a very impressive way.

After dinner, the Ambassador suddenly approached me, with a number of hoods behind him. He said, 'Mr Pinter, I think you've got your facts absolutely wrong. The reality is that we have the Russians just over the way and you have to understand the military reality, the diplomatic reality, the political reality.'

I said, 'The reality that I'm talking about is the reality of an electric current on your genitals.'

He said, 'Sir, you are a guest in my house.' And he turned away.

Arthur then appeared and I said, 'Arthur, I think I have been thrown out' and he said, marvellously, 'I'll come with you.' And we left.

The funny thing was that there was no car because we were at the Residence outside Istanbul. They had sent a car to bring us but they didn't provide one to take us back. Whereupon the French Ambassador suddenly came out. We told him we had no car and he said, 'I will give you a leeft.'

And I said, 'What an Ambassador that is' and he said, 'What a sheet!' He took us to the French Embassy and gave us a glass of champagne.

Incidentally, on the last day in Turkey we held a press conference. There were a lot of shadowy people standing against walls and we were quite clear about our findings. We both made statements and answered questions. We then went to a lunch given by writers and at the lunch someone came up to us and said, 'The military have just issued a decree for your detention.' The military were in power then. We finished our lunch and got into a car. The driver was a very reputable businessman and was against the authoritarian rule. He drove us to the airport but we didn't realise how nervous he was until we got there. There were armed soldiers. They let the car through but instead of going to Departures he went towards Arrivals. Then he stopped. He knew the airport well but was extremely tense. Then he started to reverse. We were looking back and could see one of the soldiers turn round with a gun, looking to see what was going on. He pointed his gun and I thought we were going to be blown up. But we got through and staggered through Departures. It was a very, very tense moment. We finally got on the plane and as we were sitting on the runway I said, 'Well, Arthur. We made it.'

And he said, 'We haven't gone up yet.' We were expecting the door to open at any time. They were really making themselves extremely clear. They were saying, 'Get out of here!'

I admired Arthur tremendously. It was wonderful to be with him. I think he remains a tower of strength as a playwright. I have the utmost respect for his work. When you look back, it is a remarkable achievement, and not just the earlier ones. I admire *Broken Glass*. *The Last Yankee* is a wonderful piece of work. He's done so much.

Heather Anne Prete

Actor: **Finishing the Picture**, *Goodman Theatre, 2004*

My agent called on a Sunday afternoon to let me know that I was Robert Fall's first choice to be in the new Arthur Miller play *Finishing the Picture* at the Goodman Theatre, Chicago. However, I would have to meet Mr Miller himself in New York to be approved. I promptly fell on to the living room floor, screaming.

My agent went on to explain that I was not yet cast, but that wasn't the point! I was going to meet Arthur Miller! THE Arthur Miller!

So this is where it began for me. I actually did not need to go to New York as Arthur approved me without us meeting. So my chance to see this great man was postponed. Several weeks later I entered the Goodman rehearsal space at 10.30 on a sunny Tuesday morning and took my seat at the table. Filtering in were theater royalty such as Linda Lavin, Stephen Lang, Stacy Keach, Harris

Yulin, Frances Fisher and Scott Glenn. Oh, and by the way, Matthew Modine was to play my husband Paul, not bad.

Then Arthur walked in. I had no idea he was so tall. He was a really stunning man, amazing for his age, handsome and broad-shouldered. He wore a baseball cap and his large rimmed glasses, dressed in tans and khaki, loose pants, a T-shirt and a light jacket. He was a cool, casual presence.

After a bit of chatting we all sat at the table for the first reading of *Finishing the Picture*. My seat was directly opposite his, so of course I couldn't help staring. I watched him throughout the entire reading of his play. As he listened he sat far back in his chair and laughed out loud. He closed his eyes, removed his glasses and rubbed his brow. He crossed his long arms across his chest and gently nodded. He listened, and it was true, intense, beautiful listening.

I can recount something memorable he shared about the theater and actors specifically. I can't remember what led into the conversation, but he began to compare the actor's voice with musical instruments, all different types. Some of us were string, some wind and so on. He went on to say that with different actors *Finishing the Picture* would be a different play. He reminded us to play the music of the text. I felt very soothed by these words because they seemed to reflect the heart of a writer who loved and respected the actor. In other words, he liked us! Later on in the rehearsal process he said to Robert Falls, 'They are all so marvellous and it's all so innocent right now. Make sure they don't start acting more.' I took this as encouragement to make sure our voices stayed unique and true to ourselves as artists.

I have a favorite memory of observing Arthur. We were in dress and had just begun to work on the Goodman stage. Arthur had just recently returned to Chicago to come to rehearsals. He was sitting alone in the third row watching the show, when Linda Lavin made her entrance. As soon as Linda let out her first line he just began to laugh and laugh. He laughed like a man who had never read the play much less written it. I laughed because he was laughing so hard. I loved seeing him enjoy Linda so much. That is a fond memory for me and is also the most private moment I was witness to while working with Arthur.

In the show I played the role of Kitty. She is written as a drugged-out emotionally damaged movie star who can't seem to get up from her bed and to work on the set. Matthew played my husband, Paul, the film's writer. His character struggles with trying to save Kitty from her troubled past and destructive present.

In reality, Matthew and I were playing out the final days of Arthur Miller and Marilyn Monroe's marriage as they shot his film *The Misfits*. It was brutal and sad and bravely raw before the world. However, no one was ever to use Marilyn's name when addressing the character of Kitty. We were not to acknowledge that these people really existed beyond the boundaries of fiction. Just as is indicated in *After the Fall*, my hair was not to remain blonde, I wore a brown wig in production. We all watched videos of the making of *The Misfits* but never were able to speak of it in talks with Arthur.

I recount this because it leads into what I experienced as the most powerful aspect of Arthur's personality and our play. Arthur was a man forced actively to protect his private life while, as an artist and legend, live his life in the public eye. He dealt daily with the inevitability of public commentary on the very things most people are able to keep locked away in heart and home.

Yes, sometimes it did feel like a contradiction to know who we were portraying and not publicly talk about it. I'm sure many audience members and reviewers wanted to stand up in the theater and yell, 'We know who they are!' Actually, a few reviewers did just that in print. But it was not contradiction. It read to me as pure uncompromised unapologetic strength. Here was a man who had gone through the McCarthy hearings with grace and conviction. Here was a man who almost always received negative reviews from his city's most important paper. Here was a man who had gone through a marriage that an often hungry, selfish public felt they had a right to know everything about and he simply said no and it floored me.

It floored me to hear a hint of condescension in reviews that Arthur wasn't being 'truthful' enough about who Kitty and Paul were. Of course we all knew who they were, but it was Arthur's right to refuse to participate in limiting his works to anything less than portraits of the universal man and woman, to make it less than it was. And no one in the cast broke the sanctity of the unspoken truth. We did our work as needed, then treated Arthur Miller with the love and admiration we had for his gifts and for his life.

Stacy Keach once said that being asked to do a new Arthur Miller play is like being asked to go to the Olympics. I am so grateful to have been a part of his final play, an honor, a dream, a GIFT. It is something that I will always cherish. Thank you for allowing me to record some of my thoughts and experiences for print. Thank you for asking me to help pay our respects to this great, great man.

David Rabe

Writer

My relationship with Arthur Miller started when I was young and, he mature, and lasting over fifty years, it was conducted from afar (although I did meet him twice) and was largely, I suspect, if not exclusively one-sided. It was marked by periods of adoration, of disappointment and resentment, even at times criticism verging on condemnation. I swore I was done with him more than once, only to find myself captivated again, as something new in his accomplishments overtook me.

Memory, with its magical approximations, is all I have to go by in this depiction, and memory believes my introduction to him came in the early fifties when I would have been around twelve. Sick with a cold and home from school in the late morning, I was treated to a TV program called *The Morning Movie*, and on this particular day the movie aired was *All My Sons*. I have the impression of something that touched me with bewildering power. Edward G. Robinson as Joe Keller stormed about in a black-and-white world, bringing calamity down upon trusting strangers, and then into his own family. In order to protect a lucrative government contract, he allowed defective engine cylinders to be used in military planes that must sooner or later fall from the wartime skies. In the end his own son, an air force pilot, crashed and the consequences of the greed and cowardice of his immoral act came smashing into his heart. This may or may not be an exact description of the film, but it is how the recollection exists somewhere in my brain today when Arthur Miller is dead and I'm older than he was then.

I was a Catholic child and preoccupied with the moral tests of approaching adulthood. This portrayal of the furies inherent in corruption resonated, offering, I suspect, a breath of encouragement and even sympathy to whatever unacknowledged winds had begun to stir those elements in me that would lead me to know I wanted to be a writer.

Our next encounter came years later when I was in college. An English major, I was eligible my junior year for an elective in Theater, a survey course covering modern plays from all over the world. There was no theater department and so the class was three or four students gathered in a tiny room with a young but committed teacher. At some point in the semester *All My Sons* came up for study and now I found it wanting. The moral order it venerated, together with the dramatic construction that made this order manifest, impressed me as false. The idea that Joe Keller's crime would bring about the death of his own son struck me as preposterous. The crimes of greedy men destroyed the lives of strangers. It was the early 1960s and it seemed, increasingly, that perpetrators of ruin experienced little guilt or remorse even when their responsibility was publicly and unequivocally established. Evil deeds threw their seed to the wind where randomness ruled an ever-widening ring of suffering that seemed to have no connection to, let alone repercussions for, the powerful forces standing untroubled at their root. The teacher and I argued, and I did my best to express my beginning sense of the world. The pattern that *All My Sons* exhibited with its orderly developments and well-timed revelations was something I found nowhere in the unfolding events around me, where deceptions, secrecy and wilful obfuscation seemed the rule.

Of course I was searching now for my own way as a writer. I was reading books on playwriting such as *The Theory and Technique of Playwriting* by John Howard Lawson, along with a half-dozen other manuals. The 'well-made play' was the ideal of the time and *All My Sons* seemed its perfect embodiment, as did *Death of a Salesman*. Independent of how chaotically a character might behave or speak, these plays were constructed according to the rules of reason, with cause leading to effect in perfect proportion. I saw them as expressions of the authorised model that I felt I could not fit into. I was beginning to revel in Ionesco and see a mirror in John Osborne. Though these men confounded me, they also exhilarated me, and I felt that hope lay in their dark direction. I was done with Arthur Miller. Existentialism, the theater of the Absurd, Camus, Artaud and the theater of cruelty were crowding the horizon and leaking into my thoughts even in our small school in Iowa.

But then in 1962 during my senior year in college I saw the film version of *A View from the Bridge*. In the darkened theater I watched Eddie Carbone waver, before allowing his incestuous dream to have its moment in the light. I felt the presence of his opportunity to retreat from the edge, as well as his dark appetite to jump. I remember my thoughts, as I saw the disaster waiting beyond the gesture he could not hold back. I knew that if I saw it, he did too. But he wanted what he wanted. My alarm at the onrushing consequences was matched by pity for the helpless state in which he stood before himself. I thought, Don't do it. And in those seconds I knew for the first time what so many had tried to instruct me regarding the rapturous fall at the heart of tragedy with its invocation of terror and pity in the bystander who can do no more than witness.

And yet this encounter did not return him to his original height. It may be that the play when I read it seemed cold, the construction sufficiently 'well-made' to justify my earlier rejection. Or perhaps the negative critical assessments carried more weight than I might like to admit.

I graduated college and began a Masters Program at Villanova University. Brecht, Camus, Sartre, Beckett, Genet, Ionesco and lesser luminaries were the new gods and I was eager to absorb them. But then in 1964 I read *After the Fall* when it was published in the *Saturday Evening Post* magazine. Miller seemed to have arrived where I hoped to go before I even had a chance to define that destination. The play occurred in a broken world with the man at the center, Quentin, attempting to find a new order in the wake of Maggie's destruction. A voluptuous, desirable woman, she had been a siren call of irrationality wheeling into his known world the way a whirlwind wheels into a seemingly sturdy house. Filled with forces that logic could not contain, illuminate or mitigate, she swept aside even those sensible gestures that might have guided her to safety. Her furious aims cared nothing for sanity or even survival and she shredded both Quentin's sensible strategies and Miller's ability to construct an orderly play. Play and playwright were largely condemned for varied transgressions. He was accused of sullying the memory of Marilyn Monroe, a fake indictment if ever there was one, given the way the press and public had never viewed her as anything but a sexual hot spot with her dress blown up around her head so she was faceless thighs and panties ready to rut. What there was of Monroe in *After the Fall*, and one must assume there was plenty, was furious and alive and very human. Nothing is more individual than anger with its claim of independence, its declaration of offence. She was a character of indomitable risk. He was also condemned for seeing a connective line carrying current from the most prosaic of human betrayals to the vast reservoir of human faithlessness that produced the Holocaust. Criticised and demeaned for these so-called faults, his real crime (aside from having married and slept with Marilyn Monroe) was his refusal to provide the temperate world with the reassurances of a reasonable play.

I had not at this time fully shaped my own views, though I would later devise something like a theory whose premise found that the well-made play was the theatrical face of the Newtonian universe which was said, metaphorically, to operate like a big clock. In both clockwork universe and clockwork play cause preceded effect and both were identifiable, locatable, visible, proportionate. But at the start of the twentieth century we had entered a universe in which time and place as we knew them were illusions. From Freud we had been given the unsteadying explanation that many of our deeds arose from aspects of ourselves hidden within us. Subatomic activities mocked logic and proportion, introducing a realm that one of its early initiates, Sir Arthur Eddington, ended up describing as, 'Something unknown is doing we know not what.' From the funhouse fog of nuclear physics had stepped the atomic bomb. Now where was proportion when a few ounces of fissionable material could obliterate cities in seconds, turning their population into light and dust? It seemed to me that *After the Fall* occurred in such a system. Behind every corner Maggie, with her bottomless irrationality, waited, devouring her own life and forcing those who would survive her to see that their survival depended on betrayal. In the end, when Quentin declares that even the most personal of lies contains the fissionable human faithlessness needed to multiply into Olympic destruction, it was the modern loss of proportion in human affairs that he was mourning.

In 1968 I saw *The Price* at an out-of-town try-out in Philadelphia. I had dropped out of graduate school, spending the years from 1965 to 1967 in the army, before returning to school at Villanova. *The Price* was not well received. In a sense, the dramatic construction was that of two brothers, along with the wife of one of them, struggling to create a well-made play from the chaos of their shared past. They wanted a history in which sense ruled and order could be found. They wanted agreement regarding assigned faults and attributed motivations. In the end the construction went up in smoke. They could not agree on who was at fault or even on the nature of the narrative they shared. The truth – by that I mean what actually happened – vanished as they grappled with one another to find it. Or perhaps it had vanished before their effort had even commenced. As the play spun to its ending, the very idea of a knowable truth in human affairs evaporated right in front of you while an old man, a near ghost, a junk appraiser who has been called to give value to the human belongings in an attic, laughed.

Somehow in the succeeding years my feelings for him slipped away. I think it had to do with the many revivals of *Death of a Salesman*, and the critical certainty that this was his masterwork. But my own career was rising and I was not thinking much about influences. He was away, banished to England, where his reputation persisted. He wrote new plays that I failed to see. When I finally met him for the first time, it was after a performance of a revival of *After the Fall* in New York in which Dianne Wiest played Maggie. She was a friend, and my wife and I went out with Arthur and her for a beer. He was robust and hearty while I was somewhat timid, though I did tell him how much and for how long I had admired his play. I remember that he seemed surprised that a contemporary playwright – my own career was at its height about then – could hold anything he wrote in such high regard.

That was it for contact, other than a subsequent encounter at a PEN event. A photo taken that evening of the two of us talking stands in my living room among what are mostly family images.

Somewhere along the line, as my own career faltered, I had a peevish moment or two where I was annoyed at the fact that he was still going on, even finding a kind of resurgence in America, though it always seemed to have to do with *Death of a Salesman*.

And then one night on a television news program I encountered a story about a former Navy admiral and his son, both of whom had served in Vietnam. And what the story revealed was that the Admiral had been instrumental in the deployment of Agent Orange in certain areas and that his son, who had served in those areas, was dying of leukemia with the pesticide as its cause. The story had its own power, but beyond what was inherent, I saw the arc of *All My Sons*, with the father scattering the toxins that would kill his son. I remember thinking, Damn, Arthur, you were right even in that one.

The fated scheme I had first admired and then seen as false came back with a jolt.

What further surprises did he have for me? Well, two. The first came when I returned one day from the post office and found, amid the junk mail, solicitations and bills, the February 2005 issue of *Harper's*. In it he had a short story, 'Beavers', which tells of a man who, living in the country and owning a pond with pure, nearly potable water, a surround of tall trees mixed with seedlings he has planted, discovers that beavers have invaded. In the subsequent events a failed effort to scare the beavers away with shotgun blasts into the water leads to a decision to get help. He consults with a local friend, a stone mason, and the two men decide reluctantly to kill the beavers in order to prevent the surrounding trees from being felled, the water polluted. Before the deadly shots are fired and the 'juvenile couple', as the beavers are referred to, drop lifeless on to the back of the mason's truck, the male beaver begins stuffing debris into a drainage pipe in an ingenious and determined effort to raise the water level. The project begins after the initial shotgun blasts and makes no sense because the depth of the water is already more than adequate for the lodge the beavers have completed. They were there to stay, the mason noted, probably thrown out of the tribe of beavers up at a neighboring pond. With the touch of that fact I found it impossible not to detect Quentin's warning that 'we meet after – after the fall'.

When the truck pulls away with the lifeless bodies swaying in its bed, the last pages form a haunting meditation as the man who owns the pond circles and probes, as he considers, analyses, anthropomorphises, as he imagines and projects possible motives, possible desires on to the 'beast' in order to understand its enterprising actions at the drainage pipe. Was there some 'hidden logic'? Was it done for love? For practice? From devotion to water? Sheer animal exhilaration? Like the man, Miller searches, driven like the beaver in the story, by his nature. In the end there is no answer to the mystery, other than his longing for 'daylight sense', so that the episode could 'at least feel finished then, completely comprehended and somehow simpler to forget'.

With the beauty of that story fresh in my mind, coupled with an awareness that he'd opened a new play recently in Chicago, I imagined him strong and going on for ever, so I was caught off guard by the second surprise, the report that he had died on 10

February 2005. How many deaths does the news bring us each day?
Forty in Iraq. Hundreds in an earthquake. An airplane crash.
Murders. What do we feel? In this case he was among them and
briefly it felt as if his face was on them all.

Vanessa Redgrave

*Actor: **Playing for Time**, CBS, 1979*

As a drama student, in 1956, I saw *The Crucible* at the Royal Court
Theatre. It was the first British production of Miller's play and was
directed by George Devine in the first season of the English Stage
Company, dedicated to new writing by new British and foreign
playwrights. The witch-hunt trials in Salem, Massachusetts, in the
late 1600s, the persecution, by torture and death, of men and
women innocent of any crime, was something I knew nothing about.
The play was more enthralling than any I had seen. I knew little
about the contemporary witch-hunt hearings in Washington by the
House Un-American Activities Committee, either. Citizens
suspected of being either Communists, or having political or
professional associations with Communists, were summoned before
it. I knew some had been imprisoned, some had given HUAC the
names of colleagues, while others, a few, like Arthur Miller himself,
had refused. Many lives had been ruined. It seems odd now that
these facts appeared mysterious and faraway, while Miller's writing
brought the Salem witch-hunting of some 300 years before to my
doorstep, so to speak. I now understood how a hysterical fear could
grip a community, how the wildest accusations, based on 'suspect'
activities, could be made, both by the innocent, and by those who
can and do manipulate fear and ignorance for their own motives and
self-justification.

Since that first production I have learned a great deal about what
is known as 'the McCarthy time'. I could never have understood
how that happened had it not been for Arthur Miller's play. Since
that first production I have seen my brother Corin play Judge
Danforth in London in the 1990s and Liam Neeson play John
Proctor in New York in 2002. Both productions are fixed in my
memory for all time, as is the first.

I met Arthur Miller twice in the sixties, with my husband Tony Richardson who was an associate director of George Devine's at the Royal Court. Then, in 1979, I worked with Arthur and his producer, Linda Yellen, on a television production of his script about the women's orchestra in Auschwitz. We rehearsed for two weeks and then filmed for five weeks in the barracks of an internment camp in Pennsylvania, where US citizens of foreign origin had been interned during World War Two. Arthur and his wife Inge Morath, who photographed the production, were with us throughout the shoot. I believe I still have a Polaroid somewhere I took of Arthur in his cap, standing under the scaffold erected for the scene of a hanging, grinning at me. We had many discussions about the scenes, about the Holocaust, about the war.

To my mind, whatever the shortcomings of the film may have been, his script is the deepest insight into the horror of the Nazi mentality. There is a moment in one scene between the women when one girl asserts that Fascists cannot be thought of as human beings. The pianist replies, 'Don't you see? The whole problem is that they *are* human beings?' For me, this sentence reveals the quintessence of Arthur Miller's great spirit, as a man and as a playwright.

Many crew members had accepted low wages because they wanted to work on this film. Our film extras, who had arduous days filming, drove in to the location from miles away, having volunteered to take part because they felt Arthur Miller's script would explain the Nazi Holocaust and they deeply wanted to know. They were, I know, not disappointed as we had several discussions while we were waiting for lighting and camera set-ups. I have noticed this to be a marked and specific characteristic of Americans, in general and in particular, that they have a devouring passion to discover and know more. I also remember that there were many organised campaigns from some Jewish organisations to get me off the film, or to get the State of Pennsylvania to deny CBS the permit to film there. I know that Arthur always said he felt that I was the best actress for the role he had written. I also know that the majority of American Jews always resisted my being blacklisted, or denied a role, or being threatened in any way. The McCarthy period had taken its own terrible toll of the Jews in America.

Then, in the autumn of 2002, Arthur arrived with his daughter Rebecca and Daniel Day-Lewis and their baby for lunch in the country. Dan had played John Proctor in the film of *The Crucible*, directed by Nick Hytner. He was crackling with energy and told Natasha, my daughter, and me about the recent opening of his new play *Resurrection Blues*, in Minnesota. He told us the story and then, with great pleasure, recounted the intensely excited and outspoken response of the audience, and the discussion session he had attended afterwards: 'They got really involved with the issues of the story. Things are moving out there.'

Natasha told him I had been offered the role of Mary Tyrone in *Long Day's Journey Into Night*. She knew I was hesitating, not sure that I could play this lady. Again he grinned at me. 'Well, I'd pay money to see you in that.' His look and his words decided me, and he came to the first night the next spring, and we had a great talk afterwards. They were the most prized words of praise of my life. That this giant American died when he was still writing at his peak was a massive blow. What a legacy he left, which helps me, and so many others, keep our heads straight in the present dark times.

Sheila Reid

Actor: A View from the Bridge, Perth Repertory Theatre, 1958; The Crucible, National Theatre, 1965; All My Sons, Palace Theatre, Watford, 1985

One of the most exciting events in my life was when Arthur Miller came to the first night of *The Crucible* at the National. The company were very close and we all loved the play. Olivier had been at his most stimulating and challenging in rehearsal, and we were desperate to do him, Miller and the play justice. It was a huge gala event with live music, dancing, flashing lights in the Rehearsal Room at the top of the Old Vic building. However, the company were summoned down to the distinctly insalubrious canteen in the bowels of the theatre. And it was here that we were introduced.

I remember him as magnetic; quietly spoken, very tall. I remember, too, exactly what he said: 'I have never seen *The Crucible* until tonight.'

The complexity and subtlety of his writing is unique, and his emotional power a gift to any actor.

Michael Rudman

Director: **Death of a Salesman**, *Broadhurst Theatre, New York, 1984*

Dear Arthur,

I have been asked to write something about you and *Death of a Salesman*. I found it very difficult because so much has been written already. And much of it by you. But here goes.

The first time I read *Death of a Salesman* was in an air-conditioned library at Harvard where I was a summer school student. I read it straight through very quickly. Then I cried. Then I read it again.

I am glad to say that I never cried again over the play except twice. Once when John Shrapnel, playing Biff at the Nottingham Playhouse, talked about going to 'the U of Virginia' and once when Doreen Mantle did the 'attention must be paid' speech at her audition in rehearsal room 4 at the National Theatre.

I suppose that it is fitting that I should begin by talking about crying when the only time you ever got cross with me in the eight months that we worked on the play was when I made a facetious remark about Dustin crying again if Malkovich missed a performance in Washington. You shouted at me as we were walking across the Watergate complex. You were, quite rightly, very protective of Dustin. So was I. I wanted to keep his crying to a minimum.

'That's enough of your fucking jokes' was what you said. I should have said, 'Hey, I know. I'm like Willy Loman. I joke too much.'

I remember a lot about those eight months that we spent preparing for Broadway: the endless auditions, the wonderful rehearsals, the even more endless lighting sessions, your pages of notes and, most of all, some of the really funny things you said. The funniest one can't be repeated here but the second funniest was when we had endured that terrible press night in Chicago when some local eager beaver had stacked all the best seats with fur coats who had paid way over the odds for their tickets. It was a charity performance. Their stolidity and adamant non-response was matched by Dustin being nervous. And the more stolid they became the more nervous he got, especially when laughs went missing that had been there the night before at the preview. Afterwards, I tried to make things better by saying that, after all, it was a charity performance. And you said, 'Yeah, a lot of people in there wondering why they're not out in the rain.'

I'm not going to write about your artistry and your craftsmanship. Anyway, they are there for all to see. I can only mention some of the very human things about you so that the millions of people who see you as a kind of god can see that you were, in many ways, a natural man.

Like the hours you spent teaching your daughter to parallel park in your driveway in Connecticut with that diesel-powered Mercedes. Like the little dance step you and Inge did (and I have the photo to prove it) waving goodbye to me and my daughter Amanda after our three days in Connecticut. (Come to think of it, Arthur, were you glad to see us finally go?) Like the way you walked over to Warren Mitchell, before you saw him act, and told him that he was exactly the way you had imagined Willy Loman.

We're going to miss you, Arthur. Thank God you left the plays.

With love and admiration,

One of your many directors

PS Having read this over, I think I had better add, for all kinds of reasons but mainly because it is true, that Dustin was wonderful in the end and made everybody else cry. Like those New York fur coats who sobbed so much they very nearly fell out of the boxes at the Broadhurst.

John Shrapnel

Actor: The Archbishop's Ceiling, Royal Shakespeare Company, 1986; The Golden Years, BBC Radio, 1987

'My God, eh? So many writers! Like snow . . . like forest . . . these enormous trees everywhere on the earth. Marvellous.'

The words are spoken by a dissident writer in *The Archbishop's Ceiling*, Arthur's claustrophobic chamber piece set in an apartment in an Eastern European capital (unspecified) where a group of friends are locked in a passionate debate over the writer's fate as the state machine tightens its grip. In an attempt to silence him it will face him with a compromise: emasculation, or expulsion and removal from the source of his inspiration. This elaborate dance is acted out under the strong probability that state surveillance is overhearing everything. There is a powerful sense of paranoia in the air.

1986. Five of us were in a small room in Smithfield rehearsing the play for the RSC, and there was certainly a touch of paranoia: one of the enormous trees was coming out of the forest to join us. Arthur had agreed to come over and attend rehearsals during the run-up to the opening. The play had been seen in the States some years earlier, but this was Europe and the big movements about to shake that continent were rumbling nearer the surface now. We knew about Czechoslovakia and Charter 77, and it wasn't a big speculative leap to think that Prague might have been Arthur's inspiration for the city with the Soviet tanks 'bivouacked' outside. For my character Sigmund, the dissident writer, I was finding it useful to think about Václav Havel, then suffering under constant harassment, deprivation and periods of confinement. Arthur's circumspection was understandable, though, and the broad themes of his play certainly wouldn't be served by any attempts to be specific about place or personality.

Arthur arrives, two days later than expected; hat, raincoat, tweed jacket, big, open-throated laugh. The reason for his delay has been a meeting with Mikhail Gorbachev, who had, apparently, requested it. For a while discussion of *The Archbishop's Ceiling* goes on hold. 'You know, that guy's an intellectual. I can't tell you how rare a thing that is in a politician . . .'

Over the following days Arthur is light, easy, amusing and protectively supportive of his actors. He is encouraging, enthusiastic, collaborative ('listen; you wanna cut it, cut it!'). There is no vanity, no authorial 'distance'. He is clearly enjoying himself and our anxieties evaporate as he nudges us, with no apparent pressure, towards a solution – a way to solve a problem. He's as at home in the rehearsal room as a cook in a kitchen.

There's an occasional adjustment to the text: at one point my character mentions various celebrated authors who have supported him. Arthur approaches me one morning with some additions: '. . . Beckett, Graham Greene – can't leave those guys out.'

He stays close to us through the play's opening and visits us during the run. Occasionally, we all slip off to a nearby fish restaurant after the performance and talk. And laugh.

Two years later I was doing another play with the RSC: *Temptation*, by Václav Havel. It was to be a further eighteen months before the Velvet Revolution; Havel's plays were banned and he had effectively been denied the opportunity of seeing any of his works performed for years.

A videotape version of our production had been made, and the director Roger Michell and I had decided to fly out to Prague with a smuggled copy to show to Havel. During conversations in his apartment (then the operations centre for Civic Forum) we talked about Arthur and I asked Havel if he had read *The Archbishop's Ceiling*.

'Of course.' He wanted to know about the production: which character had I played?

'Sigmund, the writer.'

'Oh, yes: that's me . . .'

Michael Simkins

Actor: A View from the Bridge, National Theatre, 1987

Like most British actors I grew up with a love almost bordering on worship for the plays of Arthur Miller. One of my earliest memories had been watching a TV adaptation of his classic *Death of a Salesman* in which Lee J. Cobb as the hapless Willy Loman almost appeared to be bursting through the screen of my parents' sitting room, such was the baffled fury he seemed to generate in the part. Years later I saw Warren Mitchell play the same role live on stage in the Olivier and he, too, was electrifying, in an entirely different interpretation; always for me, the test of great writing.

It never occurred to me that I might actually meet the man, but in 1987 I was in the cast in a production of one of Miller's other classics, *A View from the Bridge*, at the National Theatre. Alan Ayckbourn was directing a cast of largely unknown actors, with the exception of Michael Gambon, then approaching the summit of his powers, in the leading role of Eddie Carbone, the New Jersey longshoreman whose life is disrupted and ultimately destroyed by emotions he can neither control nor understand.

During rehearsals it was impossible, as it usually is, to gauge whether we were heading for a hit or a dud. We were dimly aware that Miller was considered old-fashioned back in the States, and that several of his recent ventures had been considered null and void, as he himself had described recent critical response. Miller, Ayckbourn and Gambon: for all concerned it was a fascinating if unlikely blend. We were both surprised and alarmed by the amount of humour Gambon and Ayckbourn were conspiring to extract from Miller's dark and forbidding text. Gambon also often took the dialogue at lightning speed, in contrast to what might have been anticipated in a play dealing with such profound human emotions. Would Miller approve?

Eventually we got to the technical run, the point where a dozen or so interested heads of department from lighting, sound, make-up and props come to see the play in a simple run-through in the rehearsal room. To our astonishment, several of them were weeping silently at the end of the run-through. Others were red-eyed and snuffling. We knew then we might be on to something.

Some weeks later, with huge critical success safely assured, Miller attended a performance and we were offered the chance to meet him over a glass of wine. Strikingly tall and lean, with a taut muscular body and piercing eyes, he utterly belied his seventy-two years. His comments were generous, gracious, kind, yet it was difficult to tell his real thoughts. I got the sense that even if he'd hated the production we might never have known. 'I enjoyed it,' he said simply, before offering a few thoughts on the genesis of the play. Only as we were downing the final gulps did he allow his face to break into a mordant grin. 'And by the way – it was the quickest staging in the history of the play by nearly ten minutes. Congratulations.' We heard later that in fact he considered it a consummate production.

Josette Simon

Actor: After the Fall, Royal National Theatre, 1990

Shortly after our rehearsal period for *After the Fall* at the Royal National Theatre began, our director, Michael Blakemore, informed us that very soon Arthur Miller would be joining us in the rehearsal room. He would, we were told, be remaining there, observing, for the rest of the time up to and including the opening night. This news threw the company into a spin. I can well recall the feeling as my heart lurched forward with excitement and fear, and my stomach seemed to drop to the floor with nerves. This was the British première of the play and, as the female lead, I knew that this material – not uncommon to other Miller works – encompassed very personal issues for Arthur and I was bringing to life this character – Maggie – and in doing so treading on some deeply sensitive and painful aspects of his life. In America this part had commonly – obviously – been totally associated with Marilyn Monroe and the play, a supposed dissection of their relationship. I had been told that the majority of other actresses who had played the part in the States had gone the whole way with blonde wig etc.

I always believed that the character stood up on its own and that, like many great artists, Miller had drawn on his personal experience to build this character, but that it did not mean this was a straight exposé of Monroe. If I did not believe that the character was a construction and stood in its own right, then I could not have played it. Indeed, would not have wished to.

Arthur arrived. Tall, commanding, easygoing and the only person I have ever met who fully embodied the word charisma. We were all bowled over. He was utterly charming and relaxed. People quivered around him. He said that he would sit in the corner of the rehearsal room for the duration of the rehearsal period. 'But don't mind me,' he told us. 'Just forget that I'm there!'

At first we all fell victim to nerves and self-consciousness as we worked in his presence. But it soon became clear that this was no use to anyone. So, quite swiftly, we got down to the most important job of wanting to do full justice to the work – which is always one's only criterion. Pretty soon I did – almost – 'forget he was there'. He said very little, occasionally offering notes or clarifying points, via Michael Blakemore, who would pass them on to us the next day, before Arthur's arrival. Other than this, he remained a quiet presence in the corner. To me he said little about the part or how I was portraying it. We talked of other subjects with ease and in relaxed fashion. But he offered no viewpoint about my interpretation as it unfolded before him day after day. I decided not to get paranoid about this, but to keep my focus fixed on the difficult job in hand and not to take his lack of comment on my work as a negative sign, easy though this would be to do.

Finally, with dress rehearsals, technicals and last-minute preparations over, the opening night arrived. Arthur came to find me. He took me to one side, put his arm round me and uttered one solitary, marvellous sentence: 'You're gonna be great, kid.' He beamed. And with an enveloping bear of a hug, he was off. To others, too, he spoke in glowing terms of my performance. I encountered him several times over the years. Any celebrations of his major birthdays were accompanied by staged scenes from some of his work. I was privileged to be asked to repeat scenes from *After the Fall* at some of these gatherings, before him.

He was a giant in every way and I feel blessed and proud to have met him, and to have been involved in the work of this great man.

Patrick Stewart

*Actor: **The Ride Down Mount Morgan**, Ambassador Theatre, New York, 1998*

I am looking at the famous photograph of Arthur taken on his eightieth birthday. The mouth is open, the eyes almost wrinkled shut, the lean cheeks deeply creased by the width of his laugh. His tie is slipping down as if forced out of the collar by the intensity of his reaction. Delight and energy are bursting from him. And that is the Arthur I remember. He is the only man I have known actually to slap his thigh when something really amused him. A corny, clichéd gesture on stage but when performed by Arthur, a visible, irresistible illustration of pleasure exploding through his whole body. The gesture would at times also accompany a new, important thought.

I saw it memorably during a rehearsal on stage at the Ambassador Theatre on 49th Street, New York. We were already in previews for the Broadway première of Arthur's play *The Ride Down Mount Morgan*. My character, Lyman Felt, ended the play with a soliloquy from his hospital bed. I had struggled with it in the rehearsal room and Arthur and the director, David Esbjornson, both felt it wasn't working. The play was not being properly concluded. Arthur had done a couple of new drafts. One handwritten on a piece of paper I

had read from at the previous night's performance because I hadn't
had time to learn it. At this rehearsal the piece of paper was in my
hand. (It is now safely stored with other A.M. memorabilia from
this marvellous job.) David was sitting back in the centre of the
stalls and Arthur, because of his hearing, was in the middle of the
front row. Something I had had to learn not to find intimidating. I
had just performed the speech for the umpteenth time and we were
all silent, contemplating the serious situation of a play that didn't
have an ending.

It was then that a yelp cracked out of Arthur and that huge hand
slapped down on his thigh. 'It's the wrong mountain,' he yelled. I
looked at him. The director looked at him. Arthur was on his feet
now. 'For years Lyman has been climbing a mountain – but it was
the wrong mountain. At the end of the play he should be back at the
foot of the mountain. But now it's the right mountain.' Yes, he was
right. Here was Lyman, abandoned by his two wives (Lyman is a
bigamist), his daughter, his friend, and his body smashed up by a
terrible car accident but the words of an affectionate black nurse
recounting the pleasure she and her husband and son got out of
buying new shoes has brought him to a simple, plain place of self-
enlightenment and possibility. The speech was reworked by Arthur
and the next day when I rehearsed it and spoke the final words, it
was a relief and a joy to hear once more that yell of pleasure escape
from the great man's mouth. He had put the play and all of us at the
foot of the right mountain.

Tom Stoppard

Writer

On first meeting Arthur Miller . . . most people (say half a dozen
out of the half-dozen I know personally) made the same comment:
suddenly the marriage to Marilyn Monroe made complete sense.
Quite simply, he had as much sex appeal as she did. Hers
photographed better.

This is not necessarily the best first take on writing about Arthur.
'Don't mention Marilyn,' I said to my wife when we were on our
way to meet the famous man at friends of friends outside New York

somewhere, about thirty years ago. I was not thinking so much of his wife Inge, whose attractive qualities were obvious as soon as one met her, as of Arthur himself: when you meet the author of several modern classics, you don't type him as the man who married Marilyn. My wife sensibly ignored my admonition and Arthur talked easily about his former wife for a few minutes while I listened as agog as any *People Magazine* reader. I was still taking in the size of the man. He was big and rangy with a strong body and large hands. He looked like – he was – a man who felled trees with an axe. He didn't seem much different the last time I saw him, a year or so before he died.

On neither occasion, nor on others in between, did we talk about his 'modern classics'. I took it as understood that I was still somewhat in awe of him and that awe was due. He treated me as a peer, not because I'd written plays, too, but because he embodied the given that to know yourself as a human being is to be a democrat.

Arthur was a model in more than playwriting. I doubt he thought of himself as a model for playwrights at all. Plurality, in theatre as in politics, is a virtue he held fast. But he remains an exemplum in one regard at least. He stayed at work as long as he was alive. No one in our territory had more laurels to rest on and no one clocked up as many decades as a working writer; starting from *The Man Who Had All the Luck*, disinterred by the Bristol Old Vic in the only British production I'm aware of: even that earliest work should have announced him but *All My Sons* made him unmissable.

There will be many to speak up for the plays; let me put in a word for his novel *Focus*. Mine is the only copy of it I've ever seen, a fifties paperback. I just went to check the date of publication and it's gone missing. The good news is that it was recently reprinted.

Geoffrey Strachan

Drama Editor, Publishing Director, Methuen 1961–95

When I think of Arthur Miller I think first of his vigour. An early impression: a genial, striding giant arriving at Hatchards, Piccadilly, to sign copies of his autobiography, *Timebends*, having walked all the way from his hotel north of Marble Arch with my then colleague, Nick Hern, gleefully, if a little breathlessly, in tow. His quizzical humour. A few years later, having gratefully accepted some medication from my wife, Susan, a medical herbalist, for one of the cast of *Broken Glass* who was losing her voice in rehearsal, he reported its efficacy. But confronted one night with a melissa infusion I offered him after dinner in lieu of coffee in the gathering August dusk in our London garden, he eyed it with mock suspicion: 'What's this you're giving me?' His generosity of spirit: when, several years on, I stepped down from the front line in publishing not long after he had become an octogenarian, he wrote expressing amazement, given that I was not even eighty, and said he would try to forgive, with the friendly wish that my new imaginings be as gratifying to me as my old ones had been to others.

I had got to know Arthur Miller when Methuen began publishing his plays and other books. In 1983, a couple of years after *The American Clock*, briefly staged on Broadway, had received lethally dismissive notices from New York critics (John Simon's review was headed 'A Clockwork Lemon'), the Birmingham Repertory Theatre gave it its British première, directed by Peter Farago. Nick Hern, then Methuen's Drama Editor, arranged for us to publish the text alongside the Birmingham production. It was the first new play by Miller to be staged in Britain for thirteen years. This marked something like the start of a new era for his work here. During the two decades that followed I personally saw British productions of at least fifteen different plays of his and in several cases more than one production. Professional theatre critics probably saw twice that number. I also had the disconcerting experience in New York in those days of talking to good drama bookselling colleagues amazed that anyone should be interested in Arthur's work.

In 1984 Methuen published two further plays, *Two-Way Mirror* and *The Archbishop's Ceiling* (which led to the latter receiving its European première at the Bristol Old Vic in 1985) and in 1986 a further double bill, *Danger: Memory!* By 1987, when *Timebends* was published and Alan Ayckbourn's production of *A View from the Bridge*, starring Michael Gambon, was playing at the National Theatre, there was a rising tide of enthusiasm for Miller and his work among directors, actors, playwrights, critics and playgoers around the country. During the two decades following 1983 first editions appeared in Britain both of early plays, *The Golden Years* and *The Man Who Had All the Luck*, and of new work, as it was staged, *The Ride Down Mount Morgan* in 1991, *The Last Yankee* in 1993, *Broken Glass* in 1994 and *Mr. Peters' Connections* in 2000.

The climate in British theatre in the eighties and nineties was good for Arthur Miller. But then Arthur Miller was good for the British theatre. From 1979 onwards public funding of the arts was being eroded under the monetarist aegis of a Prime Minister who once, infamously, let slip the remark: 'There is no such thing as society.' Given this bleak atmosphere, I believe both British directors and playwrights must have been grateful for the work and the example of a writer whose plays powerfully proclaim that there is indeed such a thing and that the interaction between individuals and society is what theatre is all about. He was a writer eager to warn us, in private gatherings as well as in public, that we had better stand up and be counted in defence of subsidised theatre. In my experience, Arthur certainly enjoyed seeing new British plays. Over the years I recall seeing with him Simon Gray's *Melon* (at his suggestion) and Sebastian Barry's *The Steward of Christendom* (at mine), a new play he warmed to. He never gave up on theatre.

There was a relaxed, self-confident stillness about Arthur Miller, for all his energy and vaulting imagination, that puts me in mind of Henry Moore. Both were highly original artists of genius in their chosen medium who had great struggles in their lives and found vivid expression in their work for ideas that obsessed them. Each deeply rooted in his native boyhood experiences (New York, Yorkshire) but whose work spoke to the world. Craftsmen to their fingertips, superbly well organised and professional. Both reliant, the playwright in some ways even more than the monumental sculptor, on the skills and creativity of teams of artists and technicians, whose loyalty and commitment both men won readily.

In all the dealings I and my editorial colleagues had with him, face to face, on the telephone, in correspondence, Arthur was unfailingly down-to-earth, courteous, often self-deprecating and wryly humorous. He would write illuminating introductions, for new editions of established plays, but for the first edition of *The Ride Down Mount Morgan*, receiving its world première in London, he declined, commenting that he would rather not be ushering the play in; he'd rather just drop it on the reader and run for his life.

That was in the summer of 1991. The following summer, in a letter reporting that the play had, in Stockholm, at last been 'done with its rightful complexity' and that the search was on for the right Lyman for the USA, he alluded for a moment to the troubled politics of America, following twelve years of both actual and spiritual malign neglect, but affirming that, for incomprehensible reasons, he was still optimistic about this country.

That autumn he pondered where his newly finished play, *Gellburg* (eventually titled *Broken Glass*), could be staged, given that there were no producers any more, at least not on Broadway, for straight plays. He remarked that he would give it to the National but it seemed wrong to open yet another play in England, since his passport, at least, said he was American. The play was premièred at the Long Wharf Theatre, New Haven, the following March and was scheduled to open at the National in August. In June he spoke of rapturous audiences, with nobody stirring from beginning to end except to laugh or gasp. Then, before moving on to talk about the English edition of the text, he slipped in news of a domestic matter, namely that he had just had the pleasure of emptying the compost bin, which had yielded several bushels of soil from kitchen scraps, expressing amazement that it had worked so well and filled him and Inge with such a sense of virtue.

I had met Arthur in New York, and quite often in London and elsewhere, but it was not until a wet, grey November in 1993 that I visited him and Inge in their Connecticut home. Yet even before seeing him there I had sensed that he was deeply rooted in that rural base, the old farm with the silo he had converted into a photographic workshop for Inge, the pool, the hut where he wrote, the woods where he walked, the physical trappings of the place (including the junk-filled garage – 'Europeans have cellars, Americans have garages'). He often gave us vivid weather reports. Hearing that it was raining in London, he made mention of gorgeous sunny days – just, as he said, to make us all feel miserable.

He was meticulous, but considerate (and, on occasion, both humorously contrite and teasing) over the minutiae of preparing and proof-reading texts. On one occasion he had mislaid some galley proofs. Asking for another set to be sent, he promised to return them the next day. Apologetically, he described himself as covered in dust from looking under stuff he had not touched in half a lifetime. Delivering final revisions on *Broken Glass*, he teased us that we could all relax now as he didn't think he'd write another play. The sting in the tail in brackets being that he was currently working on a novel that would require stupendous changes right up to the last minute.

Pungent comments on the American political scene continued to alternate with discussions of his work and vivid allusions to the seasons in his garden and the woods at Roxbury. In September 1992, in the last weeks of the presidential contest between Clinton and Bush, he referred to the latter as a terrible fellow, full of deception, dishonest, without insides. In mellower mood on his birthday, 17 October 1994, he spoke of a golden fall, temperatures near 70°F, hardly any wind, trees bursting with colour, the pond glassy as a sky.

In October the following year the celebrations for his eightieth birthday in Britain were widespread: events in his honour in London, East Anglia and Oxford; the publication of his novel *Plain Girl*, productions of his plays all over Britain. Benedict Nightingale's comment on this catalogue of celebratory events in *The Times* perhaps catches the spirit of defiant possessiveness felt by many of Arthur's British admirers, myself included: 'Why is the prophet more honoured in our country than his own? . . . Being old tends to be a sin in a nation that sometimes seems to regard the day before yesterday as the day before the Peloponnesian War . . . I exaggerate but have you a better explanation for the neglect of a man who can claim to be not just America's but the world's greatest living dramatist?'

Back home (where, to be fair, he was also fêted by American PEN) Arthur wrote graciously, if wryly, that the whole ten days was rather overwhelming. The Latin (at Oxford where he had received an honorary doctorate) had made him feel he was back in the twelfth century, one that compared favourably with our own. Having walked in the woods the day before, his news was that enough leaves had fallen to allow a view through the brush and that he had seen a flock of about twenty-five wild turkeys, most of them full grown, feasting on fallen seed pods. The toms, he commented, are immense birds.

In the years following 1995 (and my exit from Methuen), despite his playful promise after *Broken Glass*, Arthur Miller did, of course, go on to write more plays. I saw him again in London five years later when *Mr. Peters' Connections* was finely performed at the Almeida (I later reported to Arthur that in my view it had been even more adventurously staged in French at the Théâtre de l'Oeuvre); also in

Norwich, when he was given the freedom of the city and once more celebrated (with fireworks at the University of East Anglia) as the honorary Grand Old Man of British theatre (except that, even then, he just didn't seem old).

Breaking a long silence, I wrote to him on his birthday in October 2004, having just seen the superb production of *The Price* directed by Sean Holmes, with Larry Lamb, Nancy Crane, Brian Protheroe and Warren Mitchell (who had played Willy Loman years before), acting in perfect equilibrium. It was one of those stunning experiences that only a great performance of a great play can offer. I wrote to thank Arthur (again) for writing the play. He wrote back, glad I had seen *The Price*. He had heard it was beautifully done and had just received a birthday greeting from Warren Mitchell, whom he described as a lunatic actor who must be marvellous in the part of the furniture dealer . . . He thought I sounded content with my retirement and said he might possibly be coming to London in May for the production of *Death of a Salesman* with Brian Dennehy, hoping, after two bouts of pneumonia, to be himself in good time. Alluding to my wife's work as a medical herbalist, he remarked that he could probably have used her medical advice at that time but unfortunately was too far away.

I wrote back to express the hope that we might meet on his next visit. Reading of his death in the paper a few months later, I was incredulous. I can still hear his voice, ruminative, enthusiastic, jocular, and feel his calm, vibrant presence – whether in the same room or at the end of a transatlantic telephone line. The plays he gave us are treasure beyond price, nourishment to help us find our way through this next, difficult century.

David Thacker

Director: In his work at the Young Vic, where he was Artistic Director, and elsewhere, David Thacker has directed ten plays by Arthur Miller

Dear Arthur,

Chris has asked me to write something for a book about you. You know how much I hate committing myself on paper, perhaps because as I have spent years working on the texts of great writers, admiring and delighting in their use of language, anything I write seems stupid in comparison. And perhaps out of fear – the absolute opposite of you – that once it is on paper I can't wriggle out of it, pretend I didn't say it, use the techniques of oral communication to compensate for the inadequacy of my language, the imprecision of my ideas, or simply my inability to write anything interesting. With you it is there in print – bold, strong, unequivocal and true. You say what you mean, mean what you say, and that is it. Also, the most important things I want to say to you should remain private, so deep is my sense of privilege, honour and gratitude for having been able to work so closely with you since the first telephone conversations we had fifteen years ago when we discussed how to change the language in *An Enemy of the People* from 'American' into 'English'.

You remember you were startled when I explained the need to do this? 'As the play's set in Norway played by English actors, we can't do it in American accents.'

'Why can't they use English accents?'

Me (nervously) 'Well . . . try saying the first line in an English accent; "You sure eat fast Mr Kiil." '

A week later I described how we had spent the first week in rehearsal comparing your play with Ibsen's original and had come to the conclusion that there were some speeches omitted from Ibsen's play that should perhaps be restored. I sat in that little office above the butcher's shop in the Young Vic, the place that was soon to become your spiritual home in London, thinking, 'What am I doing talking to the world's greatest living playwright like this?'

You said, 'Well, try it, and phone me back to tell me how it works.'

Those telephone conversations prepared us for many meticulous and detailed conversations about text and language, casting, design and your intentions in writing each of your plays; right through to that wonderful telephone conversation you had with the Israeli actors on the first night of *Broken Glass* in Tel Aviv. Remember I arranged for you to phone them as a surprise? After he had realised it was you, and not some English actor I had enlisted as a practical joke, Rami (Gellburg) said, 'Oh no . . . you are God'.

You said to Rami, 'How's David? Is he killing you?'

'Yes, he's driving us mad with his dot dot dots and pauses' – alluding to my drilling them till they observed every rhythmical beat, every thought change – even in a language of which I could speak about three words. More fascinating to me was that I could tell exactly where we were in a scene, exactly what nuance was required, as long as the actors were being emotionally and psychologically truthful.

'Yes, because the language is only the exterior, get the interior right and it will work.' Not entirely true, I thought, but I knew what you meant. And I knew what Rami meant too.

I don't know how I'll manage not being able to phone you any more. Not that we spoke that often after Inge died but whenever we did I was able to get immediate orientation on the way things truly are; whether on Bush's real motives for invading Iraq, the effect of contemporary television on the sensibilities of the people, or coping with loss, just as years earlier we had discussed your optimism on the prospect of Bill Clinton as the next president, Gorbachev and glasnost, Nelson Mandela and standing firm on a point of principle, or why the Americans weren't interested in the World Cup, even when it was being held in the USA. You know you make me laugh more than anyone else but maybe you don't know you are a moral and spiritual touchstone for me, a source of wisdom, a purveyor of sanity, a beacon of truth, a fount of hope, a lover of humanity.

This is not what I am supposed to be writing about, but how can I separate the Arthur I love, from the Arthur Miller I direct. You and your plays are inseparable to me, and symbiotic in my imagination and consciousness. Perhaps that is because you have always been so inspirational when talking about your plays. Many writers obfuscate, either intentionally or pathologically, where you seek to demystify, clarify, to shed light and understanding. You have struggled to put everything on paper, carving out sentences as you carve wood in your workshop, choosing words with precision and deliberation, seeking to find a way of expressing ideas precisely through language, as you seek to reveal how and why people behave as they do. It all seems so blindingly obvious to you. I have never known you to make me or the actors we have worked with feel inadequate or foolish if we didn't understand something in your play.

Whether it is asking you if Biff forgives Willy Loman or what a Hershey bar is, you loved telling us what you meant. These characters lived in your imagination as vividly as when you first invented them. Telling us about them was like telling us about close friends. You would reveal their motives, explain their emotional life, and let us into the innermost secrets of their psychology. And because we all let you know how much we admired and treasured your work you spoke truthfully and frankly about our attempts to give life to your plays on stage. When dear Bob Peck, whom you loved and admired, was being characteristically obdurate in rehearsals for *The Price* you said, 'The problem is, Bob, I'm getting the impression that Walter is manipulative. He's trying to reach his brother – to make contact.' When asked to clarify Dr Hyman's motives in *Broken Glass*, you responded, 'He's a Doctor, he likes to heal people.' Or when Henry [Goodman] was showing too much emotion you advised, 'Henry, the guy has a heart attack because he doesn't let his feelings out.' Henry had been bringing the Holocaust to every second. When actors like these dug deep into their emotional systems in the way your plays generally demand, you treated them with the utmost respect. At the end of that rehearsal you said to me, 'The wonderful thing about these actors is that they can be pointing over there and you can say no, it's there and they do it. With American actors it will take three days to get them off the ceiling.' When I asked you who should play Beatrice in *A View from the Bridge* you advised, 'She's eaten a lot of spaghetti' then immediately qualified it with, '. . . on the other hand she could be slim . . . I wrote Willy Loman imagining him to be a little man, then he was played by Lee J. Cobb . . . then years later by Warren Mitchell . . . both were terrific.'

It was all so blindingly obvious to you that you could never understand it when, after you had explained something to an actor, it did not necessarily mean that they could make it real for you. We once spent most of the night discussing what strategies were most effective in making actors able to tell the truth. That was mysterious to you, as was your incredulity that anyone could seriously misunderstand your work. Only two premières, you told me, had ever satisfactorily expressed your plays – *All My Sons* and *Death of a Salesman*, both directed by Elia Kazan. 'How could you bear it?' I asked. I can't remember your reply, but I witnessed time and again your joy in the rehearsal room when actors truly inhabited one of your characters. You would laugh at the jokes, as if you were hearing them for the first time, marvel at the deep commitment and skill of our British actors; actors like Bob Peck, David Calder, Marjorie Yates, Alan MacNaughton, Helen Mirren, Margot

[Leicester], Henry Goodman, Ken Stott, Alun Armstrong, Mark Strong, Tom Wilkinson, known best to you from the work we did together, and those many other devoted actors in the birthday events we rehearsed with you. I think you and I must have worked together with over fifty actors. You admired their grasp of language, their ability to make lines 'land', as you put it, their intelligence, their wit, their politics, their capacity for empathy, their ability to engage emotionally, their companionship. Everywhere you looked you saw commitment throughout the casts. You knew they loved your work, they treasured any contact with you, and they would give everything for you.

They have all worked on Shakespeare, of course, and embody the best of the classical and American tradition in acting. That is why you admired them. What a company they would make! One of my happiest nights was after the press night of *Broken Glass*. We all went for a meal in Joe Allen's – a place you loved to be with actors. The cast were in heaven, you were radiant in the midst of them, laughing, joking and talking about all the things that matter. Inge looked lovingly at you and them, and turned to me: 'You've all made it possible for him to write another play.' But how did you write so many when your heart was broken so often by the stupidity of critics, the hostility of the establishment, the well-meaning but misguided attempts to express your plays?

The first time you met the cast of *An Enemy of the People*, we sat at your feet like the actors in *The Seagull* at the feet of Chekhov. We were all terrified, not least me because I wondered how you would react to the changes we had made. Tom Wilkinson, not prone to sycophancy and slow to hand out compliments, said that when he was delivering Stockmann's great speech – yours, not Ibsen's – he wished that every actor in the country could have the chance to experience what he experienced in the theatre every night. Of course, it was at the height of Thatcher's assault on everything we held dear and we all believed that we were speaking, through you, as no politician would ever speak, although Roy Hattersley, the deputy leader of the opposition, a great admirer of your work, wrote in the *Guardian* that Margaret Thatcher should see this play.

Sitting at your feet that day the women were overwhelmed by the presence of Arthur Miller, as was virtually every woman who ever encountered you in the rehearsal room. Over the years I began to discover how much your love of women and your own sexuality infused your work. Perhaps not surprisingly for someone who had loved Marilyn, sex is fundamental to many of your plays: John Proctor/Elizabeth/Abigail; Eddie Carbone/Beatrice/Catherine; Willy Loman/Biff/Miss Francis; Gellburg/Sylvia/Dr Hyman. You will have noticed that I always include *Broken Glass* in any list of your great plays, perhaps because it is the closest to my heart. To direct the première was a great joy – perhaps the most important artistic experience of my life. Yes, not strictly the première, but we both know it was. The New York production was the première in name, but the National Theatre production was the première of the *play*; the play that developed from the New York production to the play that is performed throughout the world. And our further work together with David Holman on the screenplay for the film, our discussions about the radio version, and our conversations about the production in Hebrew in Tel Aviv has meant that I have tried to get inside that play like no other.

In one of the American obituaries I was ridiculed for comparing you with Shakespeare. We both know that Shakespeare is pre-eminent among playwrights and that a comparison is of limited value. But I have directed more plays by you (ten) and Shakespeare (sixteen) than I have by anybody else so the connections are clear to me. You are both language playwrights – poets. You both dig deep into human emotion and explore the hidden recesses of the soul; you are both political playwrights; you both seek to understand the contradictions and complexities in situations; you both deal with the connection between the personal and the public; you both love human beings.

The most stimulating forty-eight hours I spent with you, Arthur, were the two days in New York when I was rehearsing *Broken Glass* and you were at the end of the New York run. When you were struggling for the right ending for *Broken Glass* we discussed Hermione's statue coming to life at the end of *The Winter's Tale*, and out of that was born Sylvia's rising to her feet with the words, 'There's nothing to blame! There's nothing to blame!' Among the many things we discussed that night many resonate vividly for me; your love of Marilyn and your pain at your inability to help her save herself. We both knew that Sylvia was, in part, yet another attempt to deal with that. You told me that Hyman was based on the doctor who treated Marilyn and I began to realise how many of your characters are based on real people known to you. Some, like Eddie

Carbone, were based on a real family. You told me how after one of the first performances you noticed a man sitting weeping at the back of the audience. When you spoke to him he told you that he knew the family and that the niece had killed the uncle. You had replied, 'Why didn't you tell me that before?' Sylvia Gellburg herself was a woman who always wore black, as if in mourning for her life.

But although it is revealing and fascinating to know that real people often provided the starting point for your journey it is no more significant that John Proctor lived than that Shakespeare based his plays on source material, sometimes involving 'real' kings and queens. Can you remember the story you told me as we drove through the countryside near your home after our production of *The Last Yankee*? You said to me, 'That's where the Last Yankee lives.'

'You mean he's a real person?'

'Yes, I met him the other day and asked how his wife was getting on.'

He told you that she was on and off the medication and that it was a real struggle for her. He said to you, 'You know, Arthur, you should write a play about it.'

So how will I cope now that I can't just phone you up and check through the design concept of a play, ask you about the qualities to look for when casting, introduce you to a new group of devoted actors, listen to you talk kindly, precisely and passionately in the rehearsal room; when I can't ask you your opinion on the latest world catastrophe we seem to visit upon each other, never learning, as you would have it, from the lessons of history; or share with you our relief at the next wonderful example of humanity's capacity to forgive, restore and move on. As with Shakespeare, I expect I will take comfort that 'this lives on and thus gives life to thee'. But there will be no one for me to take my moral bearings from, no one to tell us unequivocally 'this is what I meant', no one to send me the first draft of a new play so that I can read it, as I read *The Last Yankee* and *Broken Glass*, with excitement and awe.

'Help me, Willy, I can't cry. It seems to me that you're just on another trip. I keep expecting you. Willy, dear, I can't cry . . . I search and search and I search, and I can't understand it.'

With love,
David

John Tillinger

Director: After the Fall, The Price, An Enemy of the People, The Last Yankee and Broken Glass

When people think of Arthur Miller, they remember that magnificent head that seemed to belong on Mount Rushmore, or the erstwhile husband of Marilyn Monroe, or the Jeremiah in our midst reminding us of our moral standards, warning us of the social/politcal/economic dangers that lay ahead. This was not the Arthur Miller I knew and loved.

Our friendship began when I was asked to direct Frank Langella and Dianne Wiest in a revival of *After the Fall*. Rehearsals were illuminating, exhilarating even (having recently barely survived a difficult divorce, I found I learned more about my failed relationship through those rehearsals than I might have with years of psychotherapy).

Since we lived in the same village, the Millers and I were soon socialising on a regular basis. An invitation to dinner at their house always thrilled me for besides Inge Morath's superb cooking, the guests were fun; stimulating and amusing. I found that I was more articulate, thought clearer, expressed myself better in their company. But laughter was what I remember most. Arthur and Inge loved to laugh, epitomised by their wonderful sense of irony and Arthur's sardonic Jewish wit.

I suppose you had to be there really to appreciate Arthur's humor and timing. I remember once picking him up with my car to take him to the theater in New Haven. 'My God,' he said, 'you've still got that old car? How many miles has it got. On second thought, tell me when you've dropped me off home again.'

Later we passed a piece of property that was for sale for seven million dollars. 'Do you know how the owners made their money?' I asked. 'Pornography! Sex shops. Sexual paraphernalia and magazines.'

As I waxed increasingly more indignant, Arthur punctured my self-righteousness by asking, 'Do you think they'd give us a discount?'

On another occasion, when I arrived at their house, I found Titi, Inge's mother curled up on the sofa, reading a huge tome on nineteenth-century European politics. She was ninety-two at the time. She read faster and retained more than I ever did. 'Do you know why she has lived to such a great age?' Arthur asked. I was expecting some major insight into longevity. 'Sausage,' he said. 'She consumes vast quantities of sausage every day.' And indeed, when we sat down to lunch that day, she devoured lots of salami.

Arthur liked my work, particularly after seeing my revivals of Joe Orton's plays. And he asked me to direct a revival of *The Price* (I wish everyone could have seen Eli Wallach's definitive performance as Solomon). Then came the world premières of *The Last Yankee* and *Broken Glass*. It was a daunting assignment. As we worked on the play I would cautiously question a line, the order of speeches, a character trait. I even suggested an extra scene. Arthur would consider my ideas, rewrite sometimes, restructure and, on one occasion, add a scene. 'If that line doesn't work,' he'd said, 'just cut it.' I told him he ought to lecture young playwrights on the virtues of collaboration.

However, as I made these suggestions I became increasingly anxious. Here I was editing a play by Arthur Miller, for God's sake. I happened to be having lunch with Elia Kazan (Arthur's greatest interpreter) and expressed my concern. 'But that's what he wants you to do,' Kazan said.

On the opening night performance of *Broken Glass*, Arthur and I were having a drink in a bar nearby. I told him that I was unhappy with my production of the play and felt I had failed him. Arthur replied, 'Other than the original production of *Salesman*, none of my premières were ever successful.' And there were no recriminations on his part towards me. I told him that I was certain *Broken Glass* would receive the approbation it deserved in London, whatever the production. 'They like me over there,' he said. 'I don't understand why they don't like me in my own town.' At the time certain New York critics would not even review his plays. This was before recent revivals of his plays were hailed as theatrical masterpieces. 'Wait around long enough', he said to me, 'and they will recognise you once more.'

Arthur had an almost childlike ingenuousness. If someone wanted to revive or produce his plays, if he received accolades, he was genuinely surprised and pleased, as if he were an emerging playwright. I went to see him the day before he died and congratulated him on his short story in *Harper's* magazine entitled 'Beavers'. He entirely captured the ambivalence we feel in having to get rid of these resourceful creatures. I told him that a bank beaver had felled forty-seven trees on my property that year in less than six weeks. (A bank beaver is thrown out by the wife and lives out the remaining two or three years of its life alone.) I wondered to Arthur what then happened to the wife. Arthur, who had not been able to speak because of the extensive chemotherapy, suddenly whispered, 'I expect she creeps back to Canada and resumes her career as an actress.'

He gave my life substance and stature. He and Inge always made me believe the best of myself. I mentioned this to his daughter Rebecca and she said, 'That's what they did best.'

I miss them both desperately.

Andrei Voznesensky

Writer

In a brown sheepskin coat trimmed with white, wearing a cherry-blossom scarf, against a background of melting snow, Arthur Miller was standing raised on the porch of the Pasternak Museum, which was at last open after many years of struggle. The branches of the pine trees, which had just shed their covering of snow, waved in time to his words. A crowd of visitors, guests and local inhabitants was watching intently. I recalled the funeral and another crowd. In his oration Arthur had said, 'If Hitler had managed to get his hands on Pasternak, he would have killed the poet twice – as a Russian intellectual and as a Jew.'

Why had I invited Arthur Miller and Inge Morath to fly over for the Pasternak readings? And why had they flown halfway across the world to be there? Arthur Miller was essentially an intellectual in the Russian, Chekhovian sense of the word. In my view he was a pillar of the world's conscience in our time. Of course, it is possible to be a brilliant artist without being the conscience of the epoch. Beckett and Dali were indisputably geniuses, but of a different mould. We and our time have been lucky in that the patriarch of our theatre was also the conscience of humanity. He was scrupulous in seeking out the green shoots of conscience and, with a growl, helping them to grow.

The PEN Club writers, supporters of human rights, understood this when they appealed to Arthur for help. Our persecutors of Pasternak also understood this when they tried to win him over with cordiality: 'You can do anything . . . You tell them, Miller . . .' But his psychologist's intuition and his experience of McCarthyism meant that he immediately saw through their tiresome intrigues.

I was fortunate enough to witness the runaway success on Broadway of one of Miller's plays, staged with deliberate simplicity [*Broken Glass*]. Its subject matter was stomach-wrenching. The persecution of Jews in Germany causes a woman in America to develop an illness at a distance. This long-range conscience was Arthur's alter ego.

He also felt for Russia from afar and felt its pain through Chekhov, through the Sovremennik Theatre, which put on his plays, and through the Moscow Art Theatre. His name, Arthur, could almost be an anagram for 'art theatre', and his daughter Rebecca, herself a film director and artist, has played a Chekhov heroine. Such facts seem more than coincidental.

Together with Inge Morath, the gothically beautiful photographer who was his companion, he published the photo album *In Russia*. It was a declaration of love for our country and its culture, with psychological portraits of Nadezhda Mandel'shtam, Aksenov, Brodsky and Korin. This book appeared round the world and only in our country was it refused publication. With her lens, Inge had uncovered a terrible state secret: the number of wrinkles on the face of the USSR Culture Minister of the time. The government was furious, the pair became persona non grata and Arthur's plays were removed from the repertoire.

Both of them have been dear to me. I lived with them in town and out of town on more than one occasion. In times of difficulty they always tried to help. In her more recent *Russian Journal*, Inge published my letters to her from back then. I had forgotten that I had written them – they had, of course, not been sent by post. At that time, after my 'open letter', I had been suffering the usual persecutions.

Articles were placed, both in our own press and that of the CPUSA, to the effect that I was being 'directed by the CIA'. My letters of that time, which were secretly passed on to Miller and were not intended for publication, remind me of my state of mind then. Now, when I reread those forgotten letters, I am struck not only by my knowledge of English then, by my ability to use the untranslatable word 'fuck', but also by my understanding as to whom the word should be addressed. The second letter contains a mistake. I had not personally seen *Novi Mir* then [he states that *Novi Mir* had published three of his poems]. The third poem had not been published. The second, 'I am in crisis', again led to a furious scandal. These lines caused particular offence:

For what, my grey one, are you crying in the wind to white Vladimir?

'White Vladimir', they imagined, referred to Grand Duke Vladimir Kirillovich Romanov, a claimant to the throne living in Spain. Could anybody have imagined at that time that Vladimir Kirillovich would later officially return in triumph to Russia? And that he would be solemnly buried in a tomb in St Petersburg? My lines were crying out from a dark age.

Like many world-class writers, Arthur and Inge felt for Russia. How they longed for our life to become more humane and open! In his book, Arthur takes pleasure in the courage of the stocky Chingiz Aytmatov, but at the same time notes that his 'independent literary forum' was financed by the state. You could not catch Arthur with chaff. I remember how, immediately following a meeting in the Kremlin, he and Inge telephoned me and, to avoid eavesdropping, invited me to a café to talk. Arthur was very animated, very taken with Gorbachev, with his courage and erudition, which were quite unexpected in a Soviet leader. 'He recited your poems to us by heart, without any cues. He spoke of all-human values.' How happy these people, supposedly foreigners, were for Russia, how full of hope they were.

A few years later I was at their country house in Roxbury. We were watching the news about the Belovezhskaya Pushcha agreement. Arthur was talking about the split with the Ukraine, about the break-up of the country, as if it were a matter of his own family, his own daughter Rebecca. Our pain had become his pain.

The ideas of Miller, that great realist, are relevant to us today. We have now lost our illusions both about the Communist paradise and the capitalist one. We should understand the world as it is.

For his anniversary I portrayed him as a long-legged set of

wooden compasses, of the type a teacher might use to draw a circle on a blackboard. He is both calliper and measuring rod. His circle extends from England to China, right off towards the horizon. For me it was an honour to be in that circle, just as it was for everyone. My own story is of interest here only as an example of Arthur's solicitude for everyone – not merely in words or on paper, as so often happens, but in his life and his actions. I experienced this myself. On one occasion I had, once again, not been permitted to leave the country, and then suddenly, at Pierre Trudeau's invitation, I was allowed to travel to Canada for ten days. Arthur and Inge drove for six hours, taking turns at the wheel, along the icy highway from New York to Montreal just to meet up, find out how I was, hear the news about the country and our friends. One does not forget such kindness. It was Arthur who accommodated me in his apartment in the Chelsea Hotel, New York, on my first visit, and introduced me to the bohemian company there. From that day on the Chelsea has been my stamping ground in New York. Arthur explained a lot to me in America. When I was invited to the White House, Arthur spent several hours patiently explaining the nature of power to me: 'The fathers of our democracy, those who composed the Declaration, were highly educated men, with an excellent grasp of Latin and Roman Law . . .'

Everyone should plant at least one tree during his life. Arthur and his wife planted several thousand around their farm. They did it together, with their own hands, with only a trench excavator. These trees grew up on Arthur's land next to the houses of Alexander Calder, the Styrons, Tatiana and Alex Liberman. And he nurtured so many people – including in our country.

Arthur wrote the foreword to the American edition of my book *Nostalgia for the Present*, explaining the resonance of poetry in Russia, the land of poetry.

Translated by Francis King

Eli Wallach

Actor: **The Misfits; The Reason Why; The Price**

When I was performing *Teahouse of the August Moon* at the National Theatre in Washington DC – my role was Sakini, an interpreter for the American army in Okinawa – I felt that the second-best show in Washington was the hearings of the House Un-American Activities Committee. Each morning I would sit quietly in the rear of the hearing room to watch those who were subpoenaed. At one session two famous witnesses were Arthur Miller and Paul Robeson. Robeson's rich voice filled the room and terrified the congressmen. The prosecutor asked Miller why he wanted to go to London – his application for a passport had been denied. 'I wish to go to London to marry the woman I love,' he answered. All the journalists leapt to their feet, running to the phones to report that the woman he loved was Marilyn Monroe. Miller bravely stated that he would answer any question asked him but would not take the Fifth Amendment (the right in the Constitution which protects one from self-incrimination). That action showed plainly that Miller would not name names. I thought he was a hero.

In 1969 Miller asked actor Robert Ryan and myself to go to his home in Connecticut where we could do a short film [*The Reason Why*]. We shot the playlet [which presented a metaphor for Vietnam] in one day. Miller often wrote plays set in the past with a strong link to the present – as in *The Crucible*, which clearly referred to what was happening at the House Un-American Activities Committee. *All My Sons* was a direct link to the evil doings of World War Two, then barely in the past. *The Price*, too, linked the past to the present.

I was given a choice role in *The Price*. I played [Solomon] a used furniture dealer hired by the sons of a wealthy man who had died intestate. *The Price* involved the sons' price for the struggle of their family and the price for the furniture. Solomon was a superb role – full of humor and also pain. In one scene, for example, we learn that his daughter had committed suicide. I called Miller toward the end of the run of the play and begged him to write a new play about the dealer and his daughter. Miller growled, 'I wrote the play; now I'm busy writing a new play that has no connection to your idea for furniture dealers.' After weeks of calling him I wrote the following letter:

Dear Mr Miller,

You know me; my name is Gregory Solomon, a character in your play, *The Price*. There's a pest by the name of Wallach who wants you to write about me and my daughter who committed suicide – Don't do it – I beg you; let us stay on the printed page.

Sincerely,

Gregory Solomon

PS If you change your mind, I will give you a deal on some furniture.

Two weeks later I called Miller and asked if he had received my letter. 'Don't bother me,' Miller said and slammed the phone down.

Miller was a giant among playwrights – his deep analysis of what ailed America appeared in his plays. His heroes were Strindberg, Ibsen, Chekhov and Williams. He found in his later years that his plays were severely criticised by the reviewers. Tennessee Williams once wrote to the critic who tore his play *Camino Real* apart, 'I have to write you. You have a right to your opinion. But, silence is only golden when one has nothing to say – and I feel I have a great deal to say! Cordially, Tennessee Williams.' Miller and Williams were friends and both felt that England remained receptive to their writings when America did not. Miller's book, *Timebends*, remains an insightful, perceptive and deep analysis of the artist.

Zoë Wanamaker

Actor: The Last Yankee, Young Vic, 1992–3; The Crucible, Royal National Theatre, 1991

I first learned about Arthur Miller when I was quite young during discussions at the dinner table with my father regarding his experiences during the McCarthy period and the terrible repercussions that he had suffered during those dark days of the blacklist.

After Joe McCarthy's office had been broken into everyone who had been blacklisted, or had appeared in the publication *Red Channels, The Report of Communist Influence in Radio & Television*, was sent their file. Dad then proceeded to show us his, which was not very big but had his name down for every rally or every time he had spoken against social injustice and for world peace, and included names like Paul Robeson and Arthur Miller.

Sam Wanamaker had worked with Arthur in his early days when he had taken a group of actors to factories and shop floors. Arthur wrote a short one-act play [*That They May Win*] for this group. Sam and Charlotte, my mother, were the first students in Lee Strasberg's front room at the birth of his Method. It was a productive and exciting time for this generation who had survived the war and would influence theatre and film right up to the present.

The next time I spoke to Dad about this whole period was when I was rehearsing for *The Crucible* at the National Theatre. He talked about his decision to leave the USA. He had been asked to do a film in England and while he was there he was subpoenaed to go before the Un-American Activities Committee. With this knowledge my mother packed up the house, put furniture into storage and my sister and I came to England on the *Queen Mary*. He explained that he had a wife and two children to support. However, this decision was extremely difficult for him as he knew a lot of his friends and acquaintances, including Arthur Miller, had been prepared to go to jail for their beliefs. I suspect he had a strong feeling of guilt about this.

Being the man that he was he had directed a play called *Joan of Lorraine* starring Ingrid Bergman, which had opened in Washington in a segregated theatre; he had refused to open the show until the theatre had been desegregated. It caused a huge uproar, with people walking round the theatre with placards protesting. He also directed a play called *Goodbye My Fancy*. Ed Sullivan in a newspaper article accused him of being a 'pinko' and in his usual way Sam wrote an open letter in reply. He was also part of the Hollywood Ten who went to Washington to protest about the blacklist. These are just a few examples of his so-called Communist tendencies.

My mother, Charlotte Holland, was a major radio star at the time and always said how scary it was to know that the phone was being tapped and to fear for every knock at the door. They thought that their trip to England would be a short one but months turned to years and eventually my father's passport ran out. He made an application at the American Embassy for a renewal, which was then denied. He did not work in America for twelve years.

Arthur never saw our production of *The Last Yankee*, which opened simultaneously in Europe and at the Manhattan Theatre Club. I felt *The Last Yankee* was a jewel of a play and if Miller had died then he would have gone still writing at the top of his powers. To my mind it crystallised America, its hopes and its fears. However, he did come to see the production of *The Crucible* and I think was pleased and we talked of that period. Knowing that I was Sam's daughter, he mentioned that maybe the blacklistings had in some strange way been to England's advantage because although Sam had lost a potential movie career he had directed and produced much more in this country than perhaps he would have done in the United States. Sam had started the first repertory complex company in this country, in Liverpool, a theatre that was open seventeen hours a day – film clubs, art exhibitions, West End actors, a restaurant, kids' shows, late-night talks. Then in the late 1960s he came up with the idea of rebuilding Shakespeare's Globe on the South Bank.

Arthur always appeared to me like the American golden eagle: tall, wise, brave and articulate. Because of his and my father's similarities I was very fond of him. They both came from the same sort of background. They were both fighters, survivors and innovators.

Irving Wardle

Reviewer

In Arthur Miller's opinion his script was ready for performance. In the opinion of the producer it still needed fixing. 'Don't you realise, Arthur,' he pleaded, 'that if you get this right you need never work again?'

As Miller reported this exchange to the guests at his eightieth birthday party, it was not a funny story but a nightmare. He recounted it in a tone of horror, building up to a punchline that turned the goal of moneyed retirement into a death sentence. What was the point of being alive if he wasn't producing something?

That question has been echoing in my head ever since and it keeps cropping up in the ever widening longevity debate. British radio and television have recently devoted series to artists who continue working into old age. The Tate Modern famously opened with the statue of a giant spider by the nonagenarian Louise Bourgeois. People can carry on for bad reasons: from vanity, or reluctance to acknowledge they have outlived their powers. 'With sexual impotence,' said Michel Saint-Denis, 'they turn to religion and theorising.' Maybe grinding out another stone-dead novel is a small price to pay for escaping that fate. Aldous Huxley kept on writing because he felt dirty if he didn't. These are solipsistic justifications: why should material produced to make its producer feel good deserve to get into print or performance?

It's easier to find an answer if you restrict the question to playwrights, who have less chance than other writers to succumb to narcissism, as their work will never be seen at all unless it is of interest to other artists. Without going back to the sublime octogenarians of fifth-century Athens, the modern English-speaking theatre has a notable succession of dramatists who refused to recognise that their time was up. 'My bolt is shot,' said Shaw in his seventies, going on to write *Too True to Be Good*, *Village Wooing* and his satiric extravaganzas on pre-war Fascism. Ben Travers tried to retire on the collected loot of his Alwych farces; but after years of idyllic seclusion in Rye, attended by a devoted housekeeper ('That woman does everything for me, she is a saint. I am bored to death'), he renewed his West End career at the age of eighty-nine and achieved the biggest hit of his life with *The Bed Before Yesterday*. Christopher Fry, despite decades of neglect, returned in his ninety-fourth year with a millennium play, *A Ringing of Bells*, which was seen at the National Theatre. On Miller's side of the Atlantic, there is his older contemporary Barrie Stavis, another exponent of the politically loaded history play, who was battling on into his mid nineties to add the United States to the list of twenty-five countries where his work is staged.

Just as Shaw disparaged the work of his self-confessed dotage, I don't suppose any of these writers would claim to be working with the energy they had in their prime. On the other hand, unlike so many past their middle years, they have not betrayed their youth. Shaw at the last gasp is still presenting himself as a comic Cassandra, bearing a vitally urgent message but capable only of making people laugh. Ben Travers made his comeback to complete the world of the Aldwych farces with a sexual candour that was unavailable to him in the days of stage censorship. Fry returned to his lifelong interest in John Bunyan in a piece for Bunyan's home town of Bedford. Stavis, from first to last, adopts history as a platform for what he calls 'forged characters' from Galileo to IWW leader Joe Hill. In each case these writers are in service to an idea and a chosen art form. Perhaps sentimentally, they might echo George Peele's prayer to his Muse: 'Goddess, allow this aged man his right, / To be your beadsman now, that was your knight.'

The case is different with Miller in the sense that, whatever the limitations of physical energy, his dramatic world kept expanding. He began with ideas about social justice and emotional honesty in post-Depression America, and extended them backwards in time and outwards in space until he had connected American consciousness with the *Kristallnacht*, the Holocaust and the security-poisoned communities of East Europe: while simultaneously returning to the material of his earlier plays and digging deeper and deeper into memory. I can find little to criticise in Miller, except perhaps the title of his last play, *Finishing the Picture*. That picture was never going to be finished.

Arnold Wesker

Writer

How to encapsulate the life of a giant of twentieth-century drama. There are certain people – men and women in the arts, the sciences, politics, philosophy and sport – who, through their work and endeavour, transcend their place of birth and become inhabitants of the world. They seem able to cross frontiers and cultures, to touch us and remind us of our humanity, of the best that is in us. And we claim them. They become ours. Suddenly we can't imagine the world without them.

Certainly this playwright can't imagine the world without Arthur Miller. He was there when I wrote *Chicken Soup with Barley*, the first play of mine ever to be performed. The best artists fall into roughly two categories: those who enrich tradition and those who extend tradition, by which I mean those who make possible that which had not seemed possible before. *Chicken Soup with Barley*, an autobiographical play, ends with a line which was uttered to me by my mother in the midst of a bitter political quarrel. 'If you don't care,' she said, 'you'll die.' I don't think I would have recognised the resonance of such a line had I not encountered Arthur's play *Death of a Salesman* containing near the end one of its most memorable lines: 'Attention must be paid.' When my mother said 'If you don't care, you'll die' I knew at once that was the last line of a play because I'd heard something similar in another playwright's play: 'Attention must be paid.'

My sensibilities had been sharpened. I had been prepared, by Arthur's play, to receive and understand my own experience, and my play went on to echo his existing masterpiece. And I don't think I could have written, over twenty years later, a play called *Caritas*, set in the fourteenth century, had I not known *The Crucible*. In fact, *The Crucible* remained with me up to my latest play, *Denial*, about the frenzy surrounding the false memory syndrome.

I only refer to my plays in order to explain my debt to Arthur and I only talk about *my* debt because it is an example which, when multiplied by all the writers he touched and triggered into confidence, shows the extent to which his influence pervaded the second half of this century.

Works of art are like people. There are those you meet and say to yourself, I don't believe them. Intelligent, yes. Achievers, yes. Perhaps good husbands, wives, parents but – something emanates from them, their personality; they're contrived, put together for effect and, you say to yourself, I just don't believe them. Others you warm to at once. There's nothing calculated about them. Their pain, their joy, their advice, their whole being vibrates with a front-line honesty. So it is with works of art, or works that aspire to be art – some you believe, some you don't. Some you come away from disbelieving, some you come away from feeling you've encountered the real thing. That's what I find in Miller as a person and a writer, and what my daughter, a graduate in drama, found. In her words, 'He's timeless . . . full of heart . . . no punches pulled . . . handles reality without being gratuitous . . . and his images and energy stay with me twenty years later.'

But perhaps the most important lesson he handed on to me was that no writer should consider material to be fit for drama unless that material is more than itself. I confront much that suggests it is the stuff of drama but I don't handle it because of this lesson

Arthur's plays taught me: the material isn't more than itself, it doesn't resonate, the material is only about *itself.*

As one of this old country's old dramatists, I can say that in Arthur Miller we do not honour mere fame. He was and is a man who touched lives across frontiers and cultures. 'Attention must be paid,' said Willy Loman's wife. Honour must be paid, too, and I am proud to be part of this honour being paid to a playwright the world has claimed as its own.

Timothy West

Actor: Death of a Salesman, Theatr Clwyd, 1993 and BBC Radio; The Price, BBC Radio, 1988

In 1993 I played Willy Loman in Janet Suzman's production of *Death of a Salesman* for Theatr Clwyd, which went on to do a tour of the UK. I also performed it in a later radio production. My very first chance, though, to appear in a play of Miller's hadn't occurred until I was fifty-four, when I was rather strangely cast as Gregory Solomon, the ancient Jewish furniture dealer in *The Price*, for BBC Radio, an award-winning production which starred Richard Dreyfuss and Amy Irving.

Shortly afterwards the Arthur Miller Centre at the University of East Anglia presented a celebration of the dramatist's work, and I joined a whole host of British actors for an unforgettable performance that he attended at the Theatre Royal, Norwich.

I had met the great man earlier, when he and Inge came to England in 1985 to be involved in the final rehearsals of *The Archbishop's Ceiling* for the Bristol Old Vic Company, with which I was then involved. While they were in Bristol, a city both the Millers seemed to like, Arthur regaled Paul Unwin (the BOV Artistic Director) and me with stories of his early days around the New York theatre. Once, apparently, when desperately short of cash, he had procured a tiny part in a Broadway thriller about a smuggling outfit run by the captain of (surprisingly) a Staten Island ferry. In his single scene, Arthur was supposed to be the Customs Inspector and his task was to climb aboard the ferry at dusk, carrying a revolver, rap on the door of the Captain's cabin and thrust it to open to surprise him and his cronies in the act of hatching a further dastardly plot. Arthur duly had to announce himself, arrest them, line them all up against the wall and that was more or less that. On the first night Arthur, hugely tall in very new, very squeaky yellow oilskins and sou'wester, climbed, jittering with nerves, over the ship's rail, and made his way to the cabin. He hit the door hard with the butt of his revolver, which immediately fell apart into about eight separate components. Arthur knelt on the deck in a bemused attempt to reassemble the pieces, during which nothing at all happened on stage for a full minute.

Finally the impatient Captain pulled open the door to see the mortified yellow figure still trying to stick bits of revolver together and apparently incapable of speech. 'Are you the Customs Inspector?' he rasped. His intended Nemesis looked up in miserable acquiescence from his kneeling position and nodded.

The Captain sighed. 'Are we under arrest?' he asked. Another nod.

'So you want we should all line up against the wall?' he suggested finally. Another, vigorous, nod.

Curtain.

Arthur was replaced for the second performance and maintains he never set foot on stage as an actor ever again. [Ed.: He later claimed this incident occurred while he was at college. Either way, it was not quite his last performance. He had a walk-on part in Elia Kazan's film *Boomerang* and, many decades later, a film based on his novella *Homely Girl*.]

A little while after *The Archbishop's Ceiling*, Arthur was over in London for a few days, and Paul and I arranged to take him out to dinner in Covent Garden. We picked him up at his hotel, the Savoy, and he came downstairs wearing a very beautiful open-necked woollen shirt. I suggested a drink in the hotel lounge before we went out to the restaurant, but we were quickly intercepted by the head waiter, barring our way into the Lounge and informing us firmly that guests could not be admitted without a tie.

I was incensed about this, and was about to remonstrate with the man, when I felt a strong hand on my arm. 'Well, let's go and eat,' said Arthur cheerfully. When we got outside, he let go my arm and said, 'I know what you were going to say. You were going to say, "Do you know who this is?" weren't you?'

I admitted shamefacedly that this was the case.

'Yes,' continued Arthur, 'and then *he* would have said, "I don't care if it's Tennessee Williams, he's not coming in here without a necktie."'

David Westhead

Actor: All My Sons, Young Vic Theatre, 1992

In 1995 I was asked to participate in an event at the National Theatre celebrating Arthur Miller's eightieth birthday. The idea was that we would perform scenes from Arthur's plays to complement an informal question-and-answer session being mounted on the Olivier stage. It was quite simply the best and worst of invitations rolled into one. Fantastic – you would be one of the privileged few allowed to listen to Arthur talk about his life's work and watch some terrific actors perform excerpts from a dozen or so of his greatest plays. Slightly more perturbing was the fact that at the same time you'd be undergoing total nervous meltdown, as you prepared to perform a scene from a play you hadn't looked at for four years in front of a thousand members of the public and the great man himself.

As if just being a part of such a memorable evening were not enough, we were all offered a major incentive. The event was scheduled for a Sunday, so Arthur himself would rehearse with us on the Saturday. Imagine it, the great Arthur Miller would be in the same room as us mere mortals. He would watch intently and add his ample two-pen'orth as we scrabbled to re-create scenes from plays we had last performed several years previously.

By six o'clock on the Saturday we had witnessed a wonderful array of tightly rehearsed vignettes performed deftly by fine actors. We were all secretly pleased that the mists of time had not totally befuddled our memories of Arthur's great works. And we sat back to listen to the maestro sum up his feelings on the eve of the celebrations.

'What amazes me more than anything . . .' he began and we expectantly awaited the self-effacing gratitude that customarily accompanies such events. 'What amazes me . . .' Breath duly bated, we hung on his every word, wondering how the master would

massage our fragile egos. 'What amazes me . . . is how you all gave
up your weekend to put this on for me . . . is how British actors can
capture the quintessence of post-war America . . . is how such an
array of great talent has thought my work worthy of their
attention . . .'

Not a bit of it.

'What amazes me . . .' he gazed intently around the room, his
eagle eyes focusing on each of us in turn. 'What amazes me . . . is
how I thought it all up!'

Peter Whelan

Writer

I remember the brilliant Sunday sunshine of fifty years ago filtering
in through the dust motes of the Royal Court Theatre. The crowd
shouldering its way into the old red plush auditorium was there for
a unique event and it was a full house. It had been well trailed in the
press and the atmosphere was one of impatient excitement . . . as it
should have been. Wasn't *the* playwright from America, husband of
Marilyn Monroe, about to set foot, live, on this stage? George
Devine, who was then bringing new vitality to the Court, had
persuaded Arthur Miller to appear on a discussion panel to tackle
the subject: 'The Crisis in British Theatre'. And if that title seems a
touch dramatic now, it certainly reflected the anxieties of Devine,
who had started a theatre company for the production of new work
at a time when new work of any real substance simply didn't seem to
exist.

It was 1956. The British theatre was on the cusp of change . . .
though few believed it yet . . . and Arthur was to add his influence
to that transformation. I was twenty-four and still pretty much a
covert writer, searching for a direction. As the early fifties ticked by,
I had lapsed into feeling I didn't somehow fully connect with the
political desert of my own country's theatre. On the other hand I
wasn't drawn to the verbal pyrotechnics of Fry or the spiritual
searchings of Eliot. For me there was a brief, vibrant affair with the
French . . . Jean Anouilh chiefly . . . but then, more and more, I
turned to the Americans . . . or what I'd heard about them. This

culminated for me in the shock and awe of seeing Devine's production of *The Crucible* in the spring of 1955. Over and above the mesmerising enjoyment came a feeling of uplift. For me, contemporary, grown-up theatre had arrived.

Until then I'd only really read about Arthur Miller, never seen his work on stage, so mine was a delayed reaction. But in a year when work by John Osborne, Brecht and Beckett were all to descend on London for the first time, why did I respond especially to Miller? I suppose the answer is that, setting aside whatever I felt about the others, his was a language I might try to learn and, in some measure, use. The others spoke with tongues of certainty . . . but Miller's was the level, honest, searching tone of a man who had room for doubt.

But back to that Sloane Square Sunday. The discussion panel was ushered on stage by critic-chairman Ken Tynan. Colin Wilson, the rough-sleeping, besweatered author of *The Outsider*, was there; so was John Whiting, lone example of the British new wave in theatre writing (Osborne's *Look Back* had not long since opened). And there was Arthur Miller.

There was a moment to be savoured as the house lights were lowered to begin proceedings. Some had already noticed that the place was packed, except for one vacant end seat on the front row of the stalls. They had begun to guess who it might be reserved for. And yes . . . as the auditorium dimmed, an iconic female figure moved swiftly in from the pass door, trying to make an unobtrusive entrance . . . but not so unobtrusive that the shimmering, silver-white sequined dress she was wearing didn't manage to catch every last scintilla of the fading light. The audience rose like thunder to try and get a better view. The man in front of me almost knocked himself out on his own knee in the act of springing upright.

As Arthur Miller says in *Timebends*, he hadn't expected most of the post-discussion questions to be directed at him. Obviously many others in that audience shared my feeling that America was where the breakthrough had happened.

One question from the audience I still recall: 'Can the British theatre ever find the social awareness and political content that American theatre has?'

Arthur answered, 'Why not? You have the same problems we have.'

It must be hard for today's generation to understand how buoyed up I was by this straightforward, on-the-nail reply. Miller was quietly proclaiming the necessary connection between everyday politics and drama, in any context at any time . . . which must seem most unsurprising now, but not in the stifled, self-censored (and *actually* censored) British theatre of that era.

Brecht's work also proclaimed the same message and his political epic theatre made a big impact on me . . . but it came weighed down with theory, whereas Miller offered a more organic theatre, where the concerns and the characters were intertwined in the same tree of life, without slogans or banners.

So I date my bonding with the Miller spirit to that Sunday at the Royal Court. Yet the situation he faced in the States was very different from the task of British writers. We had not long since experienced the setting up of a social democracy and there was no such mitigation of capitalism across the pond. It has been heartening in the half-century following to see how the mammoth exploitative market-forces economy of the States was so wisely and humanely opposed by Miller, both in his person and his work. Even when America tried to forget him they knew he was there.

Gene Wilder

*Actor: **Death of a Salesman**, four separate productions over fourteen years*

When I was sixteen years old I saw *Death of a Salesman* for the first time; the Broadway production, with Lee J. Cobb and Mildred Dunnock. When I flew back to Milwaukee I fell asleep and dreamed that I would meet Arthur Miller one day and that he would give me a gold watch.

While in high school I made a one-hour adaptation of *Salesman* and played the part of Willy Loman, appearing in churches and women's clubs. At the University of Iowa I played Biff, and also John Proctor in *The Crucible*. In Summer Stock I played Willy's boss, Howard. In 1964 I played the part of Bernard in the CBS television special, starring Lee J. Cobb and Mildred Dunnock. The great change that came over me when I saw that first production of *Salesman* on Broadway was that I put all thoughts of being a comedian out of my mind and my heart; from that time on I wanted to be an actor; perhaps a comic actor, but a real, Stanislavsky actor.

While I was filming *The Producers* Arthur Miller came to visit the set and say hello to Mel Brooks. I knew that Arthur wouldn't know me from Adam so I didn't try to break into their conversation. I saw him years later at the Round About Theatre's production of *All My Sons*, and that evening was the first time he and I had a conversation of our own; very short, but a conversation.

When my wife and I were celebrating a birthday at a beautiful inn near Arthur's home in northern Connecticut, we visited our friends Tim Cole and Joyce Chopra, who were very good friends with Arthur. We walked a half-mile to Arthur's house and all had tea together. I was still too childishly shy, or too in awe, to tell him what effect his plays had had on my life. A few years later Tom Cole interviewed Arthur on stage in a large high-school auditorium in Westport, Connecticut. My wife and I were invited. After Tom and Arthur came on to the stage and sat down, Tom started off the evening by introducing me to the packed house and then asked if I would tell Arthur and the audience how *Death of a Salesman* had changed my life. (Tom knew the story.) It was then that I finally revealed to Arthur how much his plays had meant to me. After the interview was over we all had dinner together. Arthur and I sat next to each other and talked for an hour. As we talked, I realised that I was receiving the gold watch that I had dreamed he would give me one day.

Arthur Miller Remembering

An edited version of *Miller's Tales*, BBC Radio 4, first broadcast in 1995 and recorded on the back porch of his Roxbury home

BIGSBY   You were born in Harlem, in 1915. What sort of place was that to grow up in?

MILLER   Harlem was the most well-planned part of New York City. The boulevards are like Paris. They are very wide. They do not wind around. It is the highest point of the island, so that we got a terrific view of most of the island from our home. It is where people went on vacation, back in the nineteenth century. There were German beer gardens all over the place. In fact, my father remembered that there had been a German beer garden on the area where our apartment house was standing, and it faced Central Park, which was about the most beautiful part of the island. It was just beautiful. There were a lot of trees along the boulevard – big, enormous elms and maples. If you look sharp as you go through Harlem, you will see some of the best façades of buildings in our city. A lot of them are modelled by French architects, I think. They look like buildings along the better streets of Paris.

BIGSBY   And was this partly an Italian neighbourhood, then?

MILLER   It was originally German-Irish. Then the Italians and the Jews moved in and then the blacks and the Spanish, in the thirties, forties. When I was growing up it was glorious as a neighbourhood. I could tell when I was late for school because they raised the flag on the grammar school at about seven o'clock in the morning and I had to be there at eight. I could look out the back window and see what time it was. I had the same school principal that my mother did. It was a very neighbourly place.

BIGSBY   Later on you were going to move out to Brooklyn. What sort of a place was that?

MILLER   I loved Brooklyn better, because I had cousins there whom I idolised. They were terrific athletes, and they were poorer than we were. I liked that, too, because their parents bought them these awful cheap shoes, which I thought were just terrific. They were punctured with all kinds of designs in the front; they cost two dollars a pair. My shoes were eight dollars, miserable high-class-looking shoes. There was space there. Brooklyn then had empty lots so that you could play football, or baseball. You could get lost. There were areas that still had not been cut up into streets; there were woods, and I loved that. Central Park was a tame reproduction of that, a substitute for it, but Harlem was marvellous.

BIGSBY Your description of Brooklyn sounds a bit like the opening of *Death of a Salesman*, where Willy remembers what the place was like before suburbia grew up.

MILLER Yes, it was just wonderful. Every twenty blocks or so there would be a grocery store, and people bought food in large quantities, because you didn't just jump into a car and go shopping then. They bought twenty-five-pound bags of potatoes and ten cabbages, and so on; and, when I was growing up, a lot of Italian women had vegetable gardens. They raised a lot of tomatoes, cucumbers, lettuce. Brooklyn was a countrified suburb of the city at that moment. But basically it was quite lower-middle class, though there were a lot of working-class people and I guess there were poor people. They weren't poor in the way that people are poor now, though I think of the poor now as being unemployed or unemployable. They are usually on one or another stimulant. There were drunks around then, but most people were straight. They were just looking for work. Of course, it all changed in the thirties, with the Great Crash. That changed everything.

BIGSBY You were both a child and a grandchild of immigrants. In what way do you think that has influenced your life and your work?

MILLER Well, it was an immense influence. You see, the idea then was to disappear into the general American population. The first thing the immigrant groups did, especially the Jews, was to set up schools to teach English, to speak it properly, and to write it properly, and to learn about a couple of important philosophers. I'm smiling because it seems like a hundred and fifty years ago! But that is what they were after. They were led by a lot of Socialist and revolutionary intellectuals who thought that, by educating the working class, they were going to change the world. They did. They changed the world into the middle class! But they weren't looking for that. The original impulse of the immigrant was to become educated and to become an American, not, as is the fashion now, to emphasise the ethnicity of everybody, to show how different people are. There is something to be said for both, because my parents' generation were deformed by having, in effect, to conceal themselves. They tried to eliminate any accent from their speech. There was something called elocution taught in grammar school. You were taught how to speak regular English, because they were speaking Italian English, Russian English, Polish English, God knows what. However, it made for a political cohesiveness, so that in the space of twenty-five years you had leaders of the state who were Irishmen. The Irish immediately went into politics and the Police Department. So you were kept in order by the Irish and the laws were written by them, mostly. Of course, the Jews were lawyers, who were subverting the Irish, trying to get around the laws that the Irish had made. Everybody was in this game, but they were doing it as Americans.

BIGSBY   I wonder if there isn't another sense, though, in which that immigrant background is important. You always seem to me to have been very aware – acutely aware – of the promises that America makes to itself and to those who are coming into the society. In a way your father was the epitome of the American dream. He came in with nothing and then built a large company.

MILLER   I was just talking to somebody the other day about the movie business being invented by the Jews, Russian Jews especially. I have often said that my father reminded me of people like Harry Warner (the Warner Brothers chief) and Louis Meyer. They had the same taste and, by some process which I confess I don't understand, their taste became the American taste. They knew what the average male was interested in. They romanticised the country and that is what the United States population wanted. These guys really believed that you could magically transform yourself into anything you could imagine. If you could imagine it, you could do it. To imagine it was practically to do it! It is quite amazing. I met Harry Warner once, just for one evening. He reminded me of my father in so many ways: the sense of humour, the irony, and the naïveté. They really believed they were doing good when they made a picture about some Red Cross nurse. You see, it was going to be good for the country. That naïveté, of course, is long since buried, under the Second

World War, I guess, and the Holocaust and the rest of our contemporary history. But that is what built the country. One time I had a talk with George Cukor, the director, and he said something, which I heard again only in Communist China thirty-five years later: 'You don't go to the movies to see reality. If you want to see reality, you walk in the street. If we are gonna to ask you to pay money, you want to see something that is *not* real.'

BIGSBY   Your father nearly ended up in Hollywood, didn't he?

MILLER   He came close to ending up in Hollywood, because William Fox, who was in the garment industry, was trying to arrange money to make films in Hollywood; but nobody trusted him, because he was a quite ingenious operator in the clothing industry. He asked my father, who could easily have done it, for fifty thousand dollars, which would have given him a big interest in the Fox Film Corporation. My father considered it but, as he told me once, 'I might have given it to him if they were making films in New York, but to give Bill Fox fifty thousand dollars and have him disappear into California . . .!' was beyond his powers of credulity, so he didn't do it.

BIGSBY   You must have had a curious relationship with your father, because he was the head of a very big company manufacturing women's coats and employed large numbers of people, but he was largely functionally illiterate.

MILLER   That's right.

BIGSBY   Your mother, on the other hand, used to hire students to talk to her about literature. You must have been drawn much more towards your mother than your father.

MILLER   I was drawn to her culturally. You couldn't talk to my father about anything that had to do with a book. However, he loved the theatre and he loved actors. To him the most thrilling thing that could happen to you was to meet a live actor and talk to him, which he was rarely able to do. My mother read books, played the piano quite well and sang, so that between them there could be no cultural discussion excepting about a movie or the theatre. He loved to go to the theatre and they went together. He had a terrific eye for actors. He knew a phoney actor from a good one, just instinctively, and he had no patience with the bad ones. There were two kinds of actors: good actors and 'dry' actors. He hated Monty Woolley, because Monty Woolley spoke some kind of English that he couldn't understand. But he loved good actors

230

and a good actor was somebody who, to quote him, 'put it over'. Their ideal person was Al Jolson. Al Jolson minced no words; he stood up there and belted out those songs. Or Ethel Merman. They were not about to tolerate people who muttered and implied things. They wanted to be told what the hell was going on. There was a vigour in that, though.

BIGSBY Presumably he wanted you to go into the family business?

MILLER Oh, yes. At that time, before the Crash, he had a damn good business, and probably in the normal course I would have spent some time there, simply for want of anything else to do. But I couldn't have stayed. Adding, multiplying and dividing is not my forte, and that is basically what they were doing there. They were turning over money.

BIGSBY For a while you had your grandfather living in the house. Did that mean that there was another language being spoken?

MILLER Yes. My grandfather's generation regarded German, the language and the culture, as the highest reach of human culture. Everything else was really nothing compared to German culture. This was an affliction of the Jews for ever. It is ironical to say this but the one country in Europe where they could hope to live peacefully, without anti-Semitism, was Germany. Germany had less anti-Semitism than Russia, than Poland, than England, than any place. Maybe Italy was better. The Spanish were terrible. So he regarded Germans, and the German language, as really the highest accomplishment. Consequently, he spoke a kind of Yiddish, a medieval German with other languages collected into it. If you are living in Germany you speak German Yiddish. If you are living in America or in England you speak in English Yiddish. They just adapt words. Suddenly the word 'refrigerator' is in the sentence, or 'gentleman', or whatever. He spoke that kind of a language, but he was always trying to improve his English, which is interesting. Even he. The idea was to become a citizen of the country in which you lived, not to become some excrescence from it, and that was a very strong thing.

BIGSBY You were only three when the war came to an end, but were there any echoes of that war?

MILLER There were. My uncle (my mother's brother) was in the war as a driver of an ammunition wagon, driving shells up to the front with a couple of mules, which was probably the most dangerous work he could find. The poor guy got gassed on top of

231

everything and ultimately died of that. But I idealised the war, as the country did. My uncle brought back a German helmet – God knows where he got that from – and I used to walk around wearing that when I was six years old. Being a soldier was the greatest thing you could do; in fact, until I was about twelve or thirteen, I wanted to go to West Point and become a soldier myself. It was a strong thing, a very strong image, of being an officer in the army. It all got destroyed in the thirties. Everything got turned upside-down by the Depression, by the Crash. We entered the modern age then. That is when we became cynical. But I was absolutely a regular citizen until that happened.

BIGSBY   Did you have any sense, in the twenties, of the image we have of that decade now, which I suppose is F. Scott Fitzgerald's great gaudy spree? You have talked elsewhere about it being an unreal decade.

MILLER   We did. I did. My mother cut her hair and that was a great event. She, like most of the women, wore her hair long and wound it up on top of her head. Some time in the twenties she had it bobbed, which was revolutionary. It was a real shocker! It was like an amputation. She looked great. She wore a cloche hat, beaded dress and looked real slick. She looked like a real swinger! The women changed; the men didn't, as far as I could see. The men wore the same drab costumes they had ever worn, but the women! The skirts went up high and tops went down. People were bare-armed, where before their clothes were quite Victorian, and it all happened, it seemed to me, in a year. Also people started smoking. One noticed that. They had smoked before – men smoked cigars after dinner – but you *never* saw anybody smoking in the street, for example. I think it was regarded as bad form, especially for a woman. A woman smoking in the street would have been regarded as – really – a prostitute. It wasn't done. And suddenly it *was* done. Also there were suddenly these 'crooners'. Up to then, a man singing was an Irish tenor. He sang at the top of his lungs and put it over. Suddenly you had Rudy Vallee moaning into the microphone, and I can tell you that the women went nuts! Really, all these married hausfraus. I'd forgotten how it was. It was late in the afternoon that he came on, but I remember it clearly. They would all flock into one house, eight or ten of them, and sit there facing this radio, just enthralled by this guy!

BIGSBY   Is this why we very nearly had Arthur Miller – crooner?

MILLER   I wanted to be a crooner, sure. I wanted to be anything
that was going! I had a radio programme, in fact, that I sang on
two or three times. I had a good tenor voice and sang all the latest
hits. I had a blind pianist who had a lot of dandruff, and he said,
'You are the young Al Jolson!' But it got so boring that I stopped
doing it after about three times.

BIGSBY   It was one of those decades that genuinely ended with a
punctuation note: 1929 and the Crash.

MILLER   Oh, yes, it was rather sudden but I think probably it took
eight months, maybe a year, before people felt the full effect.
They could not believe that this was what it was. You see, there
had been a recession, a mini-crash, in 1921, I think it was. The
stock market had gone down suddenly; there was a lot of
unemployment for about a year. But there had been this kind of a
thing, periodically, for ever, certainly since the Civil War in the
1860s. There would be growth and then there would be collapse
for a little while, and they thought that this was another one of
those occasions, so that what they would do would be to sell off
some shares, let's say, to get some cash.

My father made the great discovery, made by better men than
he, that you could make more money on the stock market than
you could make manufacturing whatever you were
manufacturing. You could make eighty, ninety per cent on your
money in six months. You could not do that in a legitimate
business, it was impossible, unless you were mining gold. So
more and more of the capital of these businesses went into the
stock market, leaving them less and less operating capital. But
they were all relying on the ever-rising stock market. So
whenever they needed the cash, they would sell some stock. They
would sell it at a much higher price than they had bought it for,
so everybody was very happy, until suddenly they needed cash.
They would have to sell stock at a lower price than they had
bought it for, so they took a distinct loss. And then, pretty soon,
they needed more cash, because the market was drying up.

People were losing their jobs, the amount of purchasing going
on was less and less and, within a year or so, a lot of businesses
simply folded up. Some didn't, because there were a certain
number of people who were so big that they could weather this,
or, in a few cases, very few, they were sceptical of the stock

233

market anyway. So, within a year or so, they had to really change their lives. It was humiliating. My family had to get out of that nice apartment and move to Brooklyn where it was cheaper to live. They moved into a very nice house in Brooklyn which they rented, and then found another one which was even smaller, which they could buy for, oh, I don't know, probably forty-five hundred, five thousand dollars for a six-room house.

BIGSBY   Did the company keep going?

MILLER   No. It collapsed finally, just went bankrupt.

BIGSBY   There are a couple of your plays at least, *After the Fall* and *The American Clock*, in which a husband-and-wife relationship is almost broken by the Depression – accusations exchanged – does this come out of your family background?

MILLER   My mother was smart enough to understand that it was not his doing; but the frustration was so great that she could not help blaming him anyway. She blamed him and she pitied him at the same time. It is one thing when everything is going great, and both people are feeling absolutely secure. That is one relationship. But when suddenly they do not know from one week to the next where the money is going to come from, the recrimination begins and a loss of respect, loss of mutual toleration. It went up and down the street, and there were a lot of suicides. I remember three on that little block. These people were not fallen giants of industry. They were just ordinary middle-class people and they could not cope. The impact of that disaster was incalculable.

When I was doing *The American Clock* I did some research, just to remind myself of what it was like. So I went back through the New York Public Library and got out some issues of the *New York Times* for those weeks and months. In one article, a news story on the front page, a couple of reporters had gone out and interviewed people; they estimated that about a hundred and fifty thousand people in New York City who, a year before, had had good jobs, now were not only unemployed (there were many more unemployed than that), but considered they would never work again because of the psychological trauma that was the impact of the Depression. See, it was not just the money. This is what is important about it. It was the illusion. These people were profoundly believers in the whole American dream and, when that stopped working, the day the money stopped, their identity was gone. They did not know who the hell they were.

BIGSBY That must have created a curious tension between the generations because, if you are in a family, the father is in a position of some authority and confidence.

MILLER Sure.

BIGSBY All that must have gone.

MILLER The cleavage was sudden and terrific between the generations. At one point – I was, let's say, fourteen, fifteen years of age – I thought nobody, none of us, would ever go to a synagogue as adults, or Christians would never go to a church again. I wondered what would happen to these buildings, because Brooklyn was full of churches and synagogues. It was just a passing fantasy, as though the whole thing was over. I did not know that some of my friends would end up being on the managing boards of synagogues, and that they would be more devout than ever! But at that time it seemed the end of it. That was a real cultural shift, as one imagined it. Much less changed than met the eye, in the long run.

BIGSBY In *The American Clock* the family, which is based very obviously and squarely on your own, has starving people come to the door. Was that part of your life?

MILLER Oh, yes. I still, to this day, do not understand it, but we had a house which was in a small neighbourhood like one in any city – London or Toronto, New York or Pittsburgh. There was one little row-house after another, and you would see these guys come around the corner, walk down the street and turn into our house. And I often looked around to see if there was a mark someplace! My mother was a sucker. She would give them whatever was going on the stove, a bowl of soup or a piece of bread with butter, whatever. They were genuine victims, these guys. They came from all over the United States. First they would look for work. There wasn't any. There was a great joke in the old days. There are two cars. One is heading east, the other is heading west. They meet in Arizona and stop, and the occupant in each one yells at the other, 'Go back! Go back!' Everybody thought it had to be better in California, and a lot of them in California thought it had to be better in New York. There was a mass migration going on, on the buses, on the roads, of people dreaming. That is where the dream came back. I don't think that would happen in another country. They couldn't give up the

235

dream. The dream was 'elsewhere'. Elsewhere had to be better! And, believe me, it was in the minds of thousands of people.

BIGSBY Do you think America has ever really got over the Depression?

MILLER I don't think it ever got over the Depression because I don't think there is any real basic confidence in the economy. I think there is a certain lingering expectation somewhere in the back of the brain that the whole thing can sink without a trace at a moment's notice. A few years ago I was in a restaurant where I went for many years. I knew the guys there, and occasionally I would eat there if I were in the city alone. On this particular occasion I noticed the prices of what I was ordering (it was a good Italian restaurant) and for the first time I realised how expensive everything had gotten. When Pepe, the waiter, came for my order, I said, 'When the hell did the prices go up like this?' He said, 'Oh, they went up about three years ago' (this was about four–five years ago), and I said, 'Jesus! A plate of spaghetti, nine dollars?' He says, 'Yeah!' and I looked around in the restaurant. They were perfectly ordinary people. This was not an elegant restaurant; the food was damn good but there were accountant-clerks and so on. I thought, how in hell do these people afford this, because it cost me about twenty-three dollars to have dinner, alone. I had one little glass of wine. I said, 'How do they afford all this, Pepe?' He said, 'I'll tell you something. Years ago on our menu we had one or two fairly expensive dishes, and those you hardly sold. Now they do not look at the prices. It does not matter what everything costs, they order it!' I said, 'Well, how do you figure that?' He says, 'They feel that the ship is sinking, so they might as well have a good meal!' That was an expression not of confidence, but of the opposite.

BIGSBY That is a common thread in almost all of your plays, the sense that all this could go away and that, therefore, what is important is to get down to some essential which is to do with the relationships between people, individuals.

MILLER I think whatever lasting qualities the plays have is because of that. It is because everything else is ephemeral. It is going to blow away, excepting what a person is, and what a relationship really is, which, of course, is almost impossible to define, but you can work at it. Somewhere along the line, all the visible world became unimportant, because it could vanish. It was not there for very long. Maybe that is why I live among trees, which also have their seasons!

BIGSBY   But that conviction might have led you in another direction, which is towards religion.

MILLER   It did, and it does. I think about religion a lot, but I do not make much of it, because I usually detest organised religion. It just seems to me that it is always so close to fraud that I cannot bear it for the most part.

BIGSBY   How Jewish was your own upbringing?

MILLER   My grandfather would have described himself as orthodox. As a child I had a mystical feeling about religion. Most children do, I guess, and I kept it. I have never lost it, really. But I never could arrive at where I could stand with other people in a congregation and bow my head to some deity. It just seemed embarrassing. I have felt wonder about life and about nature especially, but I can't do it in chorus! I am in the early stages of a religious evolution, I suppose.

BIGSBY   Do you remember your Bar Mitzvah speech?

MILLER   No, but I probably did a very good one, because my father said, 'Boy, you put it over!' He was quite sceptical about religious things, principally because the beggars who came to the door very often were from religious organisations, both Christian and Jewish. My father believed that people ought to earn a living – that is all he was ever doing in his life – and should not go around begging from other people who did earn a living, especially when they leaned on their religious identity as a reason for you to give them money. Something in him rebelled. But, at the same time, he was dutiful and orthodox, and he regarded the whole thing with respect. He never could keep his place in the prayer book, however. His mind kept wandering and he would keep asking me where it was, as if I would know.

BIGSBY   You went to university in 1934 but, in order to get there, you had to raise five hundred dollars, which meant that you did a number of menial jobs. Did you learn anything from that?

MILLER   I was happy doing those jobs. They were jobs requiring some skills. Maybe you had to drive a truck, so you had to know how to do that (and people did not drive that much in those days). I didn't have a driver's licence, but I was driving anyway, because I loved to drive; and I always believed in my luck, that I wouldn't get caught. I worked in an auto–parts business and various other things. I was a waiter. I delivered bread at four in the morning on a bicycle. The thing was, by the time I got to the university I was already a year or two older than most of the kids and the teachers immediately recognised, when we started to write little pieces for the English class, that I had something to write about, because I had met all different kinds of people and I knew what the score was. So I was quite proud of the fact that I was not one of these rosy-cheeked kids who didn't know anything. It gave me a certain amount of confidence, having been forced to do that, and I am very sympathetic to young people who do not want to rush off to school. There is another kind of school, especially in a city like New York or London, a lot of things you can pick up.

BIGSBY   How radical was the University of Michigan?

MILLER   They used to say it was the most radical university in the country. Where somebody teaching birth control at, say, Columbia University (which was the great university of New York) was fired for so doing, they would end up at the University of Michigan! It is weird. I haven't thought about this in years. There was another man who was preaching the use of condoms to avoid unwanted pregnancies. He was thrown out of some place in North Carolina and ended up at the University of Michigan. It was a collecting point for all these so-called radicals. They weren't particularly political radicals. I am talking about the twenties now; this antedates the Depression. By the time of the Depression I was of the generation that took over the school newspaper, the *Michigan Daily*. It had a quite large circulation for a college newspaper, and it had its own building, its own printing presses and its own staff of printers. It was put out like a small-town newspaper. However, it was in the hands of the fraternity guys. They were the upper class of the school and did nothing but sit around and drink. I was of that generation that came in in 1934, who were already Depression kids. The other guys were kids out of the twenties, the Jazz Age bums, as we called them, so we took over the paper and turned it into a real radical newspaper. We had the Associated Press, we had Reuters, we had all kinds of news agencies and became the newspaper for that whole area, not just the school. The thing was that the whole orientation of the paper was very liberal and nobody would think of having breakfast without finding out what was in the *Daily*.

BIGSBY   How radical is radical? Do you mean liberal or Marxist?
MILLER   I wouldn't call it Marxist. They were concerned with
issues of the New Deal. The New Deal was fighting one court
case after another to try to push through the social legislation that
was being obstructed by the Supreme Court, which was basically
Republican and right-wing. So there was one case after another
where they were calling something unconstitutional, because it
had never been done before. I was running around all over the
campus interviewing historians, economists, sociologists,
psychologists, about their views of this legislation, as though, if
the *Michigan Daily* published something, we could force it
through the Supreme Court. I think the Peace Movement was
invented there, the whole idea that we were not going to have
World War Two. Little did I know! We were basically trying to
fight the last war, as usual, that is, to stay out of the last war. We
were agitating about the Spanish Civil War. That was a big thing.
I knew five students who went. One was killed, the others
returned. One was badly wounded. I was tempted to go myself,
but I probably did not have the courage to do it, or maybe the
conviction, finally.
BIGSBY   What got through to you?
MILLER   It was Fascism. You see, by this time – 1934, 1935, 1936
– Hitlerism especially (Mussolini was rather a joke) was the
replication of everything we were fighting against in Michigan.
Michigan was the heartland of the new trade union movement.
We were forty miles from Detroit, where the big war was going
on. It was literally a war, with guns shooting off. Mr Ford, Henry
Ford, had gas piped into his sprinkler system, so if there was ever
a sit-down strike he would turn on the gas. It was murder. He had
real, Fascist-type storm troops running that factory. In fact,
Harry Bennett, who was his chief operator for the company
police, literally took over the factory from that decrepit brain of
Henry Ford Senior and came very close to destroying the Ford
Motor Company altogether as a going business. And they were
killing people. They killed a lot of workers. They beat their brains
in. So the workers started to agitate for a union.
BIGSBY   So Spain wasn't a remote foreign policy issue, then.
MILLER   Spain was in Detroit. We knew what that was about.
Spain was a battle of very rich people against very poor people.
That is the way we saw it and we could see it on the streets of

239

Detroit. I covered the first sit-down strike for the *Michigan Daily*.
I went up to Flint, Michigan, which was a good distance from
Ann Arbor. That is when the sit-down strike broke General
Motors. They would not recognise the United Automobile
Workers' Union, no matter what, and it was almost a classical
situation. There was a road: on one side was the company
administration building, and on the other was the factory where
Fisher Body Number two Plant lies, which made the Chevrolet,
Pontiac, Oldsmobile, Cadillac bodies. And there was an overpass
between the two buildings, a covered overpass, a kind of a bridge.
The workers took possession of the factory. They wouldn't leave
and the company tried to get police to come in through that
overpass. There was a major battle. A lot of people were hurt.
They called out the National Guard, which set up machine-guns
in the street, and one morning they shot two guys dead, who were
stupid enough to come out on a parapet to get some air and were
knocked off by these soldiers. So the workers welded three
Chevrolet bodies on their side in the overpass entrance, to block
it. This went on, I can't remember now how long, until they
caved in and recognised the union.

BIGSBY   How deep did that radicalism go in America at large?
Most people, after all, were not joining the Communist Party or
watching Clifford Odets's plays or fighting battles, were they?

MILLER   The country was divided, in my experience. The majority
probably were for Roosevelt, which means they would have been
against General Motors. They identified themselves with the
underdog.

BIGSBY   Would your father have been for Roosevelt?

MILLER   No. My father probably would have thought they were a
lot of troublemakers, because he was always battling the union in
the coat business. But he was a minority. He was a boss and most
people were not bosses, so they did identify with the workers in
those situations. On the other hand, it is important to remember
that there was a large population, larger than ever afterwards,
who were not involved in industrial production. The number of
actual workers in factories was minimal, compared to the rest of
the population: farmers, people in small towns, in small
businesses and the rest of it. So you have a sizeable group of
people who thought that this was un-American for these people
to be fighting such a wonderful company as General Motors.

BIGSBY   But even those who suffered in the Depression seem to have blamed themselves and not the system.

MILLER   That's right. Studs Terkel did a book [*Hard Times*] on the Depression and he interviewed a psychiatrist who said, remembering his life in the thirties, that he thought that the difference between what was happening in psychology in the thirties and in 1975 was just that, that in the thirties people blamed themselves, whereas in 1975 they were going to blame the system. Well, I do not think that happened. I thought it was happening, but I do not think it did. Americans are still loath, by and large, to blame the system. The ones who do are not the Left, but the Right. It is the right wing that has become revolutionary, and it is the liberals and the Left that are trying to conserve the government as a liberal force. The right wing is trying to dismantle the federal government. They have their own agenda and that agenda is also to dismantle, for example, all the environmental laws which prevent industry from dumping its poisons into the rivers, that protect child labour, defend standards of health and distribute food in schools. They want to do away with all that and go back to 1924, or maybe earlier than that. It is odd. It is interesting. Things have completely turned around.

BIGSBY   But you can see why, in the thirties, they would have blamed themselves rather than the system, because the whole point of an immigrant society is that this is the place you came for things to be better. If you start blaming the system you have to start undoing history and the justification for coming to the country in the first place disappears.

MILLER   Right. Also, you have to eliminate hope. If the system is so bad, what the hell is there to hope for? Americans hope, even when it does not work. You keep the hope alive. That is why the movie industry is always so good. It generates some kind of illusion that the sun is coming up tomorrow morning. It is, after all, only a few years ago that we began to make sceptical or negative movies, and those do not sell. The ones that sell are where you generate the idea, again and again, that the country is OK and things are going to get better tomorrow morning.

BIGSBY   William Dean Howells once said that what America wants is a tragedy with a happy ending.

MILLER   That is exactly right!

BIGSBY   That may be one of the problems you have with the American public, that you do not write tragedies with happy endings.

MILLER   That is right. Archibald MacLeish said that America is promises; Robert Frost said, 'I have promises to keep.' The idea of rejecting the evidence in favour of hope is profoundly Whitman. This is what he is about. After all, he lived through the worst war in our history, some people think in any history. The casualties were stupendous; the brutality on both sides was unbelievable. Then he comes out of it, saying 'I sing the song of myself'.

BIGSBY   In the thirties you wrote a series of plays at the University of Michigan, which won awards. Why plays? You had seen hardly any and did not even know how long an act was.

MILLER   Two reasons occur to me. One was that suddenly, when I was growing up in the thirties, the theatre became the cockpit of all literary activity. There was the audience, here were the actors, and you could talk directly to the audience and radicalise everybody. That was one reason. Whereas a book, prose, you dropped it into the well and you heard the thing go 'plunk' in the water, and that was the end of it. You had immediacy in the theatre and we were working against time. Everybody thought that either the Second World War was going to happen, or we were going to have Fascism so, whatever you are going to do, you had better do it quick. So there was that. But the other thing was temperamental. I think I have always thought that playwriting is an oral art. I heard language and could reproduce what I had heard, with variations. So it was a thrill for me to write down what I was hearing, whereas to reduce it to prose was to formalise it, and the blood left it, the pulse left it. With drama you pick up the real language. It was thrilling to write that and I think that is probably why I was more excited about theatre.

   Finally, I cottoned on to two things. One was the Greeks, the other was Ibsen. Here, for the first time, was a structure that was architectural. A play was like a sculpture; you could walk around it. Prose was like a painting: you looked at it, but you could not really get behind it. I am rather a sculptor myself, or I would have been if things had been different, and I like to make things, objects, furniture mainly, and create as I am going along, improvise designs. I never make a drawing. I just get a couple of pieces of wood and start to fiddle around with them until something happens. It's an improvisation, but it is something you can walk around or sit on, or you can hear it if you drop it. A play is a real object, whereas prose has always been more evanescent. I must confess I have read far fewer plays than I have stories and novels. The idea of sitting down and reading a play is a chore, compared to reading well-written prose, or poetry for that matter.

BIGSBY So when you started writing, it was with this sense that you could intervene in the world, you could change the world.

MILLER Oh, definitely. That was what it was for.

BIGSBY Does that remain your conviction?

MILLER I have given up the idea, objectively, that anything I wrote was really going to get somebody elected, changing the world in that sense. However, I do think that, in a very small way, probably historically of no importance, what one writes can change people in the sense that it gives them a new image or revises an image they already have of themselves. My evidence is simply that I have been around a long time, and I have mounds of mail, as well as conversations, indicating (and I must confess I am a little embarrassed when I hear it) that something changed the life of somebody because he saw something he had not known before as a result of seeing a play of mine. I guess that is about as far as it goes. In other words, you will shift the consciousness of a certain number of people, and I do think that that happens.

Whether it is politically significant or not, I doubt. People do not go to the theatre and decide they are going to vote one way or another, or go on a demonstration. It is very rare for a work of art to change things. It happened with Harriet Beecher Stowe's *Uncle Tom's Cabin*, or John Steinbeck's *The Grapes of Wrath*. That was a book that all the congressmen read. It had a quite definite concrete effect on the way agricultural workers were treated, but it takes a particular kind of a crisis, and a particular kind of a writer to address that crisis, for that to happen.

BIGSBY You left university in 1938, at a time when very interesting things were happening in the American theatre. One of your plays was very briefly performed by the Federal Theatre, a remarkable organisation.

MILLER The Federal Theatre was our abortive attempt to create a national theatre. However, it was based on welfare, let's not forget. We had a lot of writers, actors, set designers, folks of talent, all out of work, so the government set up a project that would employ them because otherwise they would have to be paid, anyway, to stay on welfare, so why not get some art out of it? It was a brilliant idea. It was also total chaos, but out of it came the one theatrical invention of that era, namely the Living Newspaper, which was an American invention, a new dramatic form. It was not written by one guy, but by a committee, by a lot of people, as movies are written. They would take a subject, like the electrification of farms, which is quite a subject to write a play about, and they would approach it from various points of view, one of them being the personal. However, the personal one was incidental. They might take a family and show the effects on that family of having electricity in the country, out on the farm somewhere. And then they would trace the conflicts that arose from the government going into the electricity business. Usually they would blame the privately owned utilities companies for trying to block this, which indeed was the case, and you would get a real conflict going. There were songs, music; it was rather Brechtian before Brecht.

BIGSBY   A key thing about that theatre was that, though it only lasted for four or five years, in that time the audiences amounted to the equivalent of a quarter of the population of the United States. You could get in for a few cents. We tend to think of theatre as appealing only to one per cent or two per cent of the population. This was popular theatre throughout the country.

MILLER   Orson Welles did a production of *Doctor Faustus*. He went up to Harlem with it and played in empty stores. Harlem was full of them where people had gone out of business. Some of those stores were quite large, and he played to the black population, or largely black. They charged twenty-five cents. If you did not have the twenty-five cents, they would let you in anyway! It was a smash hit. It was a gigantic thing in Harlem. It could have gone on for two years up there, but only played a matter of weeks. Interestingly, there were very few black people involved in it, because the idea of black actors playing anything but black parts was not accepted. Nobody even thought of it. But still, it was very unusual. Anyway, I was on the Federal Theatre project. They invented a project for playwrights called the Federal Theatre Playwrights Project and I had just gotten out of school in June 1938. In order to get on to the project you had to prove you were impoverished. I, of course, could have lived with my parents, but if you could live with your parents you could not get on welfare. You had to be on welfare and you had to show you were totally desperate. You could not have a place to lay your head, so I had to fake an address. A friend of mine, who had just joined the police force, had a little pad in the middle of Manhattan and I pretended that was where I lived. I got on and I was on for about six months. I wrote the Montezuma play, *The Golden Years*, while I was there. I got twenty-two dollars and seventy-seven cents a week, which was real heavy pay! But you could live on that; I could, anyway. Congress killed the whole thing, finally. We were heading into World War Two, anyway, not officially, but everybody knew something was up, something was in the air, and Congress was becoming increasingly anti-New Deal. They had had it with these liberals. The South was raising its head against the unions and against blacks, and the nativist American reactionaries were gaining strength again, so they shot it down.

BIGSBY   What was the impact on you and the people you knew in 1938 of the Hitler–Stalin pact?

MILLER   It was devastating. The Hitler–Stalin pact was the first of the great moral dilemmas, I would say. You see, Spain was simple. For most people the worst struggle a person would have about Spain was if he was a devout Catholic, because the Church was on the side of Fascism and Franco, and if you took a position against the Church it might trouble your conscience. Otherwise, if you were pro-democratic, you were in favour of the Loyalists. There was no problem that way. But throughout the thirties, the Russians were the flag bearers of anti-Fascism. You certainly did not rely on the British, who apparently had a strong group of reactionaries among the upper classes who were really pro-Hitler, or were certainly tolerant of him, and did not see what all the excitement was about simply because he smashed a few heads here and there. The American State Department was very ambiguous, very pro-British. It was also not known for being at all opposed to Franco or any of the right-wing movements in Europe. They rather loved Mussolini and all the trains running on time, and the rest of it.

The one reliable source of anti-Fascist strength was Russia. Russia was the cat to the dog of Fascism. Suddenly they were in bed together. Well, you can imagine! Life collapsed. Political orientation was impossible. Then the rationalisations began that, after all, the Russians had tried to make a pact with the French and the English against Germany, but they had refused, or they had been piddling around for three years trying to negotiate something but never could, and the Russians decided that they were not going to pull the West's chestnuts out of the fire. Otherwise the Russians really would not be helping them by sending in oil and supplies. Well, that turned out not to be the case, either.

Nobody, and I was among them, could really face the fact that, in one sense, Hitler was a version of Stalin. To say this was immoral. The whole Socialist movement in England was based upon sympathy with the Soviet Union, because there was an antipathy towards the Fascist Right. None of us, I think, understood properly what dictatorship meant. We had a systemic view of it, that it was all based upon economic determinism. We completely wiped out the idea that there were personalities in the world, like Hitler and Stalin, or Franco, who were in themselves so powerful, in terms of generating illusions in the human beings around them, that they could be related, even though their countries, their nationalisms, might have been opposed. It destroyed the systemic idea of Marxism. German Fascism was an expression of the capitalist class in its last throes, as it tried to survive. Socialism was the systemic expression of the working class. How could both of them come together in the same bed?

So it was catastrophic, the whole thing, and I do not think ideology, as such, ever recovered. The charms of ideology really died there, but it took a generation to confront the signs. For the right wing, ideology has never died. It is alive today. They have a systemic view of life. There are such things as Left, liberals, Communists, devils, and they are all together in league. It does not matter whether they are nice fellows or not-nice fellows, they are out to destroy *Us*. They still believe that.

BIGSBY   How did you and your family, a Jewish family, react to the news coming in from Germany in the late 1930s? Was there a conviction that this would just simply blow over?

MILLER   My father was politically nil. He did not know what the hell was going on. My mother read the papers every day; she knew what was happening in a general way. My grandfather had memories of being an adult in Germany, in Austria and in Poland, so he had an idea of what was happening. He was convinced Hitler would last six months. Why? Because the Germans were too intelligent. This oaf, this Austrian border oaf, who could hardly speak correct German, how could he lead that country? It was impossible. His view was shared, of course, by a lot of people who never believed that this kind of thing could happen to this country. But then we would get news that the army was being built up, and there was a paralysis, that was the idea, paralysis. Nobody could stop it. This demon was gathering force from somewhere.

BIGSBY   That has echoes of your early play, *The Golden Years*, and a more recent one, *Broken Glass*.

MILLER   That's right. *The Golden Years* is the story of Montezuma and Cortes where it is quite obvious to Montezuma that this invading group of white people from somewhere had to be gods. No ordinary humans could dream of overthrowing him, since he had armies of fifty, sixty thousand in one division; he could have swamped them simply by the numbers. There were less than three hundred guys among the white people. Three hundred! So he was paralysed by his wish to placate these gods and to earn the approbation of heaven, because he had conquered the world and the only thing left to him was to become a god. He had, after all, been a priest himself, before he became a political figure. So, between the wish and the curiosity and the desire to participate in this virile religion, or whatever the hell they were bringing to him, he was effectively brought down.

BIGSBY   So there is something seductive in the mere implacability of the force?

MILLER   Look, Charles Lindbergh, our great national hero, went to Germany in the thirties and returned to say, 'It is the wave of the future.' Nobody could possibly catch up with their air force, which was the most advanced air force imaginable. They were neat, clean and white, and you had better get out of their way because they knew how to deal with life, unlike us and the British and the French, who were schlopping around, didn't know anything about nothin', all mixed-up politically. And Lindbergh's attitude was very widely held.

BIGSBY   But weren't you also isolationist, at that time?

MILLER   Yes. I would have thought, in the thirties, that we should never go sending troops anywhere. We had a Marine, a Brigadier General Smedley Butler, who came to Michigan. He was going round all the universities making speeches advocating a law which would have prohibited the sending of American armed forces beyond a ten-mile limit around the United States. The reason? He had spent his whole career in Latin America leading Marines and, of course, what they were doing down there was making life safe for the United Fruit Company and Standard Oil, but he was too stupid to know this. This was his story as he wrote it and as he told it to me, because I interviewed him for the *Michigan Daily*.

He said he was – where? Nicaragua, I guess – and they had been called in because there were brigands who were murdering people on the roads, and the first thing they do is call the United States Marines, which was a police force for Latin America. And he was in charge. He went down there, got off the boat and a man came to greet him, a civilian, who said, 'General, come with me and we will orient you about what is going on here.' So he went. He said, 'They took me to the office of the National City Bank, which seemed OK. I had been there many times before, in similar situations. It was usually some bank or an industrial place where we had our headquarters.' He said, 'I went in there and they had a map of the country on the table, and there were these guys saying, "Now, look. There is oil right here, and we would like you to clear the people off that area; and there is more oil over here, so you can get them out of that area. Once you have got them out of there, your job is over."' He said, 'It then went through my mind that some of us might get killed in this thing, and what I was doing was making those areas safe for their exploitation of the oil.'

He put his men back on the ship and ordered them back to the United States, and he was like Paul of Tarsus. He was struck by lightning, and he left his commission and resigned from the Marine Corps, and carried on with propaganda for the rest of his life against the use of American troops in order to secure land for these corporations. Therefore, one was very loath to send troops out of this country, and that was what my attitude would have been.

BIGSBY   So what was your road to Damascus? When did you abandon isolationism?

MILLER   Hitlerism. When it started to move into the Ruhr and it began to break out of Germany, and especially when they went into Czechoslovakia and Austria in 1938. Then, the stories of their murdering of the Jews, a methodical murder, which had not yet been seen in the West, began to come out. Then I realised that we were up for grabs. This was a whole new way of thinking. I did not know at the time what Stalin had done with the so-called kulaks. He had killed far more people, but, you see, that was inside Russia, a case of Russians killing Russians. When they start killing foreigners . . . ! More alarming.

BIGSBY   We are right at the end of the 1930s now, 1939, 1940, you are two years out of college and not working for your father. How did you see your future then? Did you have a plot for that future?

MILLER   I was either going to be the best playwright in America or I would go into another line of work. I knew a lot of people, by this time, who were would-be playwrights who were already turning into their thirties, and I did not want to join them. I knew screenwriters and I was not interested in that. What that other line of work might have been I had no idea, but I did not want to hang around trying to get on to the stage indefinitely.

BIGSBY   In 1940 you got married for the first time. You were Jewish, your wife was Catholic. Did this cause ructions?

MILLER   For a while it did not go down well, but pretty soon they got used to her and she to them. She, in any case, was not a practising Catholic by then. It was far more difficult for her parents, by far, because they were still very devout and I was a heathen. Actually, that is part of the ceremony. There are special ceremonies for Mohammedans, heathens and Jews who marry Catholics. You are not married in the church and you have to get a special dispensation from the church in order to do that. That was not always easy to get.

BIGSBY   How did you earn your money in the early 1940s?

MILLER   The only way you could earn a living in those days was to write for radio because, of course, American radio was completely commercialised. Everything was sponsored. They had four, five, possibly more, dramatic programmes and they hired people to write them. So I got on to the Dupont Cavalcade of America, which was probably the most widely heard one and the most popular. It was basically a programme of half an hour mostly on American history. I got paid, I think it was two hundred and fifty dollars per script, which was a decent piece of money, you know, because the rent of the apartment was forty dollars per month.

BIGSBY   December 1941, Pearl Harbor. You were turned down for the military because of an old football injury from school and went into the Brooklyn Navy Yard. Why did you do that?

MILLER   Well, I was writing these radio shows and it was so futile. Here was the greatest war in history going on, and I was writing this piddle just to make a living. I wanted to get into something that had something to do with the war, and the Navy Yard was ten minutes from where I was living. I thought maybe that was a way to make some contribution to the war effort.

BIGSBY   But it must have been a very curious atmosphere, because it was full of Italian workers building ships for a war against Italy.

MILLER   That was always the problem in the Navy Yard. You see, the Italian workers were all pro-Mussolini, and we repaired a lot of British cruisers and destroyers and battleships, which were being banged up all over the oceans, and the Italians hated the British because they felt that they had betrayed Italy by declaring war on Mussolini. They were very patriotic Americans, though, so they beat up English sailors on Sand Street, next to the Navy Yard late at night. The sailors would come back drunk to the ships. They were easy prey for these idiots to beat up. We were fighting several wars at the same time. World War Two was just one of them! We had a lot of German workers in there. The Chief Machinist in the Navy Yard was this German who could hardly speak English. We had the *Iowa* in there (I think it was the *Iowa*, or the *Missouri*, one of the big battleships), and he armed that ship, meaning, you know, these sixteen-inch cannon. Quite a piece of thing to pick up, and that thing has got to be mounted with an exactitude that is hair-raising, because that is what the whole ship is for: it is just a floating platform for these cannon. I will never forget the day I was standing there. There were these higher officers, admirals, everybody standing around as this one lone machinist with a black worker's cap on – he looked like he was right out of Bremen – marched up the gangplank with about five 'ducklings' behind him, his assistants; and he never touched a tool. He just stood over the hole as they lowered this cannon. It took about a day to do this. He was the king of the ship and I heard him speak with a distinct Deutsch accent. The whole thing was crazy.

BIGSBY   In 1944 your theatrical career finally began on Broadway

with a play called *The Man Who Had All the Luck*, which turned
out to be a somewhat ironic title.

MILLER   Not 'somewhat'! Totally ironic!

BIGSBY   But fifty years later the same play was successful. Why
was it a failure the first time?

MILLER   That play was more like most of the plays I had written
before, that is, I became noted for an interest in the well-
constructed play, but, in truth, that did not interest me; it never
really did. I had been writing rather lyrical plays, crazy plays, and
The Man Who Had All the Luck was really a metaphorical work,
completely, from beginning to end, although I tried to make it as
real as I could. But basically it was the story of a young man in a
small town who, unlike all his friends and relatives, succeeds in
everything he tries to do. No matter what he does, it turns out
good. Most people have some kind of a cross to bear, but he does
not, so he conceives gradually that there is some force up in the
sky that is waiting to beat his brains in one of these days. It has
got to come out of somewhere and explode in his face, and he gets
paranoid and begins to wonder where it is coming from, until he
finally decides. He marries this girl he has always loved, and she
loves him and is going to have a baby. It is a very simple kind of a
tale, which has no plot, really. It is just a story. Finally the end of
it is that he is certain that the child will come out crippled or
defective somehow, because she has taken a fall in her last month
of pregnancy. Anyhow, it comes out perfectly well and the issue
then becomes, 'Well, do I go on doing this or do I take charge of
my life?' I never could find the right answer to that question;
neither did Job, as a matter of fact! Nobody ever has. But I did
not know the history of this idea; I thought it was a brand-new
idea when I wrote it because it was based on a guy in Ohio who I
knew about, though I had never met him. You had to stage it as a
kind of mythological, metaphorical story.

BIGSBY   Why did it not work, that first time?

MILLER   I think the whole idea was so weird to the critics. They
could not follow the mode of this play. It is a kind of epic play,
you see; it is not a play about real people. It is a play about a
philosophical situation, basically. It is a fable, and fables were not
what you did on Broadway! And, of course, there was no off-
Broadway then. It was all Broadway. It only succeeded in
England, because in England, I think, the actors were able to

assume a kind of fabulous approach to the whole thing, since they had done Shakespeare, they had done all kinds of classical work, where also the people are not real in the movie sense of real. I suppose it might work here in America, I don't know. There might be actors around now who could handle it; I suspect there are. But we do not have a theatre that is experimenting that way. That is the only explanation. I think it was a formal problem more than anything else.

BIGSBY   Anyhow, the failure of that play sent you away from theatre entirely?

MILLER   I decided I would never write another play, for the simple reason that nothing on that stage that I saw resembled anything I had had in my mind while writing this play. It all became totally materialised. It became real. Well, I had no interest in a real. Anyway, I then wrote *Focus*, a novel.

BIGSBY   Yes. *Focus* is concerned with anti-Semitism. Why that subject?

MILLER   Because it was rife in certain sections of New York City before and during the war. People were blaming the Jews for the war. There was an organisation called the Christian Front, which was a branch of a group of Catholic priests in Detroit, Michigan: the Church of the Little Flower, in Royal Oak, Michigan. Father Coughlan had the largest radio audience in the United States – larger than Jack Benny's. Jack Benny had a pretty big audience, but you could not go anywhere on a Sunday without hearing that dreadful voice coming out. He organised the Christian Front, which was an armed group. They were put out of business finally by Roosevelt, who got the Church to stop him. They arrested about thirty of them in New York City, many others in other cities, armed with machine-guns! It was a Fascist organisation. He finally ended up making speeches which were direct translations of Goebbels's speeches (he was the Minister of Information for Hitler). As the war approached, and during the war, we had a very dense anti-Semitic movement, certainly in New York, which I knew about personally. I ran into it all the time. It was strong in Chicago. The Midwest was very much that way. So this whole theme became dominant in my mind.

BIGSBY   *Focus* was, in fact, very successful. So why didn't you stay with the novel, which had been successful, after a play which was not?

MILLER   I don't know. I think it was that instinct for acting. You know, a playwright is really part actor, as most of the playwrights I know about are, either openly or secretly. Shaw was an actor, certainly. I think most, if not all, of the British playwrights are manifestly actors, whether they admit it or not. That was part of it, and also that I was more at home with the idea of succeeding in the theatre. That was the challenge of my life. And the other reason was that even though I was successful with that book, well, you could not see the audience. You wrote the book and it disappeared! That was not much fun; I think it was partly that.

BIGSBY   The war in the Pacific was ended, of course, with two nuclear bombs. I assume, at the time, however, that your response would have been unalloyed delight?

MILLER   Well, I had a lot of friends in the army going East and I figured never to see them again. See, the scuttlebutt was that we were going to lose, I don't know, some fabulous number of troops and, indeed, the battles that were fought in Okinawa and on the islands on the way to Japan were some of the bloodiest battles in history. They were remorseless. They would never give up, and one imagined that if their home island was attacked they would kill a half-million people on our side. So, naturally, the idea that the war was over was just marvellous. The fact is, you know, we killed more people with firebombs over Tokyo. Everybody has forgotten that. The casualties were much greater.

BIGSBY   Do you think 1945 marks a line across American history, that something stopped then and something else began?

MILLER   I think that things like that, and the Holocaust, maybe the whole of the Second World War, which was extraordinarily bloody with forty million dead on all sides, can't happen in a generation without having a deep psychological effect on everybody. It cheapens human life in ways that we never thought of. It has affected the culture. The culture now is extremely anti-human. People get killed on television like rats in a cave. They go 'bang-bang', and thirty are dead. They have got these weapons, now, which do not exist in reality, Hollywood weapons. They shoot like Gatling guns; you kill ten, twenty, forty people. I think that it desensitises the human race, frankly. In the West. Of course, it has been going on for ever in the East. We used to say that the Chinese didn't value human life. Of course they value human life, but human life has been so cheap there for so many generations that you can say that they accepted this kind of thing in the way that we now accept it. But think what US forces have done, for example, in Nicaragua, places like that, where thousands of people have been killed by our representatives. And we knew it. There has been no secret about it. Then there was the Vietnam experience. That is why I feel endangered now, not personally, but in terms of civilisation.

BIGSBY   In the 1930s there was a certain idealism, and again during the war itself there had to be. But what was it that drove America after the war?

MILLER   We really felt that the last bad people had been killed. The rest of the people remaining were victims of the bad people. But now there was a world that we could raise up with our generosity, which, indeed, certainly turned the corner in Europe. People were riding around Paris burning wood. This was 1947, two years after the war. Down in southern Italy there was real starvation; I was talking to some people down there and every Monday the Americans landed a liberty ship full of food. We had a lot of liberty ships and it was explained to me that that grain could last a week if the election selected the Christian Democratic government. If that had gone the other way, and they had elected a Left government, those ships would have stopped and everybody knew that. Indeed, the Communists were telling the people to vote for the Christian Democrats because the Russians could never send any food. And they had a week's supply of food. So why wouldn't America feel pretty great? I mean, here we were, feeding the world, for the moment, and lifting up the wounded. There were good reasons to feel that way and, on the part of the people (I am not speaking of the politicians in Washington), a feeling that they had a duty to help the rest of the world. The average American certainly felt that it was his job to help do this.

BIGSBY   Then your first really successful play, *All My Sons*, which was 1947, presented America with a kind of accusation. It presented a radically different image of America.

MILLER   That is right, because I wrote that play during the war and I thought the war was going to continue. That is what we were told. Certainly the Japanese part of it would take, maybe, eight years. That was the general idea and, God knows, without the atom bomb it probably would have gone on at least a year or two. So I thought the play would be produced in wartime and if it

254

had I would have been hanged! That never occurred to me, of course! There are lines in the play which were pretty strong. For example, the father defends his own crime, saying, 'What did they do in Detroit? Did they ship a gun or a truck until they got their price?' In fact, the corruption was massive, but it was overlooked. Well, it wasn't altogether overlooked; there were prosecutions and one of the chief prosecutors, I would remind everybody, was a fellow named Harry S. Truman. He had a Senate committee that was trying to chase these people who were stealing right and left, and really sabotaging the war effort. He would have liked the play, I think.

BIGSBY   There was something strange about your reaction to the success of the play, though, because here you were, suddenly become very successful, with money coming in, and what you did was go and work for wages in a warehouse.

MILLER   Yes, I couldn't stand the idea that I was making money without working. It was morally disgusting. So I presented myself to the Employment Bureau of the State of New York, which parcels out jobs, and I got work in a factory making beer boxes. But I couldn't go past a week! It was not the work, it was the boredom.

BIGSBY   Were you driven by those old values of the 1930s?

MILLER   Sure, and Christian values, if I may say, of the earlier sort that do not exist any more. I wanted to be with the salt of the earth and the salt was in that factory. But these people were totally depressed. It was just awful being there and I would have gone crazy there finally. So I lasted about a week.

BIGSBY   Then, in 1949, came *Death of a Salesman*, which was awarded a Pulitzer prize and was made into a film. Yet it is also a play that seems to be attacking the very values that were most loudly asserted at that time in America, the revival of materialism, the American dream, or at least a version of it.

MILLER   I wrote *Death of a Salesman* at the beginning of what was probably the greatest boom in world history. I knew the boom was going on, but I was not alone in thinking, when I was writing about it, that what we were saying earlier was the case, namely that the reality was Depression. The reality was the whole thing coming down in a heap of wood and cinders. Truman, who was never my ideal, had the same idea. He thought we were going right back to where we had been when we were rescued by the

255

Second World War, namely a lot of unemployment and deprivation and general decline. A lot of us did not think that the boom in America was really going to last. What happens when everybody has a refrigerator? What happens when everybody has a car? We turn out this stuff so fast, it has to end. So those of us who had passed through the Depression – I suppose the majority of the people, since the Depression was not that far back – were very chary about this and Willy Loman's situation would have met with a lot of understanding by the audience. Somebody once asked me, when we were doing the play the first time, 'When is this play supposed to be happening?' Well, I had never thought of that. I said, 'I don't know. Now.' He said, 'There's something about it that's like the Depression.' I said, 'Well, maybe it is the Depression, except that the two boys have been in a war, so it is after the Depression.' So I figured that what is happening is in my head, in never-never-land. It is not tied to the history book. It is the attitudes that are tied to history. Within the play, in the figure of Charley, I already a creature of the boom. Charley and his son, Bernard, are on the make, they are on the up. They are cheerful, confident and, indeed, they make out. It is very strange.

BIGSBY   They not only make out, but they are also humane.

MILLER   Very humane. They don't have to cut throats in order to make a life and this is a-historical, or non-historical. I don't know what it is, but it is quite strange to me.

BIGSBY   How early did you become aware of the increasing and dangerous right-wing element in America that was going to lead to House Un-American Activities persecution?

MILLER   It was always there in my lifetime. It was there, if I really wanted to go back, in the twenties, when the Ku Klux Klan was extremely powerful in the United States. We have all forgotten that. I remember my mother noting that they were anti-Semitic. Nobody was particularly troubled that they were anti-black; what was worrying was that they hated the Jews and that they were in New Jersey, across the river from where we were living. It was a very strong Ku Klux Klan territory. As far as my own consciousness was concerned, it was really during the thirties with the rise of Fascism. One connected Hitler to these reactionaries here. We had a few in Congress. There were a number of Senators who were real outright racists. There was a Senator from Mississippi who would rant about Jews, niggers and wops. I suppose you would call it American nativism. It exists in every country: the French have it, the British have it, Russians have it, Germans have it. It explodes periodically here. If you want to look at it benignly, it is as old as the country.

BIGSBY   But what didn't happen in Europe after the war was this institutionalisation of that right-wing version of the world into something like the House Un-American Activities Committee. Why was that?

MILLER   I don't know, maybe some of our fellows saw a great opportunity to get elected that way! We must not underestimate that. It certainly accounts for a fellow named Joseph McCarthy, for example, who got elected with the help of the Communist Party in Wisconsin. He was a left-wing guy then, but he caught on that the pot of gold was in the anti-Communist thing and I wouldn't underestimate that at all, that sheer opportunism. However, the liberals were more likely to be passionate on principle because they saw in Stalinism a menace to liberty. But a guy like McCarthy couldn't care less about liberty. It was not his line of work. I think that maybe the fact is – and this is my reading of it, I may be wrong – that the whole thing, from an American viewpoint, is so far away that you can afford to have all kinds of fanciful explanations for things. For example, in 1949 China goes Communist. Well, people, with straight faces, said, 'We lost China.' It is like an elephant being lost by a mouse! I mean, what an idea! You could only think that because you were six thousand miles away from China.

BIGSBY   But, domestically, there is nothing more un-American than the idea of an Un-American Activities Committee, is there?

MILLER   You would think so, excepting that under Jefferson they had the Alien and Sedition Acts. Only a year or two after the revolution they started to hunt out foreign influences, anti-American influences.

BIGSBY   It is bizarre, isn't it, in an immigrant culture?

MILLER   It is crazy! Well, maybe it is because it is an immigrant culture. There is no sense of rootedness in a lot of these people. As Willy Loman says, he has always felt very temporary about himself! Maybe they feel temporary about themselves. You know, up here on this road, in the fifties, at the top of the ridge about half a mile from this house, they built a cabin about ten feet by twelve feet, with windows on four sides. I passed it one night. I came back about two o'clock in the morning and there was somebody in there. I had not paid much attention to it and I looked and there was somebody reading a book inside this cabin. So I stopped and I recognised the person, a young man. I said, 'What's happening, what are you doing?' Well, it was a watchtower for Russian bombers!

BIGSBY   In Connecticut?

MILLER   In Connecticut. And the breath was simply knocked out of me. He was otherwise an intelligent guy. They were manning that thing day and night, twenty-four hours a day, to spot Russian bombers coming over Connecticut! And if you said, 'You know, I don't think there is ever going to be a Russian bomber coming around here' they would look at you with a certain amount of suspicion. After all, what right have you got to say that? Can it be that you want to disarm us in the face of the enemy? That's how bad it got.

BIGSBY   But what it means is that when, in 1950, you adapted Ibsen's *An Enemy of the People*, in which a central character stands up against the general opinion of the day, and three years later you wrote *The Crucible*, you were poking a stick into a wasps' nest, weren't you?

MILLER   Oh, yes. By that time I knew what the pay-off was going to be; but I have to say that I still had confidence that there was a sufficient number of people like me out in that audience who were simply scared to speak or uncertain what to say about this situation and who I thought would respond to this kind of work; and I turned out to be right and wrong. They rejected *An Enemy of the People*, but that was partly due to the woodenness of the production, and it was quite wooden, despite Fredric March playing the lead. He played it like Jesus Christ, terribly seriously, when the fact is that the character of Doctor Stockmann is that of a semi-lunatic scientist who is really a very frantic kind of a person. He is not a professor. *The Crucible*, likewise, had a wooden production. In fact, I have not been blessed with good productions the first time around, on the whole. However, in the case of *The Crucible*, another production was done about eight months after our production closed, by young people. They told me it was the first off-Broadway production of any kind in the ballroom of a hotel, which was not something done in those days, and that was a great success.

BIGSBY There were those then, were there not, who rejected the notion of a parallel between the witch-hunts of the seventeenth century and those of the 1950s?

MILLER Yes. They would say to me, 'This is all fraudulent. There never were any witches, but there are Communists' and I could only say, 'In 1692, if you had stood on the Main Street of Salem, Massachusetts and said, "There are no witches!" I wouldn't want to be your insurance man; because the Bible says there are witches; the King of England said there were witches; every legal authority in Christendom said not only that there are witches, but that it is the obligation of the state to wipe them out, and all who sympathise with them.' But, of course, you could not talk to anybody.

BIGSBY One element you introduced into *The Crucible*, which was not there in the original trials, was the idea of a sexual liaison between John Proctor and Abigail. Why did you introduce that idea?

MILLER First of all, I suspected there *had* been a liaison between the two of them. There are hints in the literature of something like that. She was thrown out of the house by Elizabeth Proctor and she was, by one person, called lascivious, which was a fearful charge in those days. It was next to the worst thing you could say about somebody. Hawthorne wrote a whole book about this. Then there were certain things in the testimony. There is a wonderful description by Reverend Paris, who is the villain of the piece, in which he describes his niece, Abigail, about to make a charge against her former employer. It is a marvellous piece of descriptive writing. She claims, in court, that Elizabeth Proctor's spirit has come out of Elizabeth Proctor and is, right now, torturing her, and she has got her fists closed, according to the Reverend Paris, and is about to strike Elizabeth Proctor when her hands open and, instead, she simply embraces her, touches her. The whole struggle of that girl not to kill that woman, who was the wife of the man who, in my opinion, had had an affair with her, is fascinating. It is a wonderful piece of psychological writing. Now, he wasn't making any point. He was just describing something he had seen. His point in writing that was, you see, that she *was* being attacked by Elizabeth Proctor's spirit.

BIGSBY If you had been writing for Hollywood at that time, you would certainly have lost your job and not been re-employed for a long time.

MILLER   Oh, yes, sure.

BIGSBY   Why was the theatre immune?

MILLER   There is a very simple answer to that. First of all, the theatre affected very few people. Who the hell in Indianapolis gave a damn about what was happening in a theatre which nobody was going to go and see anyway? They had never heard of any of the actors or the directors. So there was no national pay dirt here for a politician. That was the primary reason. Secondly, Hollywood was controlled by a few banks and a few production companies. If you could control those few, or get them to agree with you, you could control the whole industry. New York production was in the hands of little businessmen who raised maybe five hundred dollars at a time among innumerable people. I think we had something like thirty backers for *Death of a Salesman*. The whole cost of production was about thirty-six thousand dollars, so, if each guy put in twelve hundred dollars, you had the thing made. It was very hard to control that kind of disorganised production system and that was the reason. They did try from time to time. They would hold hearings in New York City and call up an actor for a day or two; but everybody in New York was hip; they knew what the score was. They couldn't get anywhere, so they just left. This happened two or three times. The Committee would come, call up some guy, start calling him names, but everybody in the city was against them and they smelled it, so they would pull out.

Where they made progress was in radio and television. Television, of course, was still young and did not matter much, but the radio programmes were devastated. Why? They were all subsidised by a few big corporations. So they would get to the corporations, threaten a few of them and five radio programmes would be affected. They hit some company like Proctor and Gamble (incidentally, Proctor was a descendant of John Proctor), they hit the soap operas, so called because they were selling so many brands of soap through radio. All you had to do was hit three-four important patrons and you had the whole industry sewn up.

BIGSBY   What was it like to be a liberal intellectual in the mid-1950s, with absolutely no leverage on the system?

MILLER   It was hell! I felt completely isolated. The trade unions
were all roaring anti-Communists; they would have nothing to do
with any of us. There was absolutely no part of society that would
welcome you. It got so bad that a group of writers, I think about
twenty of them, got together, editors and reporters. One of them
had been the editor of the *New York Herald Tribune*. These were
very respectable people, I thought, and they asked me to join
them, which I did, in an attempt to generate articles (these guys
wrote for the major magazines, normally) which would oppose
McCarthyism, because no such articles were being written. They
would discuss what they could write. One guy would say, 'I've
got an idea, I will write about this and that, and no doubt
something else.' So we would meet once a week in the home of
Jack Goodman, who was an editor at Simon and Schuster, one of
the biggest publishers in New York.

In six months or whatever, they could not place one single
article! Now, these guys were star reporters, they were big shots.
These were not beginning writers. Nobody could get anything
published of that nature. It all paid off, finally, when the House
Un-American Activities Committee summoned the host, this
editor from Simon and Schuster. I don't even think he was a
liberal; he was just a guy who was disturbed by all this and, boy,
they scared the living daylights out of him and the whole thing
simply vanished. It wasn't doing any good, anyway, so everybody
stopped coming.

It started with six or eight people, of whom I was one. William
Shirer, who wrote *The Rise and Fall of the Third Reich*, was
another. There were several American reporters who had worked
in Europe and seen Hitlerism, and they were goddamned worried
about this. Anyway, it blew up because they could not effectuate
anything and we just stopped coming. But before that his living
room was packed; there were forty people in it. We started off
with six and the meeting grew very lively. I did not know anybody
there by that time. Clearly there was an informer there, because
we had no publicity. Not a line appeared in any newspaper about
these meetings and then, suddenly, Goodman is in front of a
Committee in Washington and somebody had turned us in.

BIGSBY   But that raises an interesting question, because your next
play, *A View from the Bridge*, takes as its central character an
informer and treats him with real understanding.

MILLER   Well, of course, that was part of the irony of all this. A lot of the informants were very honest, straightforward, worried people. They really thought that Jack Goodman was going to destroy the United States and that we would be leading in the Red Army. You see, it is not all mendacious, by any means. Had it been mendacious it would have exploded in a very short time.

BIGSBY   In 1955, the year of *A View from the Bridge*, you got divorced and married Marilyn Monroe.

MILLER   The first marriage was collapsing gradually over a period of two or three years, so that there was nothing much left of it finally. I met her in 1951. I was in Hollywood with Kazan to get a movie produced that I had written about the Brooklyn waterfront [*The Hook*], which we thought we could do independently, because no studio would ever buy a script like that. It was the story of a corrupt labour union and a rebel group within the labour union which was trying to overthrow the leadership. It was later the basis of *On the Waterfront*, the movie that Kazan made after we had parted but which had certain vital differences from my script. However, I was there to try to get Columbia Pictures to do it, and that is when I met Marilyn.

BIGSBY   Were there any evidences then of the problems that were eventually going to destroy her?

MILLER   If I had been sophisticated enough, I would have seen them. But I was not. I loved her.

BIGSBY   Can you recall what that first impression was?

MILLER   Yes. She was standing in costume on a set in Twentieth Century-Fox. They were making a silly comedy [*As Young as You Feel*] and she had a fairly unimportant part in the film. She was talking to Kazan, who had met her a year or so earlier, and was weeping. She was so striking. I was standing some feet away, so I couldn't hear what they were saying. It turned out her man and protector for the previous several years [Johnny Hyde], an agent who had really tried to create her career, had just died. He had had a long-standing heart disease and he had died only some short time before. So that was the first time I saw her, and she was weeping.

BIGSBY   When you began to get to know her, were those problems that were eventually going to destroy her evident to you?

MILLER   They were, and I felt for a long time that they could be resolved, that she did not have to be destroyed by them, but gradually it became clear that, if she was going to remain an actress (which she should have done, because she was very good, she was a surprisingly adept comedienne, as *Some Like It Hot* certainly proved), she was going to have these problems. They were basically unresolvable. You could not live a life and be at the mercy of that industry. You see, they did not regard her as an actress. They regarded her as a sexpot and, indeed, she had not had much of a chance to act in anything. But Billy Wilder understood what she was able to do for the first time.

BIGSBY What was the nature of the problems?

MILLER They were self-inflicted, mostly. She had very little confidence in herself. She had been exposing herself as an actress (which an actor or actress has to do) and this brought to a head all her sense of unworthiness. She felt she was being a faker and this led to a feeling that one was looking at somebody who, while she might be witty and funny and so on, had some profound sadness. I think that depth was what captured the world, finally.

BIGSBY Did you ever get to the bottom of that sadness?

MILLER Oh, yes. It was partly that she had a crazy mother. That is not a good start; her mother was quite mad. She was a paranoid schizophrenic who ended up spending half her life in an institution. The mother tried to kill her three times and she was convinced that she was a worthless creature because she was illegitimate. I am not sure she was illegitimate, to tell you the truth, but she was brought up to believe that, which meant a lot more then, incidentally, than it does now. She was characterised as an orphan; of course, she was never an orphan and always tried to convince the world that she was not, which is ironical. But she was put in an orphanage. It was a terribly mixed-up situation, with the whole idea that she was worthless being at the bottom of it. And, of course, the religious side of it played an important role. They were fundamentalists – the mother was, all the people around the mother were. They believed in hellfire and damnation. Sex was bad, any self-displaying was evil: beauty itself was evil.

BIGSBY So she felt guilty about the very role she was playing?

MILLER She was guilty by looking in the mirror! She felt guilty, because she was so attractive and beautiful. The devil is always the handsomest creature in the cosmology, isn't he? Milton tells us that.

BIGSBY   The image of her that you get from the parts that she played was of a sexuality concealing a kind of vulnerability, naïveté, almost innocence. Was there anything of that about her, in reality?

MILLER   Oh, yes, she was just that way. She wasn't acting very much. Off-screen she was a lot like on-screen excepting when she got angry. She wouldn't show that, excepting I had her do it in the last scene of *The Misfits*, when she was furious at them for capturing the horses. Then she was quite a different person, and she became herself: quite paranoid.

BIGSBY   In 1956 you were yourself called before the House Un-American Activities Committee. A lot of your friends had already appeared before it, Elia Kazan (the director of *Death of a Salesman*), Lee J. Cobb (who played the original Willy Loman), Clifford Odets (the playwright of the 1930s, whom you most admired). They all named names when asked to do so. You refused. Why did they name names? Why did you refuse?

MILLER   I had never thought of myself as being dependent upon the public. My mindset was such that I figured I was writing for the future, maybe. I was never on a salary, excepting when I was writing radio. I never worked for a company. The others all worked for companies. They had to behave, or they'd get fired. Nobody could fire me, because nobody had hired me, consequently I had this delusion that I was invulnerable that way and, in a way, I thought that they were. I thought that they were great enough artists, most of them, that they could have made their way without the approbation of these big studios, because that's what it was all about. If you did not do that, you could not work. It was all about work, about employment. You had to do that as a condition of working in Hollywood. They made that quite clear, and Hollywood was the only place in those days that movies were being made. It was the age before the independent film, by and large, in America anyway (in Europe it was quite different), so that if these guys wanted to work they had to face up. So there was that element. But the other element was that I felt that life was one continuous moving stream, and the water was the same water going over the rocks and going into the shallows, and I did not want to cut off the earlier part of my life from the latter part of my life. It was one energy, good, bad or indifferent. I simply could not walk around saying that everything up to now had been a mistake.

BIGSBY   If that whole episode was, as you have suggested, about careerism, on the part of McCarthy and also of Richard Nixon, who was involved in the same business, was it also a revenge on the 1930s, a revenge on Roosevelt, do you think?

MILLER   Yes, and they have never stopped taking revenge; they are doing it right now, in 1995. They are dismantling the government as Roosevelt constructed it. They are deconstructing the government, or the agencies of the government, the philosophy of the government, which was diametrically opposite to what is believed today. Since 1934, roughly, when the New Deal began, there has been a building-up of a revanchist feeling in the Republican Party, which is unbelievable in its viciousness. Really a philosophy: it is pettiness beyond belief.

BIGSBY   Do you think it is possible that America could ever again witness something like the House Un-American Activities Committee?

MILLER   As such, probably not, because the propaganda against it has been enough to inoculate people against it. But you should never say 'never' in politics. What they lack now is a foreign enemy. If we had a foreign enemy, you would have it back in ten minutes, because the whole basis of the Un-American Activities Committee was that they were calling people secret agents of Russia, or Communists. Since neither exists any more, it is not going to be possible until they find another threat from a foreign power. I question whether you could reproduce that again at this stage of the game. However, if you get people scared enough about anything, you can go a good distance with this kind of thing. Politicians like to live off the fears of people. They will crop up as soon as people are scared enough. You could, for example, if there was enough terrorism in a country, get something going about that. People would be scared to go downtown, scared of being in office buildings, scared of going on the subway, and if you nailed somebody and said, 'He is part of this big conspiracy,' you might get something going for a while. It would not have the exact same function as the other one did, because just about everybody is against terrorism. What you would have would be, maybe, some civil libertarians. That is happening now, to a degree, in 1995. They have got the people who allegedly bombed the World Trade Center, killed half a dozen people, and of course did a lot of damage. There is an

265

incipient hysteria there, provided there is another explosion that you could lay at the feet of Moslem fanatics. Then I could see where any Moslem would have a problem, or anybody related to them or defending them. But that still is not quite the same thing.

BIGSBY   In 1956 you suddenly found yourself sentenced to prison.

MILLER   Yes. When you refuse to answer a question of a Congressional Committee you can be cited for Contempt of Congress, which is what happened to me, and then there is a trial in the Federal Court charging you with contempt and you can then defend yourself. Normally, these cases take a morning. They were really pro forma cases, because the evidence was clear and nobody ever mounted a really strong defence against the charge. In my case Joe Rauh, who had been a very experienced civil liberties attorney for years, decided my case would be a good one to defend, so we were in court for five days, which was unprecedented. At the end of it all, as we knew would happen, I was pronounced guilty of contempt, despite everything, but we built up a record during the trial. These cases were based upon the government bringing in so-called experts on Communism. These experts would say, 'I have examined the writings and speeches of the defendant and, as an expert on Communism, I can tell you that he is a Communist, or he is under the control of the Communist Party.'

In my case, for the first time, we brought in a counter-expert. This was a guy who had been a United States Senator, an ex-Marine from the Korean War, who had turned against the whole business after having been elected with the help of Joe McCarthy, who was a good friend of his from Seattle in the state of Washington. He was appointed by Eisenhower to guard against Un-American activities in the federal bureaucracy. He discovered, after a time, that large numbers of these people were either cases of mistaken identity or actually just liberals, or just people. When he tried to get reviews of these cases from the Eisenhower administration, they fired him. This planted a bomb in his head and he then began to examine the whole business of loyalty. He ended up having a television programme in Florida of a liberal sort. He learned how to be a liberal by being a reactionary.

In any case, we called him in. He had read my plays and he said, 'I do not see any sign of this guy being a Communist.' It did not matter anyhow, as we knew it would not; except there was

266

one cute thing during the trial. I was accused, among other things, of violating the terms of the United States passport by going to Czechoslovakia when it was a forbidden territory to Americans. On each American passport was a stamp saying Not Valid for Travel inside a certain number of countries, all Eastern countries. Well, my lawyer Joe Rauh said, 'When were you in Czechoslovakia?' I said, 'I have never been in Czechoslovakia.' When the time came for the prosecutor to repeat what he had said once before, namely that Miller went to Czechoslovakia in violation of the United States passport, up jumped Joe Rauh, who was six feet three inches tall, an ex-basketball player, and said, 'Your honour, he has never been in Czechoslovakia. This is all some kind of mistake or a sinister attempt to blacken him.' And then the prosecutor would go right on. This happened four times and the fourth time the judge, McLaughlin, having heard Joe explicate four times now that I had never been in Czechoslovakia and that therefore this whole conversation was simply moot, said, 'Oh, I think it covers the four corners of the indictment.' I turned to Joe and said, 'What does that mean?' and he said, 'Oh, nothing at all!' At the end McLaughlin said, 'Do you have anything to say for yourself?' I said, 'No, not a thing. I have said all I wish to say.' He said, 'OK, you get a year in jail, suspended sentence, and a five hundred dollar fine.

Anyhow, that was over and thirty years passed (this was one of the reasons why my autobiography was called *Timebends*) before I get a letter in the mail one day from a Professor McLaughlin of the University of Wyoming, or Montana, or someplace. 'I am the nephew of Judge McLaughlin who sentenced you, and I just wondered what you had felt about him, because I know that he regretted that very much. He was a very decent man, and he did not really understand why he had to do that.' I mean, the farcical nature of this thing is beyond belief. So I wrote back and said, 'Well, I can't tell you that I fell in love with him. I just felt it was a bureaucratic thing from beginning to end. He was a good Democrat, old McLaughlin, and his party told him that is what you have to do, and that is what he did.' I said, 'I really did not think much of him, but I am glad he had these feelings.'

BIGSBY   And you could have avoided this whole thing if you had allowed your wife to be photographed with the Chairman of the Committee.

MILLER   Yes. The head of the Un-American Activities Committee
sent a telephone message to Joe Rauh, my lawyer, saying that if
we would arrange for him to have a photograph taken with
Marilyn, he would forgo the whole hearing. Whereupon, when I
said no, he walked into the hearing room looking as though he
was trying one of the great Russian revolutionaries. And I was
supposed to take this seriously, and people *did* take it seriously!
And it was a fraud and a farce, except it cost me a fortune for
lawyers and a year's time lost in the bargain, worrying about it
and figuring out how to react to it. When you have a thing like
that hanging over your head, it is not easy.

BIGSBY   But, in another sense, it was pure theatre.

MILLER   The whole thing is theatre. It is produced, directed and
acted, no differently in any way from theatre, except that the
effects can be deadly. You can end up behind bars.

BIGSBY   Meanwhile, back in your real career as a playwright, *A
View from the Bridge* went to London. But it was not the same
version as that which had been produced in America in 1955.
Why did you change it?

MILLER   I had seen the original production in America, which was
a bad production, as usual, with the wrong people in it – very
good actors, but completely miscast. As an Italian longshoreman
on the Brooklyn waterfront we had a very good actor out of
Oklahoma, who had never heard this kind of language. He could
not handle the speech; it was a foreign language to him. But I
changed it partly because, even then, I realised that I had not
done justice to the women in the text. They were underwritten. I
was more interested in them than the play would indicate and
that was basically the reason why I began to add to their roles.
Then the thing got unwieldy as a one-act play, because it was too
long to be in one act. There was a natural break in the middle and
we simply used it.

BIGSBY   There was another difference that came from it going
across the Atlantic. When it was performed in London it could
not be performed on the public stage. We had the Lord
Chamberlain censoring plays, then, and it had to be put on at a
theatre club. The reason for that is to do with the sexuality of the
piece and there does seem to me a stark contrast between
American theatre, whether it is O'Neill or Tennessee Williams or
your own plays, and British theatre of that time, in that sexuality

268

was not really a part of the British theatre. There is a sexual frisson in your plays, and in the plays of your contemporaries in America, which was not there in Britain.

MILLER   Well, the British were even more repressed than we were, much more, at that time. They broke loose, at least part of British society did, just about at that time, with John Osborne and the others. But I remember a gathering at the Royal Court Theatre. The theatre was packed with theatre people, hangers-on, critics and everybody else, and I was one of two or three speakers. The question was, 'Why is the British theatre in the condition it is?' And I brought the startling news that, maybe if they started to reflect the real life of the British people in the plays, something might happen. Of course, Osborne had just opened *Look Back in Anger* some months before this meeting. Anyway, in those days the American theatre was regarded as being the most advanced, certainly.

BIGSBY   When you staged *A View from the Bridge* in America, it had a companion piece, a play called *A Memory of Two Mondays*, which was really about what in Britain would have been called working-class characters. It was not really a nostalgic piece about your own past. In many ways it was talking about the mid-1950s as well, surely?

MILLER   What it was saying to the mid-1950s, which the mid-1950s chose not to hear, was that this was the bedrock. While we were busy doing the boom, there were a lot of people in warehouses who were condemned, as though to death, by an economic system from which there was no recourse for them. They were not what you might call important people. They were not supposed to exist, so it was news from the netherworld. That was what I had in mind. Of course, nobody could be less interested in such events in the mid-fifties, when the tail-fins were going on to the cars, television was roaring up, Eisenhower was in heaven and all was well with the world. Why bother with this kind of nonsense? That was what that play was addressing.

BIGSBY   What did the Eisenhower years mean for you, aside from the episode with the House Un-American Activities Committee?

MILLER   Well, it was as though Newt Gingrich got elected President. Things did not grind to a halt. That would have been too noisy. They sort of fell asleep.

BIGSBY   And yet you had the Korean War, the beginnings of the
Civil Rights movement . . .

MILLER   Well, they came out of that, yes. They were reactions
against it, in a way. But this is the American pendulum. It goes
from one extreme to the next. In Eisenhower's time a man had to
have short hair, or none. The women all had these print dresses
down to just below the knee, and white shoes on Sunday.
Everything was proper; but we do that. We are going to do it
again, but now it is a little more difficult, because of the drugs,
which have, I think, had probably the biggest effect on politics
that has never been reported. We did not have the drugs then.
We had booze, but that was a different thing.

BIGSBY   Did you feel, in the mid-1950s, or from there on to the
end of the decade and beyond, that you had lost some sort of
connection with an American audience?

MILLER   Yes, I suppose I did. I wrote *The Misfits* during that
time.

BIGSBY   Yes, but no new play appeared for about nine years.

MILLER   No. I was busy trying to keep Marilyn afloat, but I also
feared dislocation for people of my generation. You had lost any
orientation, politically, or socially, for that matter. I could not
think of myself any longer as being allied with some working class
or with the oppressed, because the oppressed were being middle-
class. We were developing the classless society. The end of
ideology was announced. We were not going to think any more in
terms of rich and poor, high and low, nothing like that. Life was
going to be an oblong blur, and, indeed, this was what it was
turning out to be until it exploded in the sixties. I knew it was not
true, but I did not know what was true, and I simply could not sit
down and write some entertainment. *The Misfits* was an attempt
on my part to deal with the dislocation, with the sense that there
was no root to anything, that we were a wandering tribe that was
looking for some sense of values that was very difficult to locate. I
do not think the picture succeeded in locating them. All it did was
to succeed in conveying the feeling that nothing was really
connected to anything. And that is about the way I felt.

BIGSBY   So there was another sense in which that title, *The Misfits*,
applied to you as well, in the context of American society?

MILLER   Yes, sure.

BIGSBY   It was quite a jump for you to make, turning away from the theatre, which you loved, towards Hollywood, which you deeply distrusted.

MILLER   I would not have written it except for Marilyn. I wrote it for her. It was the only time I did write anything for an actor and, had I not known her, I would not have begun such a thing. She had lost a child in early pregnancy, which really upset her a lot, so it was a kind of a gift. It was also the expression of some kind of belief in her as an actress, because it did require a lot of acting, which was not something she was called upon to do very often. When I wrote it, *Some Like It Hot* had not yet come up and her other pictures were really indifferent variations of the same character. *Some Like It Hot* required her to be an actress and showed that she could do it. So I did a film because she was there to do it.

BIGSBY   And yet, as it turned out, it was a film that was hedged around with a certain sense of doom when things began to fall apart in the process.

MILLER   Oh, yes. By the time we got to make the film, and the whole process must have taken over three years, we were no longer really man and wife. The film was there but the marriage was not.

BIGSBY   Why did it disintegrate?

MILLER   Well, it was a whole complicated long story. I really could not manage that kind of life, finally. I live a very quiet existence, despite appearances, and that whole show business thing was more than I could take. And she was on her way. She wanted to do other things. She could not quite be happy settling down into a domestic kind of situation – nor should she have. But I think it was also that her attitudes towards herself were ripening, so to speak. There was a very destructive thing going on in her.

BIGSBY   Part of the problem, surely, was that everybody wanted a part of her in some way, didn't they?

MILLER   Yes, I suppose it is a condition that goes along with all the rest of it; one is especially open to that as a performer, because you are exposed. You are out there alone doing it, and that is different from being a writer.

BIGSBY   And yet isn't there a paradox in what you are saying, because you are writing plays about the need for people to understand fundamental values, to face the reality about themselves and their relationship to other people, and yet you move in a world that is about artifice and pretence.

MILLER   It is very hard to put those together. That is why so many performers, actors, players, directors, are up to their eyebrows in psychoanalysis, trying to find a way through that underbrush. It is quite different from being a writer or a painter, somebody who works alone and does not have to confront production, other people, the public, personally. A writer can bear all these contradictions because he can control them, but when you are dealing with actors, directors, producers, and so on, you are in action. You are not just alone in your study with plenty of time to figure out where you are. It is the difference between training for a war and being in one.

BIGSBY   You met your wife, Inge Morath, on the set of *The Misfits*.

MILLER   Yes, she came out with a lot of photographers from New York. They were all members of Magnum, a co-operative, and they came because Gable was in it and Marilyn was in it, along with Montgomery Cliff; and I had written it.

BIGSBY   So, when did the romance begin?

MILLER   Oh, not until later. Marilyn and I broke up at the end of *The Misfits* and that was when Inge and I got together.

BIGSBY   This was going to be your third marriage, and her second one. Did you mutually have any doubts about taking this step?

MILLER   Oh, yes. I did not believe that I could ever relate to anybody for very long any more. I was already a middle-aged man by that time. But she is terrific, that she could even bear being with me for that long. She has her own life, her own art. She does some amount of travelling alone, still, working on projects. She has a very strong character.

BIGSBY   But has the fact that she is a photographer changed the way you view things at all?

MILLER   I have got more acutely aware of art, of painting, and of images in movies and so on. I've met some of her friends who are terrific talkers about this, like Henri Cartier Bresson with whom she worked for many years and who is, of course, a master of this. We have had marvellous talks together. I was educated by Henri about how to look at things. He does not know that, but it is true.

BIGSBY   In *After the Fall* the central character is about to marry a woman called Olga. There is a sense that this woman is potentially his redemption. That is Inge.

MILLER   I think it is true, to some degree. Without her I do not know what the hell would have become of me. She helped me construct a whole existence that had never existed before in my life, including this whole domain I am sitting in, which I probably would not have done without her. She is just a tremendous force for good in my life. She has kept me sane (as sane as I am!). She has a wonderful combination of aesthetic sensibility and a practical view of life.

BIGSBY   There is a vulnerability for the playwright that does not exist for the novelist in that you are completely dependent on the productions of your plays. People's reactions to you as a writer are derived entirely from individual productions.

MILLER   Absolutely. And individual actors. You can fall down dead because the wrong actor is in the part; maybe a perfectly good actor, but the wrong sensibility, the wrong personality for the role. Then some other actor picks it up ten years later and says, 'Geez, I never knew that was in there.' It was always in there, but the actor was not there to do it. It is true of all the performing arts. In music, if you listen to a recording by a conductor like Toscanini of a Beethoven piece, and then to another recording, you are listening to two different pieces of music. The tunes are the same, but the spirit behind it is completely different. One is dramatic, full of necessity and organic sensibility, and the other is, well, just notes. They are the same notes, but . . . ! This is one of the terrible things about any of the performing arts. This may be one of the reasons why there are comparatively so few playwrights who outlive their time. Maybe they did not get the production that was required at the time; maybe that helped to destroy them.

BIGSBY   You have said that a play is a kind of psychic journalism, a mirror of its time, before it is art and, in a way, that is how your plays are. They do pick up a lot of what is alive in the culture; and yet, if that were all they did, they would die with the moment, like Clifford Odets's *Waiting for Lefty*.

MILLER   You have got to have more than that. I think the play needs to have that in order to arouse our interest sufficiently, but a play is about people, finally. It is always interesting to have people confronted with a certain kind of social problem but the dilemma of the person facing that problem is really the reason that you are going to the theatre. You read newspapers for a different reason, but the theatre is involved with human beings and the mystery behind their relationships. You see, a play like Ibsen's *An Enemy of the People* is about a social problem. He wrote that after he had been called a demon and an idiot and God-knows-what after *Ghosts*, because he had raised the issue of syphilis and inherited disease, and had offended the sensibilities of the hour and so was regarded as a monster.

In *An Enemy of the People* Ibsen made his metaphor out of a man who discovers poison in the town's water supply. Now, if that was all it was, that would be the end of it. What makes it of any interest – and it is probably the least interesting of his plays – is that there is a character there who, properly acted, has a certain charm. Doctor Stockmann, who is really rather a silly man, makes this discovery and is foolish enough to think that the town is going to thank him for telling them that their main industry, which is the baths, is full of poisoned water. He thinks he will be cherished; there will be statues to him. So there is a certain charm about the character. Had there not been, I do not think you would ever have heard of that play, despite the fact that the issue is still tremendously important; the issue of public responsibility on the part of officials, on the part of government and on the part of individuals. We have got it here all the time – people manufacturing dangerous medicines and saying, 'Well, if I do not do it, somebody else will do it' and selling it to a gullible public. The issue is always there, but this play would not have been there excepting for that; plus the form of the play. The storytelling is very good. But it is grounded in reality and it is about people, finally.

BIGSBY In 1960 the mood changed as we moved from Eisenhower to John F. Kennedy. Was that a change only of mood and of style, or do you think it was a change of substance?

MILLER For me? Well, it certainly was a change from twenty-five or thirty years before, in the thirties or forties, sure. You see, I was in a bit of a dilemma in the sixties because I did not believe there was a revolution going on. My idea of a revolution was quite different from the one they were advertising. I thought the kids who were out on the streets throwing rocks at the cops would, in five years, ten years, be behind desks selling stocks. That is the way it looked to me. Why? Because they had no viable alternative, economically. There was no economic statement. They despised economics. They were contemptuous of political planning of any kind; they were not into that. Everything was personal, completely personal, and I thought that, when that got exhausted, nothing would have changed, except that some people would have become dope addicts, others would have been killed by it and others would have been burned out by it. But it would not have changed anything because they really did not have a political plan of any kind.

Some did. They were influential in this country for a time. I think they had been underestimated. They helped stop the Vietnam War, which is no mean trick; for that in itself they deserved a lot of credit. But that was the issue and, once that issue passed, there was no ongoing scheme of things. I can't blame them because I did not have any, either! I am not criticising anybody, I am just stating a fact. You can't have a revolution if you do not have an alternative vision and the only alternative vision they had was Flower Power. I started to write a little movie script, which I never finished, called *The Love Drug* and, by God, there is one now! Some young guy discovers a drug that makes everybody affectionate. He feeds it to the cops and he feeds it to the army. He stops wars. It is all great except that the aggression implicit in industrial production, which makes people get on the train in the morning to go to work, was stopped, too. They loved one another so much they stopped working! We are damned, it seems to me, by our human nature. It requires a certain aggressiveness, if you are going to carry on an industrial system.

BIGSBY   That seems to me to have surfaced in your 1968 play *The Price*.

MILLER   *The Price* was a kind of summing up of the balance of forces. There is a policeman on one side who is a dutiful, socially responsible human being; on the other side is his older brother, a surgeon, a very aggressive, money-minded guy who, however, is an extraordinarily good surgeon. Nothing less than perfection is what he is after, and it is a form of aggression against people and against himself. It drives him nuts. Now, which one do you want? Well, I'm afraid you have to have both of them, and that is what that play is telling you, which is not good news for the human race, I guess, but I thought that that was the balance of forces.

BIGSBY   But, before *The Price*, you re-entered the theatre after this nine-year gap as far as theatre was concerned, with *After the Fall*, a play that is close to certain aspects of your own experience.

MILLER   The plays are my biography, really. I can't write
something that does not seem to be summing up where I am. So
it is not really any more autobiographical than *The Price* is. *The
Price* deals with people whom I manifestly do not seem to be like,
but I am in all of them. You have got to be; I do not know how
else to go about writing.

BIGSBY   It is also a play, like all of your work, in which the past
bears directly on the present. In fact, the past is not separate from
the present; it is contained in the present.

MILLER   The present is simply the part of the past that we are
confronted with at the moment. That's all.

BIGSBY   You followed *After the Fall* in 1965 with *Incident at Vichy*.
Both of those plays touch on the Jewish situation during the war.
Why were you writing in the early sixties about that particular
subject?

MILLER   Because that play is stating that there are values, that
there are things people must commit themselves to. Mind you,
that was written in a time when all values were up in the air.
People were saying, 'Well, you believe that, that's good. You're a
Nazi. And you have as much right to be a Nazi as I have to be a
vegetarian.' The principle is that everyone has the right to be
what he wants to be. In other words, there is no society is what
that message of that time was.

BIGSBY   Is that also why you reacted against the theatre of the
Absurd?

MILLER   It seemed to suspend all values, and it was a fake because
we rely on certain values when we walk into the street. The value
I rely on when I walk into the street is that, if I have a wristwatch
on, you are not going to come with a big knife and cut my arm off
to get the wristwatch, at least you should not, and that is what I'm
relying on. Even if I am absurd, I am an absurd author with a
wristwatch. I am still relying on that value when I am out. That
has always caught me sideways. I always felt there was a
fraudulence at the bottom of that attitude towards existence. It
seemed to be overlooking the fact that we do rely on these values,
as long as you are not living alone in a desert or a forest. When
you are involved with other people, there have to be certain rules.
Maybe you do not like it, but you are relying on it. That is the
point. In *Incident at Vichy*, this is presented in a fairly abstract
way, but not altogether. The human being's sense of himself

depended upon separating himself from an evil that he saw was an evil, and he could not go on being himself until that separation was effectively made. That was true of the Prince in the play who, in effect, sacrificed himself for another man. That action combined self-sacrifice with the assertion of some kind of value that is at the bottom of that play. The Jewish side of it is important, of course, but it was the framework. It was the occasion, not the theme.

BIGSBY What was your attitude to theatre in America in the 1960s, with its emphasis on actors and directors? One group, for example, took a copy of *The Crucible* and cut it up.

MILLER Right. That was a revolt against authority. When they did that production, they were all very young people, sixteen, seventeen, eighteen years old, it seemed to me. They sat on children's swings and recited the whole play that way at about four times the speed of normal conversation, so that all you heard was this sort of hubbub. I asked them, 'Why do you do that? How does anybody understand?' They said, 'Well, everybody knows the play, and they are very moved by this.' I objected to it. Anyway, some young fellow called out to me and said, 'Why are you opposed to this? It's a great honour. They are regarding *The Crucible* as a sort of found-object.' I said, 'Yes, but it's a found-object that nobody lost. Why should I be happy about this? You labour over something and create it and put it in place, and then somebody goes and takes the scissors and runs them across this play. I can't be happy about that.' But, of course, they were looking at it from an entirely performance viewpoint. They had learned not to care about the text at all. I don't know, maybe that is good. Maybe they will find their way to some other art form. But it certainly has not got anything to do with the theatre that I know anything about.

BIGSBY In the mid-1960s you became President of PEN International, which is the writers' organisation. What did you learn from that experience?

MILLER I learned a lot. When I became President of it, it was falling apart. They came to me and said, 'There will be no PEN if somebody does not take it over who is well known.' PEN started out after World War One as an organisation developed by mainly British writers – George Bernard Shaw (admittedly an Irishman) and a whole long list of wonderful people, plus a few French and

277

one or two Germans. The idea was that they would abort another war if all the writers of all the countries got together all the time, to create an international community that would prevent nationalism doing what it had done in World War One, namely, to pit the cultures of the various countries against one another. The cultures could prevent the politicians from driving populations against one another. Finally, it broke apart, to a degree, when the German writers were expelled, in 1934 I think it was, for defending the Hitler Reich, the persecution of the Jews and the destruction of various intellectuals in Germany. Anyway, up to World War Two it had a symbolic function of sorts but, once the war was over, it seemed not to have any function except as a general gathering place for writers to talk. It was devolving into a tea party of sorts, excepting that one side of it was becoming part of the Cold War.

By the early fifties it was enlisted pretty deeply, probably in the CIA, and the rest of the Cold War. By the late sixties, though, the Cold War was in bad odour among intellectuals. It was starting to get rancid and PEN really had nowhere to go. What could they do except fight Communism? So they came to me and I said, 'Well, you've got a lot of people in jail for various reasons all over the world. How about that?' I had never become a Cold Warrior and I was still somewhat acceptable in the East since I had battled with the Cold War in the West; and the West really did not give a damn what I was, much. So I took it over out of curiosity, partly, and I am glad I did. I think I invigorated it; it now became a place for people of any ideological conviction, provided they could subscribe to its libertarian constitution. It believed in liberty for everybody and that PEN had to enlist itself to support the liberties of writers, no matter what the system. So there was no a priori judgement about Communism involved there and, consequently, we got a lot of help to people in the Communist world, the black African revolutionary world and various parts of the world, and gradually we attained some kind of respectable standing. But the main thing for me was meeting all these folks from various cultures who were so different, one from the other, and yet seemed to be sharing a set of values despite everything. It was quite reassuring. We were talking the same language.

BIGSBY   You say that governments all around the world put writers into prison, which they do. Do they flatter them when they do that? Do writers really have the kind of power that makes them a threat to the state?

MILLER They do in illiterate societies. The West is not illiterate and that is why the writer has a difficult time being politically significant. In Eastern countries like, for example, parts of Yugoslavia, which were dominated by the Turks at one time or another, or by the Russians, or the Austrians, the native language was suppressed and you could go to jail for writing something in Serbian. The Austrians would put you in jail. In fact, they shot one of their great poets, back in eighteen ninety-something, because to speak that language of an oppressed people was a declaration of opposition to the dominating force. The writer was in charge of the language. He was keeping the language alive and, therefore, the nationalism alive, a prohibited nationalism, and that is why they looked to the writer as the soul of the country. On the other hand in the United States, England, France, Germany and the rest of it, where such a condition does not exist, you can't expect the writer to have that function; and he does not. I do not think he ever will. So, they are flattering to them, but at the same time they are scared of them. Implicitly the writer is describing, or outlining, the ethnic definition of that people, by merely writing in that language in a noble fashion.

BIGSBY And, in some senses, the theatre has played a significant role in that. In order to view theatre, you have to come together in a crowd, in a group.

MILLER Very dangerous!

BIGSBY Often in circumstances which otherwise would make you liable to imprisonment.

MILLER That is right, and I saw it when I went to Russia when Brezhnev was in charge. The attitude of people inside the theatre was completely different from what it was out on the street because here they had, so to speak, a licence to be themselves. You could laugh at jokes that, if told in the street, would embarrass you with the authorities. But here you were allowed to do that. Repression makes it important and we do not have that kind of repression. We have a kind of parody of it here, the Gangster Rap, which is a kind of street talk in the ghettos that they have made music of. People are scared of it; in effect it has almost been outlawed in various places, on the radio and so on. Why? Because it echoes the black rebellion, the very fact that they are using a language that the whites do not quite understand. It defines them, in a way that indicates that they are thumbing their noses at the white culture. It is very important.

BIGSBY   There is obviously a politics to many of your plays but, in 1968, you stepped directly into the political arena because you went as a delegate to the Democratic National Convention in Chicago, which turned out to be an absolute bear pit.

MILLER   Oh, that was a terrifying experience! That was a scary place. I'll never forget the look on those Chicago cops. I think they were on the verge of attacking us, the delegates, and it was very frightening. I got elected because I live in this village here and I had no idea I was being elected. They had a Democratic caucus here in town, which elected me without telling me.

On the one hand it was a demonstration of American democracy at work and on the other hand it was frightening. The Vietnam War was going on. I had made speeches against the war and was openly against it. I was part of a group of delegates who were against it. We were trying to get the national party to declare against the war, which was impossible, but between us and the young people, we brought down LBJ. He could not run again and they put up Hubert Humphrey, the Vice-President, because LBJ did not dare come into Chicago! Can you believe it? The Secret Service and the rest of them would not guarantee his safety, such was the ferocity of the hatred for him because of the war, carrying on this dreadful, criminal enterprise that they were engaged in. He could have been the greatest president of the twentieth century. He introduced more wonderful reforms in this country than anybody, including Kennedy and the rest of them.

BIGSBY   He was an old New Dealer.

MILLER   He was fantastic; he had more courage than anybody. Then he went and destroyed himself with this madness in southeast Asia. It was a real tragedy. It was a hubris business for which I do not know the full explanation. Anyway, it was terrible, but it showed a side of American civilisation that one would rather not think about, because the violence underlying that thing was manifest.

BIGSBY   Vietnam was a very curious war. First of all, it was an undeclared war. Then the Americans were told that they were winning until it was lost. When the troops returned there were no parades. Later, Robert McNamara, who was Secretary of Defense

280

at the time, said that he never really believed in it, even though he was sending thousands of Americans to their deaths. It was then, and in some ways is now, about denial, and denial has been at the heart of your plays.

MILLER   Oh, yes, that is what they are about. But I think that is what a certain kind of tragedy is about. A lot of Ibsen is full of denial and the explosion of denial by circumstances so that it is untenable, finally. Yes, I understood that when we were fighting it. During the Vietnam War I was called by the Commandant of West Point. He wanted to know if I would make a speech there. I said, 'Are you sure you have the right person?' He said, 'Man, I know who you are.' I said, 'What would you like me to talk about?' He said, 'We read in the paper that you have just come back from Cambodia,' which Inge and I had visited as tourists. We were, in fact, the last European-type people out of Cambodia before Mr Kissinger decided to bomb the hell out of it and destroy civilisation. That was one of his little tricks. We were now sending troops there to become part of the theatre of the Vietnam War. I said, 'Well, I think you know my attitude about this.' He said, 'Oh, we'd like to discuss it.' I said, 'Well, I'm flattered. Sure, I'd love to do it.'

So I went down there, and I was trembling a little. There was this whole class of cadets and their officers, a lot of medals all over the place, and most of these officers had served in Vietnam. What I was going to tell them was that the war was absolutely hopeless and pointless, and that the sacrifices being made were simply too horrifying to contemplate, because they were not in a good cause. So I got up there and said, 'I've just come back from Cambodia and all I'm going to tell you is, you can't win. We're on the wrong side and, if you did win, it would be sand that would simply pour through your fingers.' The army was losing people and I thought that since I was not in the war then the least I can do was say this. Then I told them why, and what I thought of what I had seen.

At the back of the room stood this man with a big red moustache and a bald head. I have never seen such a person. He had big bushy red eyebrows and a big red moustache and no hair, and he had four rows of medals. He was a colonel. I said, 'Are there any questions? I'd be happy to answer them, but let's not fight about this. You wanted me to come and tell you what I thought, so I've told you.' He raised his hand and said, 'I was a military attaché in Phnom Penh, Cambodia, for nine years until last year, and I just want to tell you all, everything he has told you is right.'

The alienation of the army was unbelievable. I was up until three o'clock with these officers, all of whom had been in Vietnam. There was not one of them, not one, out of the eight or so sitting around drinking, who felt any differently. They said, 'It's the politicians who have created this war. The thing is unwinnable. We should not be there. We are wasting ourselves and destroying the country, and this country.' They told me that West Point is about an hour above New York City, but on leave they did not go down to New York in uniform, such was the hostility to the army. These guys are like priests, in a way; they belong to an order. Many of them are very honourable people who care passionately about their army. It was one of the saddest days of my life. They were caught in this dilemma. They were not prepared to revolt, and they had to go on training people to be sent into what they knew was a hopeless and wrong situation. It was terrible.

BIGSBY   So the sixties ended with the war raging in Vietnam and with Richard Nixon back in the White House, the man who had been part of the anti-Communist witch-hunt of the 1950s.

MILLER   Yes, it was a great time to be alive.

BIGSBY   Can you recall what your feelings were?

MILLER   Oh, yes, hopeless anger. How can you write in anger like that? It was just like being caught on fly-paper. You went from LBJ to Richard Nixon. The terrible thing is that, if you believe the American people are hopelessly reactionary, that is one thing, but I do not believe that. They support these guys with the delusionary idea that they are going to lead them towards some progressive future, you see. I suppose the country gets the leadership it deserves, in the final analysis. Maybe I am wrong. Maybe I am too naïve and idealistic about it; but I still believe in the American people. There is a democratic instinct here that is powerful, if you can call it up, but it gets betrayed all the time. It gets shilly-shallied around; it is awful, and they lose their sons that way. They lose their peace. Oh, dear God. Well, it will go on; this struggle is not going to end tomorrow. But I am still alive and working on it.

BIGSBY   Then came a new decade, the seventies.

MILLER   I have no memory of it at all. I sometimes doubt whether it really happened! I could not tell you what was going on in the seventies. It was a terrible waste of time, the seventies. If we can, we should send them in and exchange them for something good! The Vietnam War was over and Carter was coming in. So that was nothing happening in a big way. Who was writing stuff then? I wonder. Probably we are missing a whole epoch. It certainly escapes my memory.

BIGSBY   One thing that was happening in terms of theatre, from the sixties into the seventies, was that the audience was fragmenting along racial and gender lines.

MILLER   Yes, *The Price* went on in 1968 and I remember thinking right then that something had happened in the culture, because I felt that the audience was dividing between the young and the old. For one thing, the off-Broadway theatre was getting more interesting than the Broadway theatre. Mind you, the Broadway theatre was always where things were started. Whatever you want to say about it, it was the commercial producers who took the risks. The small theatres, in universities and little towns, the so-called resident theatres, or whatever you want to call them, simply reproduced what was going on, by and large, on Broadway. Now that current began to back up and reverse itself. I remember that very clearly. I remember being very discouraged when *The Price* was going on, that something deadly had come into the so-called professional theatre. It had stopped moving forward, good or bad, it just was lying there rather helplessly.

BIGSBY   You had always been a Broadway writer; that is where your plays opened. Were you tempted, in the seventies, to put on plays off-Broadway, or to associate with a regional theatre?

MILLER   Well, I did work a little bit with the Long Wharf in New Haven which is, of course, outside New York. I did not do it, I suppose, because I could still find a cast in Broadway theatres and there was still a willingness to back my plays up to a point. But I felt the hostility there, too. I remember Walter Kerr, who was otherwise a valued critic, writing a piece about *The Price* saying that if I were to continue to dominate the theatre, I would destroy it. His reasoning was that the theatre is really about enjoyment and being happy, and that I was introducing all kinds of elements that had to do with death and disfigurement and the rest of it, and that this would drive the audience out of the theatre.

He may have been right, because, of course, what really happened was something quite different that he knew nothing about, I think. A large piece of that audience moved out of New York and became suburban people, and the same thing happened in many other places. But it took years and years for a theatre to be developed that would serve that kind of audience, and it never did really develop on a high level in most places. From the middle-to-late sixties onwards, you no longer had a coherent middle-class audience, which was what had supported the theatre from time immemorial. There were a lot of visitors from out of town, there were boatloads and busloads of folk from villages outside who were getting cheaper tickets because they were buying them en masse, and there were a lot of business people who were given tickets or who had bought tickets who were in town for two days. Those people are not your audience. They are not interested in life; they really want to escape. They are busy all day making money. In the evening they want a good time. They want to go to a nightclub and, if there is a big hit in town, they want to see that hit because that is the thing to go to. But that is not the audience that I had known.

Also, the city became dangerous. That was a very important element. In the late sixties we had all kinds of incidents on Broadway and around Broadway. Certainly there had to be guards at stage entrances. We had never had a guard at the stage entrance. It had been open to the public and the public simply did not come in during the performance. But more than once, when we were doing a production of *The Price*, some hoodlums would come in and raise hell and really disrupt the performance. And where we had taken for granted a certain unity in the audience, which I think probably existed, it was now gone.

Then, accompanying that, we had the intellectualisation of criticism, which had not been quite the case before. A lot of academic critics poured in from Harvard and other schools, who really had no sympathy for American theatre anyway. They were people who thought that nothing good could come out of the American theatre in terms of thoughtful, profound drama. They barely acknowledged that O'Neill had lived. They thought he was a melodramatist, a hokey writer who had no literary qualifications, and that Europe was the thing.

BIGSBY   Or the American avant-garde.

MILLER   Or the American avant-garde. If you could follow the thing with some reasonable ease, it could not be any good. They worshipped obscurity and so-called revolution, which was nothing more than a way of looking down on blacks by making them unique. They were no longer part of the human race. But it was basically a European slant to the theatre which, of course, is where we came in. Washington Irving, who lived right after the American Revolution and was probably the first professional critic the New York theatre had, was complaining all the time that some of his fellow commentators regarded anything British as being automatically better than anything American. The irony was that when I went to England in the fifties, they would ask me, 'How come the American theatre is so great and ours is so crappy?' If you tried to explain to American critics they would look at you with blank eyes, thinking this could not possibly be the case. The sneer at American theatre was total, just about total, and this did not help either.

BIGSBY   You have never had a national theatre in this country. Maybe you can't; maybe it is just too big a country.

MILLER   I never took this argument seriously, but there are people who think that our national theatre, or the equivalent of it, are all these theatres in universities and regional theatres. I do not believe it, because I have seen enough of the productions and, with all due respect, they are not on a high level for the most part. There is some good work in Chicago on a very high level, occasionally something in California, but on the whole, they cannot keep actors long enough to create a high-level theatre and the reason is very simple. If somebody makes a remarkable debut, he is on his way to the movies before you can say Jack Robinson. There have been a few exceptions, like Malkovich, who stayed with the Chicago company with which he began, but it is hard to ask an actor to turn down two million dollars, or five, or eight, in an interesting movie, in order to play eight weeks in a moderately interesting play to an audience of hundreds. I am not sure we have a right to do that. So there is something systemic that is very wrong with the situation. It was beginning to really roll us up in the late sixties.

I had a problem with Lee Cobb in 1949. Lee opened in *Death of a Salesman* and within five weeks he was wanting to get out and go to Hollywood, because his stock had risen so high. He was being offered a lot of money, but finally he was such a pest that we let him go. He immediately got on a horse and became a sheriff. From *Death of a Salesman*! He kept saying he was going to do *Lear*. Years went by, but no *Lear*. He finally did *Lear*, and it was lousy, because he no longer had the concentration that you need. You can't just do *Lear* after doing fifteen Westerns and some melodramas. Well, that was the end of him as a serious actor. This was back in 1949, before allegedly all our problems began. So it has been going a long time. There are very few people who have stayed with the theatre. There are a few, Jessica Tandy, Hume Cronyn, people like that, who could mix the two successfully. However, they had independent money; they were not desperate for the next dollar bill, and maybe they were not offered such fortunes in the movies that it got to be an outrageous temptation.

BIGSBY   In 1977 you wrote a play called *The Archbishop's Ceiling*, which is set in an archbishop's palace in Europe. What led you to write that play then?

MILLER   I had been President of PEN and I got to know some of the situation in Czechoslovakia, so I wrote the play about the idea of the government, any government, listening to us. But more important than that to me was that this play is about a group of writers who socialised in the former home of the Archbishop of Prague. I did not identify Prague but it was quite obvious to anybody. It was now the home of a Czech writer and nobody was quite sure that he was not an agent of the government while, at the same time, he himself had been imprisoned in the past for several years. Of course, that was no guarantee. You could be imprisoned and then come out and make a deal with the government in order to get out of prison, and inform on your fellow writers. In fact, they used to bring a lot of girls there and have a fine old time, some of the writers. The scuttlebutt was that this place was bugged by the government, by the secret police, and nobody was ever sure. They still loved the whisky, the girls and so on, and they all went and fooled around there, but finally the government arrested, or threatened to arrest, their best writer.

They all, even those who disliked him, had to admit that he was their one genius and in him the spirit of the country resided.

So now it became a crisis, how to approach this writer who owned this apartment to try to get him to intervene with the government. It wasn't certain that he could do that, but it seemed likely that he could. Like everything in Czechoslovakia at that time, it was covered with cobwebs. You never knew who the hell you were talking to, what side he was on, whether he was your friend or your enemy, whether you were digging your own grave by raising certain issues in certain environments. So the whole question used to occur to me: how do we define ourselves? When are we talking to whoever we are talking to, and when are we partially talking to authority, whether it be the authority of the university, or the city administration, or whatever, or the actual government? So there were two listeners in every conversation: one was the person you were talking to, the other was some authority or another. So how do you wiggle through that maze and what is left of you, finally, when you have wiggled through it? Can you identify yourself any more? The nature of human reality began to come into play, what it was, what it entailed, and whether, indeed, you could even speak of sincerity any more, since everybody had to engineer his speech in one way or another, even with the best of motives. That was really what lay behind that play because I thought that, in a different way, it applied to the United States and probably everywhere else where there was a government.

BIGSBY   This was post-Watergate and Nixon bugged the White House.

MILLER   Right. Now, curiously, I went to Washington two or three years ago. This play was, as you said, in the seventies. I went there at the behest of the Authors' League to try to influence Senators to support the National Endowment for the Arts. I was, of course, assigned the most reactionary right-wing Senators to talk to. I got finished making my pitch to Senator Lugar, who listened quietly, and he said, 'You know, the best explication I have ever seen of the problem of the government and the suppression of literature and the arts, and so on, was a play I saw called *The Archbishop's Ceiling*!' I said, 'Where the hell did you see that?' He said, 'In Washington', and he went on and on about that. He got it. He understood the whole thing very well, but, of course, he is a practised politician so he knows the dangers of being that close to power, where you have to watch everything you say and be alert even to bugs and the rest of it. The idea of just talking to somebody out of the goodness of your heart is a very remote thing to these people.

BIGSBY   Of course, you yourself are not unfamiliar with the notion of bugs and eavesdroppers because you were followed by the FBI for a number of years.

MILLER   Certainly. I got my FBI file. Of course, they blacked out ninety per cent of it for what they called 'security reasons'. They meant embarrassment reasons. One item they forgot to black out was a dinner party I had in the fifties in Brooklyn. One of the guests, un-named, left and was trailed by their agent! Imagine! They blacked out why, or who the person was, so I could not identify him, but he was followed in the street by an FBI man! Imagine paying somebody to follow somebody like that and how many thousands of idiots we must have had roaming around doing that? Because I can't recall ever having dinner in my house with somebody who was worth following! I mean, we had all kinds of maniacs, but nobody you would want to follow.

BIGSBY   You ended the 1970s writing a play called *The American Clock*, set in the 1930s. It was very close in some respects to the very first play you ever wrote, in Michigan. Why revisit the 1930s just as the seventies turned into the eighties?

MILLER   I think it was because I wanted somehow to remind myself and the people in the audience – if there was to be an audience – about a totally different America. It seemed to me that we had completely lost any historical sense. I had talked to young people; they knew nothing whatsoever about the thirties or the forties or the fifties. We continually seem to devour or wipe out the past. Consequently there is always a groping for some kind of handhold on reality. A lot of neurosis comes out of that; it is very unhealthy. I think we just do not give a damn about what happened. It is mildly interesting, occasionally – you see an old car and think, oh, that's the way they used to make cars, or an old train. But any old idea, or any old way of life, is of no conceivable use. It simply has no utilitarian value. I really do think we do that.

So I thought it would be interesting to paint a canvas of life thirty or forty years ago. I set up situations which would be completely new to the current audience of the 1970s, whenever I was writing it. It failed in New York. It was a big hit in London, but the London director, Peter Wood, found the key to that play.

I have always been cursed by people who think I am writing some kind of realism, or naturalism, which is the last thing in the world I have any interest in. Peter understood immediately that this was a kind of vaudeville show, and he directed it like a real vaudeville, different acts coming on, a circus atmosphere. It was marvellous. It was plodding and documentary in New York, and I simply could not get it off the ground. This can happen, of course, in the theatre, as we discussed before. You are at the mercy of your interpreters. In that case, I had some very fine actors, but there was no real thrust to the whole damn thing.

BIGSBY The reputation for realism comes from one play, *All My Sons*.

MILLER Yes, and *All My Sons* was a sport among all of the plays I had written. I had never written a play like that before and I have never really written a play like that since. It is laziness, I'm convinced. It is not just my problem; everybody's problem with the press is that they have got a morgue. They look you up in the morgue and repeat the last thing said. Nobody is going to sit down and read something new. They just remanipulate the old shibboleths and reissue them. It's sad.

BIGSBY There is another curious thing, though, about your reputation in America. You are celebrated as the author of *All My Sons, Death of a Salesman, The Crucible, A View from the Bridge*, but not too many people show an awareness of the sixties, seventies, eighties and nineties, whereas in England there have been outstanding productions of those plays.

MILLER Sure. Well, one of the reasons is that I was unfashionable. Theatre is largely fashion; it always is, always was, probably always will be, and certain things at any one moment do not seem to be 'with it'. It's a bit like clothing. Skirts go down, they go up. Lapels get wide, they get narrow. Suddenly you look at your shirt and think, I can't wear that, the thing dates me by ten years. If I was labelled as somebody from the fifties, or forties, or thirties, or whatever, it's hard to get through to them. I think principally it is because we had no high-level, non-commercial theatre; none available to me in any case. All the productions you are referring to occured in either the National Theatre, the RSC, Bristol Old Vic or the Young Vic in London. These are all non-commercial theatres.

BIGSBY If you had had such a theatre in America, with which you'd had a working relationship, would your career have been different?

MILLER   No question about that. For example, *Broken Glass* should never have been done on Broadway. I did not want it done on Broadway. The producer's an old friend of mine. We did the thing first at Long Wharf, which was perfectly fine. That was a non-commercial thing and it should have gone from there to a non-commercial theatre or an off-Broadway theatre. That play did not belong competing with musicals, with *Cats*. It's not built for that. It can't exist alongside those shows. But he persisted in thinking that he could beat the rap, beat the system with that. I never believed it, but I went along, thinking, well, I do not want to stand in the way. But, curiously (this I got from one of the co-producers only last month, in Paris, who knew it better than I did), we were sold out all the time that play was running. All the seats were not necessarily paid for at the top box-office price, but there were never empty seats in that theatre. That's about eight hundred and ten seats; that's a big theatre. But we still had to close the play. Why? Because the costs were just a little bit greater than the income from eight hundred and ten people. Well, clearly, there is something wrong with a system where you fill eight hundred and ten seats a night and can't keep the play running. That is not the play's fault. That is something wrong with the relationship of the theatre to its audience, to its play and so on.

BIGSBY   In 1984 you had the chance to explore another theatre and another culture when you went to China to direct the production of *Death of a Salesman*.

MILLER   That was a great adventure for me, because, of course, I know no Chinese and, at the time, it was the first time that a foreign director had worked in China. So they did not know how to deal with me and I certainly did not know how to deal with them. But all was made possible by Ying Ruocheng, who played Willy and was an actor you may have seen in *The Last Emperor*, that terrific movie. He played the main Communist. Ying is a very good actor, very literate. He knows more English than I do, which is not difficult, and he could play Willy and interpret. I had an official interpreter but she knew nothing about the theatre and she was too slow, so Ying gradually moved into interpreting for the other actors.

BIGSBY   And you were staging this play in a society that really knows nothing about the concept of a salesman?

MILLER   Well, there is an interesting thing about that. Before we started, I had lunch with Ying and a couple of other people in the cast at the American Embassy. The American Ambassador at the time had been born in China and, of course, he understood, read and wrote Chinese. The question came up: 'Are the people going to understand this play' – among other things the form in which it is written, which is full of recollections where people come out of nowhere and perform on the stage like real people, but who are memories? A lot of people on the embassy staff thought the Chinese people would never get it. They said that the Chinese audience is very primitive. They were sophisticated within the Chinese context, but their idea of foreign cultures was incredible.

The only one who was confident was the Political Officer. His job was to estimate what was going on politically in China. He said, 'Ridiculous! Of course they are going to get it. They invented the whole thing.' I said, 'What are you talking about?' He said, 'Well, they knew business back here two thousand years ago. The Communist era is, what, forty-five years old. You are dealing with a culture here that is six thousand years old. They were buying and selling before Marco Polo thought he invented the whole thing in Europe.' So it was a question of whether he was right or the other people were right. The interesting part of it was that I found quickly that the equivalence existed in both cultures for the same thing.

There is one scene in which Happy Loman and his brother are trying to pick up two girls in a bar, and the question was how should he behave. The actor playing Happy tended to be very severe, serious, with these two young women. I said, 'No, he has got to be far easier than you are being.' Of course, they were dealing with very foreign ideas. Happy boasts that his brother is a great football player, a member of the New York Giants. None of these things have any meaning; they have never heard of these games. I was trying to explain to him the atmosphere of a bar and a young guy trying to pick up these girls. In Communist China, at that time especially, this would not have been a common occurrence. So I said to him, 'Do you ever pick up any girls?' He said, 'Well, I haven't, but people do.' I said, 'What would you be likely to say to impress a young lady with how important you are, so that she would go to bed with you, maybe, later?' He said, 'Well, I would say, probably, that I have a brother in Hong Kong!' That implied that there was all kinds of money available, television sets and so forth. As soon as he raised that image in his own mind, he went ahead and played that scene beautifully. So he did not have to know about the New York Giants, football, or anything. He said those lines, but he was thinking of his brother in Hong Kong; and it's the same idea.

BIGSBY   And did the Chinese audience interpret the play in the same way as an American audience?

MILLER   I am sure a lot of them did. They interpreted the family situation perfectly because family, of course, means an enormous amount in China. Moreover, they understood the situation of Willy's sons. As they say, 'Every man wants his son to be a dragon,' meaning a dominating figure. So they understood Willy and Biff, and that was absolutely obvious to them. However, the younger people – I think there was evidence for this – thought that Willy was right and Biff was wrong in this argument about the economy and about life. CBS had a television crew there, interviewing people when they came out of the theatre. A couple of them could speak English. One young man was in tears as he came out of the theatre. They said, 'What did you think of it?' He said, 'Oh, it's wonderful. It is exactly right, what Willy says. Everybody wants to be Number One Man. And Biff, he is wrong. He is like the cultural revolution.' Indeed, during rehearsals, the actor who played Biff said, 'Now, tell me. Does he belong to some organisation?' I said, 'Well, no, what organisation could he belong to?' He said, 'Well, he sounds like a Cultural Revolutionary. He is absolutely against the profit system, against competing with people, against asserting himself, and he wants to embrace society, mankind. It is strange that he is not part of any organisation. How could any one guy think that way, all by himself?' And that involved a long discussion about American civilisation.

This shows you that the Chinese, at least that generation, could not really conceive of himself alone. He was an element in a society, very consciously. Indeed, under Communism everybody belonged to an organisation of some kind or another. Even if it was a housewife, she belonged to some association in the village. The idea that somebody alone could do this was quite hard to understand. Anyway, I had a big education about China as a result of directing that play.

BIGSBY   The shadow of the Cultural Revolution also fell, in a different way, over the production of another play of yours in China, which was *The Crucible*.

MILLER   Oh, yes. That was quite different, though. That was done by a director who had spent quite some part of his life in London. He was a Chinese, a very elegant man. Anyway, I met, as it happened, a year after we were in China, a woman who wrote *Life and Death in Shanghai* [Nien Cheng]. She had been in prison, in solitary confinement, for six years. They had killed her daughter, who had been a Red Guard. But times change, politics change. She told me that, when she got out, the director of *The Crucible* wanted her to see the play he had just directed, which she did. I had this conversation with her in New York, at my publishers, because the same publisher published both our books. Tears were coming into her eyes as she was talking to me. She said, 'When I saw that play, I said to him, "who revised the play?"' He said, 'Nobody. We've made a very literal translation of this play.' She said, 'But Miller is not a Chinese name.' He said, 'No, no, he is American.' She said, 'I simply could not believe the fact that exactly the same questions were asked in the Cultural Revolution of people under suspicion as were asked by the witch-hunters in your play. And when I got home to America I got a copy of your play in English, and it devastated me, the idea that we had been through something that had already taken place in 1692! I was so grateful to you that somebody finally had said this.' Can you believe it? So the same thing goes on and on and on for ever. That is the lesson of that conversation.

BIGSBY   In the mid-1980s the world was already beginning to change quite fundamentally. You were one of a number of writers who went to meet Mikhail Gorbachev. Can you recall what your impressions were when you met him?

MILLER   I had grave suspicions about him, because I knew enough to know that nobody gets to be the number-one man in what was then the Soviet Union without being vetted by the Communist Party and the chiefs. For him to be talking about democracy and so on, you had to wonder what the hell was going on. Surely he could not be reflecting the ideas of the people around him? However, notwithstanding all that, I was very impressed with him because, while he described himself as a Leninist, whatever that might mean, meaning that he was convinced of Socialism in their form, at the same time he would say things like 'Marx lived in the nineteenth century. He knew nothing about jet planes; he knew nothing about modern dynamics in the scientific world. He took certain things for granted as being unchangeable, and we know that they are changeable, that we have to have new ideas and we have got to shake up our whole system of beliefs. Nothing is sacred any more, and we have got to create a new relationship with capitalism.' That was very important. There was no longer to be any hostile relation with the West. That is what he felt. Technology was looming as the ruling force in the world, rather than ideology.

Incidentally, I was not there as a reporter, I was there with six or seven writers. We had been invited to come because we were all attending a conference on the Chinese border, as far east as you can go in the Soviet Union, and suddenly there was this invitation from him. They flew us to Moscow. We met him in the headquarters of the Communist Party in the centre of Moscow, and so I realised that I was at a historic occasion, suddenly. So I began to take notes, with his permission. He was delighted that I would take notes. There was nobody sitting next to him, no assistants, nobody whispering to him. There was a translator and that was it.

Anyway, I left and came back here, and a friend of mine, Harrison Salisbury, one of the editors of the *New York Times* until some years earlier, said, 'That is a major scoop! You have got to write that!' So I wrote a piece just saying what Gorbachev had to say. He then had it sent down at his own expense to the *New York Times*, expecting it was going to be a front-page story. They were not interested! He could not believe it. So he called the *Washington Post*, where he had buddies, and they said, well, send it along. So he sent it to them – no interest. Could not get this piece published anywhere! Nowhere! Nowhere!

So I said to Harrison, you know, we have a party line in this country. The head of the Soviet Union's not supposed to be saying these things! What do they think, I invented this? It was months, four or five months, before the great news began to leak out that somebody different had taken over in the Soviet Union. So my faith in reality as reported by the press is nil! I open a paper and the first question I ask myself is, I wonder what really happened today. Because that was a lesson.

BIGSBY   In 1987 you published your autobiography, *Timebends*, which is structured almost exactly like *Death of a Salesman*.

MILLER   I guess it is, yes. It is the idea that the past is in the present, that the present is simply that part of the past that has emerged, momentarily. It is neither more nor less than that; that you are always speaking to your past, and out of your past. You are up to your neck in the same stream that you were always in.

BIGSBY   Is there any element of self-discovery in writing your autobiography? You have lived that life, after all, so nothing should be a surprise.

MILLER   It is a surprise, when you start digging it up and realise the length of time, for example, that you put into things that have no issue, that are completely pointless. Most of what we do in our lives is trivial and of no significance. That comes through when you work to try to resurrect the things that seemed important – and were important. I look at myself, probably, as another person a lot of the time in writing a thing like that. I was writing about the first time I wrote a play, thinking of myself as this kid who was doing this stuff. Then as a young man trying to make his way. The most mysterious thing we have is time. I do not understand it. I am in the same body, I am the same human being, as I was seventy years ago. How is that conceivable? I do not know the answer to this: that I could contain in my head, in the same head that is reading today's newspaper, images that are three-quarters of a century old. Weird! So time is a gelatinous substance that spreads itself over everything. It is not a column or a block or a triangle or a geometric thing. It is a Jello.

BIGSBY   You have always taken as a central assumption in your plays the existence of something called 'society', the individual being responsible to society, and society being a reflection of the individual. That was exactly what was under assault in Britain and in America in the 1980s. Suddenly it was a world of competing individuals with no social responsibility. Was that what was behind the play you brought out in 1991, *The Ride Down Mount Morgan*?

MILLER   *The Ride Down Mount Morgan* is a play about relativistic values. If I feel it, I ought to be able to do it. If I like two people at the same time, I have a right to betray both of them at the same time.

BIGSBY   The central character is a bigamist.

MILLER   Yes. It was an attempt to examine the morality of a man who has tremendous passion for two families. He tries not to betray either, but betrays both of them. There is no production of that play in the United States, yet [it reached Broadway in 1998]. Wonderfully enough, it is very successful in Germany. They know about this kind of ambiguity. The French have done it.

BIGSBY   It is surely partly about the eighties, in the sense that it is about a man who believes he can have everything.

MILLER   Sure, he can have it all. Choices are unnecessary. Choices are for the sluggards. The poetic truth of life is that you can't have everything. The result of having everything in this play is the dilemma of somebody who does, indeed, have everything for ten years. He has it all, and it is driving him nuts. I had a lot of fun writing that play, because it is very funny to me. It may not be funny to other people, but it is to me.

BIGSBY   You wrote another play in the early nineties, called *The Last Yankee* which, apart from anything else, is about the price that can be paid for failure in America. That is something that echoes through a number of your other plays.

MILLER   Yes, because we live in fear of falling, in fear of losing status. At the present moment, incidentally, it's the first time in our history, according to the statisticians, that the younger generation is doing worse economically than its parents. It has never happened in this country. This descent from the middle class is unheard of in this country. I think it probably accounts for a lot of the political dislocation that's going on and the spiritual confusion that's rife in this country right now.

BIGSBY   But *The Last Yankee* is also concerned with the corrupting power of the American dream.

MILLER   Yes. See, the Yankee is somebody who has stepped off the train. He is not running after the brass ring any more; but his wife is on that train. She can't see happiness unless it is accompanied by economic success. He makes a perfectly good living, but has got to go to work every day. He works in overalls and does not have an unearned income, which is the evidence of success. She feels that he has disserved himself, and her, by failing in that respect. I love the line when she says, 'You're never on the end of the line' and he says, 'Because I'm on a one-man line. I'm at the head of it and the back of it at the same time.'

BIGSBY   O'Neill used to say that he thought the American people had a biblical conviction that you could possess your soul by inheriting the world, that in some way, material possession places you in possession of your life.

MILLER   It's Calvinist. Calvinism was a kind of bookkeeping operation. The more you made, the more you deserved to make by the laws of God. The fact that you were rolling in money showed that you were in the favour of the Lord. If you did not make it, you were in His disfavour.

BIGSBY   In 1994 came *Broken Glass*, which is set in 1938, the year of Kristallnacht, when the persecution of the Jews became overt. Why, in 1994, turn to that particular period of history?

MILLER   To be candid about it, the woman in the play always fascinated me because there was something magical about her. Here is a basically non-political person, living in an era when women really had no place in politics whatsoever, receiving an impulse over three thousand miles of ocean as a result of seeing a photograph in a newspaper, which could enter her soul and explode her marriage – which was really a false relationship anyway.

BIGSBY   This is a photograph of elderly Jews scrubbing the streets with toothbrushes, with the Nazis standing over them.

MILLER   That's right. She sees that photograph of these old Jews with beards, on their knees, and people around them on the street laughing as they are forced to scrub the sidewalks with toothbrushes. The shock of that vision explodes her life. I suppose, just in itself, the mechanics of that operation fascinated me. You could enlarge on that by saying that it shows that mankind is one thing, that her body is partly in Germany, because she suddenly becomes paralysed, losing the use of her legs. She becomes a hysterical paralytic.

BIGSBY   But you had known that story for decades. Why did it suddenly get earthed?

MILLER   Because we are living in a time when nothing has any relation to anything else and, just for my own sanity, I wanted to write about something that showed a relationship, even across the ocean; that 'A' led to 'B'. That is really the inception of that. It is in relation to a culture that has severed all connections. We are now one individual and another individual and another individual, in the face of the fact that it is perfectly obvious that there is a society, that we are all in the grip of various forces that are raging around us. The reigning philosophy is 'you are on your own'. As Mrs Thatcher said, there is no society. That was breathtaking. It was quite wonderful that somebody would actually say that. It is Brechtian, isn't it? A character in a Brecht play might say that, and you'd listen and say, 'Brecht is a real poet, so he interprets life instead of just reporting it.' But here you could report life and interpret it. That is really the genesis of that play.

BIGSBY   It is a play, though, that has faint echoes of that very early play you wrote, *The Golden Years*, also about paralysis.

MILLER   Well, of course, the idea of being paralysed in the face of overwhelming forces we do not understand is the mark of our time, maybe of all time. We are little ants climbing up and down a gigantic structure. We are not big enough to see what the structure is. All we see is the next ant, or that grain of wood. I like to think it is art that can give us the structure, the vision, of the big thing we are crawling up and down on. That was one of the impulses behind writing *Broken Glass*.

BIGSBY   Did the re-emergence of Nazism play any role in the genesis of this play?

MILLER   In a way, yes; but I do not believe that that play, or any play that I could write, could put a stop to, or slow down, the neo-Nazi movement, if you could call it that. I do not think that art works in such a direct fashion. All it can do is give us a counter-image which, depending on individuals, would lead them to oppose such things as neo-Nazism. It is part of our atmosphere. I would not say that it meant nothing to me, but that alone would not have done it. It is the memory of that lady. Without that I could not have written it and would never have thought of writing it. I remember at the time how mysterious it was. Afterwards, for years later, I would think of her and think what an amazing event that was. It was not as if you had some activist woman who was accustomed to thinking in world terms about Jews or herself or morals or whatever; this lady was a bookkeeper who led a very sequestered life. You could pitch a tent in the middle of those small streets in Brooklyn and nobody would bother you for months. It was quiet, quiet, quiet. No disturbance of any kind, except some kids playing ball or riding on a bike.

BIGSBY She was not paralysed, though, only because of what was going on in Europe. In a way she had been paralysed for much of her life. As she says, she looked after her shoes better than her own life.

MILLER Yes. She gave away her life. She ignored her life. She did what was expected of her at all times. Suddenly it became impossible to accept this any more.

BIGSBY And the process of the play is one whereby she takes possession of her life, takes responsibility for her life back into her own hands.

MILLER Exactly. It has been a pleasant surprise to me that people catch on to that so nicely. I saw the play in Sheffield, a long way from London. It was a matinee audience. I would say ninety per cent of them had grey hair and they were women. And they dug that play! They knew all about that! You could tell from the reaction. They were really sweating bullets, watching that. It was quite wonderful watching it with them on a sunny afternoon in Sheffield. That is the great thing about theatre, isn't it? It really can reach out, touch people and bring them together, somehow. So long as you have got theatre, you have got a society. Thatcher was wrong. You can prove Thatcher wrong that way. They react together, sharing something that normally they would not be doing.

BIGSBY Has your Jewishness become more or less important to you over the years?

MILLER It's not any more important than it was. What has happened to me, like a lot of other people, is that I recognise more as I grow older. It is not a recent thing. It has been going on for a quarter of a century, that a part of my mental equipment, my emotional equipment, was influenced by my being Jewish. I would not have thought of it in those terms before the sixties, maybe. It does not make me different from anybody else, it is just that certain things are emphasised. For example, to me, as a Jew, the world can end, it can literally end. You know this myth of the ten just men: if there are not ten just men left, the whole thing is gone. That is a very Jewish idea. It means ten just Jews. If they disappear, it is all over. God just goes out to lunch and never comes back. It puts an emotional responsibility upon you. You have got to hold up the tent pole, otherwise the tent is going to collapse.

I am sure other people, with a different ideological background, feel the same way. Armenians probably figure they are about to be wiped out, because they damn near were. I thought of them because I got a letter the other day from the Armenian Holocaust Museum. The Jews have a Holocaust Museum in Washington, but the Armenians, of course, were damn near wiped out by the Turks back before the First World War. I know one or two Armenians and they are always on the verge of imagining that it is the end of Armenians. I understand that. It is why I understand what is going on in Serbia and the rest of those places. Each one of those peoples figures they are on the verge of oblivion. It is hard to understand if you are part of an empire or part of a large nation, but you can count the number of Serbs, Moslem people, Croatians, whatever, and an unprincipled politician can work on that fear, as these fellows did and are still doing there. They raise the threat of obliteration. If you do not destroy all your enemies, you are next. This is at the bottom of that struggle, the fear of obliteration by small groups.

BIGSBY   You once said that you never wrote anything good that did not make you blush. What did you mean by that?

MILLER   It has got to be a feeling that I am exposing feelings that normally I would not, through these other people. After all, what is a play? A play is a projection, through so-called autonomous characters, of what the author is feeling. There is no other way to define a play. You have to confront that fact, whether it's Shakespeare or just an ordinary playwright. This is the wonder of Shakespeare, that he could put himself in the position of so many different types of people and feel what they feel, apparently. So, if I reveal something in a play, even through another person, I have to feel the tension of the person who is being revealed. If I am not being revealed, it probably is not worth writing. It means that nobody else on that stage is being revealed.

BIGSBY   You are almost eighty. Looking back, what, outside of the theatre, has given you the greatest pleasure?

MILLER   I think my children. As simple as that. You spend so much time raising these animals and, when they turn out decently, it is rather a miracle, given the hazards of existence. I have taken a great deal of satisfaction from them. One daughter lives down the road here, one mile away. Another is going to move in here soon. I have a son out in California. The fact that they are floating, surviving, living pretty decent lives, is a gratification for me.

BIGSBY   What do you think the theatre has to offer now, because we are living in a totally different world, are we not, of cable, satellite television?

MILLER   This is a real question. I am not so damn sure that I am optimistic about this. The reason is simple: to create theatre on a high level is like creating an orchestra on a high level. You can't go into the street and find thirty fiddlers and put them up on the stage, even people who know the music. They have got to work together; they have got to be trained together. There has got to be a tradition of playing together. Now, how do you do that when people come into a play for six weeks and vanish? I've just seen a play [*Sylvia*] by Pete Gurney, who is a neighbour here. It is a big success, about a dog and two people; a very funny play. That cast has played, I think it is eight weeks, and they are gone next week. Now, Gurney's in California, the director is in Japan; so a whole new cast is going to be put into that play by the stage manager. Those actors have never met one another. It would be a miracle if they could get up on the stage and do this comedy with the spirit and the technique and the finish of that original cast. And yet the play is a success; endless numbers of people are going to be seeing it from now on. Will they be seeing a top-level production? I do not know how long an art can go on at a high level that way.

BIGSBY   Getting eight or nine hundred, let alone a thousand, into a theatre on a regular basis is getting increasingly difficult.

MILLER   Oh, you can't do that. I think there will always be theatre because it is fundamentally relatively simple, relatively cheap. In other words, if you have got a barn, there are always people who want to act, especially girls. Girls love to act. It is always easier to find good actors among girls.

BIGSBY   There are twice as many women actors as men, and half as many parts.

MILLER   That shows I was right! The beast can continue breathing, but I would not call it a healthy situation. Finally what has to happen is that the scope of the plays gets smaller and smaller. You play to three hundred and fifty people in a small theatre. Well, you can't do *The Crucible*. *The Crucible* has something like twenty people in it, of which half a dozen at least are major roles. You have got to have some background. You can't just pick up a kid off the street and do this properly. He has got to be able to handle the English language. I worry about it. I think that maybe we are being flooded out and that it will end up an art for a few people, fed by a few writers and actors who are on their way somewhere else. Ninety-nine per cent of the plays written either do not get produced, or they fail. That is nothing new, but the alternatives are new. A writer who can handle dialogue can get a job in the movies or television and make a living.

BIGSBY   Yet, in the face of all this, you have written three new plays in the nineties. A fourth is beginning.

MILLER   But what would I have done if I were twenty-five now?

BIGSBY   But why have you done it now?

MILLER   Well, I have a bad habit: I sit down here and I start writing plays! The great thing about a play is that I am sitting here with a typewriter or something, and that is it. If I agreed to write a movie, I would be here with a veritable army of producers, actors, mechanics, God-knows-what. I have just done a screenplay of *The Crucible* and I will bet you there are already three hundred people involved in this thing. They have got trucks coming from California carrying big turbines for electricity on this island where they are going to build the town of Salem. They are building the whole town off the coast of Massachusetts, on an island. They have got to build a pontoon bridge on to that island. That is because I sat down at a typewriter in my innocence and wrote the screenplay. You have probably got aeroplanes going there and armies of people. You see, in the theatre, it is me and this machine and a couple of idiots who want to get involved.

BIGSBY   But in spite of this jeremiad about the theatre, *The Crucible*, in the last twenty years, has sold seven million copies from one publisher in the United States alone. You continue to write plays in the faith that they are going to be produced.

MILLER   Well, maybe there will be enough people like me who will come along as time goes by. I am sure there are going to be writers. What bothers me is whether the longevity of the plays is great enough for most of those people. There are people like Terence McNally, who writes a play every year or two. He is

produced all over the place. Gurney is going well good. Wendy
Wasserstein is another. These are people who seem to have made
a life in the theatre. So maybe it is not as bad as I imagine; except
that, last year, they had one straight play on Broadway, I think. It
was *Angels in America*, and that failed to make its money back.
With those reviews they could not make the investment back.
Something has got to go wrong.

BIGSBY   If you look back over your professional career, do you
have any regrets?

MILLER   I do. I regret one thing only, that I was not lucky enough
to have had a living connection with a theatre, a group of actors
and so on. In the few instances when I did have such a
relationship, I was very fruitful. I tended to write for that group.
That was when I was working with Kazan. I finished *All My Sons*
and I immediately started to work on *Death of a Salesman*. But
that exploded because we parted ways. Kazan was not really
interested in the theatre any more; he wanted to make movies. So
there was a moment when I felt the connection. We used a couple
of the actors from *All My Sons* in *The Crucible* and in *Death of a
Salesman*. Arthur Kennedy played in all three of those, for
example. So this connectiveness helped, to a certain degree. I
would not write any parts for them. It is just that somebody
needed material and there was a living connection there. Once or
twice there were the British people. For example, that lovely
production David Thacker did of *The Last Yankee* was a
tremendous pleasure for me to see. Here in the United States
they had a perfectly good production, but the thing was on, I do
not know, six weeks and then swept away – not for any other
reason excepting that this was put on by what they call an
experimental theatre. Their normal run is that, unless they get a
tremendous demand by the audience; then they will perhaps shift
it to another theatre. But nobody wanted to move it. *The Last
Yankee* in London had a tremendous charge to it, tremendous
internal energy, partly, I think, because that theatre existed, the
Young Vic. There was an audience there that was passionately
interested in this kind of thing. I do not see that here in America,
right now. I could be wrong, but I just do not see it.

BIGSBY   When you are not writing plays . . .

MILLER   I am making benches and I am reading a lot of books.

BIGSBY   You are quite a carpenter, in fact. If for some reason you had not been allowed to write plays, could you have lived a happy life working with wood as a carpenter?

MILLER   It would not have been happy because the real carpenter's life, in this area anyway, is very risky. You build a house and then you have got to get another job! They love it when they are working, but we go into recessions here where nobody is building a house, and they go around having to borrow money to live. Just the economics of it are very worrying, so I would not have been happy that way. While I was working I might have been happy. Look, there is no rest for the weary. One way and another you are going to get trouble. Man is born to trouble as the sparks fly upwards. It would have been one thing or another. But I can't really believe, given my nature, that I would have stayed away from writing anyway. I would have written in the basement.

BIGSBY   And what is the greatest pleasure that working in the theatre has given you?

MILLER   The writing. I am not sure I get a hell of a lot of pleasure out of the production process. You see, almost never do you get lucky enough to have an actor who is exactly the guy who should be playing that part. There is always some element missing, or some element there that should not be there, so you worry about that a lot. I am not crazy about the production part of it. I do it in the hope that it will work; but, when I am in total control of that page of manuscript, that is a different story. The pleasure ends, really, when you bind up the play and say, well, that's it, it's finished. The rest is labour, work, and that has got its compensations because, if it reaches people, then you get that feeling of power that you have accomplished something. But most of the time you are in flight away from it. You wish to hell you did not have to have it. You wish you could just give the play to somebody and have him do it and then write you a letter and tell you whether it worked or not, like Chekhov used to do. When he was sick, he could not hang around Moscow in the wintertime, so he would give the play to the director, Stanislavsky. Then he would go see it and tear his hair out, saying, 'You screwed up this play!' It was like the first production of *The Seagull*; they destroyed that play the first time around. The great Stanislavsky screwed it up good. Chekhov must have gone out of his mind when he saw that the whole thing had been completely misconceived. I have had that happen, but I do not get second chances. I have to go to England, or nothing. It is a different world.

BIGSBY   But when it works?

MILLER   When it works, it is marvellous. It is always unbelievable. You carry some of those moments the rest of your life. David Burns played the furniture dealer in *The Price* in New York, that was 1968. I can still hear him, twenty-seven years later. He was one of the funniest men who ever laughed, and a piece of humanity that was unbelievable. He was a real creation, that man, and had never played a real part in his life. He was always in musicals. He would invent little mispronunciations of words all by himself. Some of them were just precious. He would look at his furniture in the attic and say, 'Looks a very nice family.' So you have that, a few voices left in your head, and that is not nothing.